Alan Sinfield lives in Brighton. H
Studies at the University of Susse
the masters' programme: *Sexual I*
He has lectured widely in Europe and the United States, and held
visiting positions at the University of California, Berkeley, and
Northwestern University. He writes regularly for *Gay Times*.

By the same author

Faultlines: Cultural Materialism and the Politics of Dissident Reading (California University Press and Oxford University Press, 1992)

Political Shakespeare: New Essays in Cultural Materialism, ed. with Jonathan Dollimore (new edition: Manchester University Press and Cornell University Press, 1994)

The Wilde Century: Effeminacy, Oscar Wilde and the Queer Moment (Cassell and Columbia University Press, 1994)

Cultural Politics – Queer Reading (Pennsylvania University Press and Routledge, 1994)

Literature, Politics and Culture in Postwar Britain (new edition: Athlone Press, 1997)

Gay and after

Alan Sinfield

Library of Congress Catalog Card No: 97-069090

A catalogue record for this book is available from
the British Library on request

First published in 1998 by Serpent's Tail,
4 Blackstock Mews, London N4
Website: www.serpentstail.com

Set in 10pt Sabon by
Avon Dataset Limited, Bidford-on-Avon, Warwickshire

Printed in Great Britain by
Mackays of Chatham PLC, Chatham, Kent

10 9 8 7 6 5 4 3 2 1

Contents

Acknowledgements

I have benefitted from conversations about topics in this book with too many people to name here, including colleagues and postgraduate students at Sussex. I hope they found it half as rewarding as I did. I am specially indebted to those who read and commented on partly coherent drafts: Rachel Bowlby, Laura Chrisman, Wei-cheng Raymond Chu, Jonathan Dollimore, Murray Healy, Gowan Hewlett, Robert Howes, Hans Huang, Stephen Maddison, Vincent Quinn, Pratap Rughani, Ashley Tellis. Several of those people lent me or told me about useful materials; so did Zackie Achmat, Carrie Bramen, Peter Burton and Rachel Holmes.

Some parts of some chapters have appeared in other forms, in *Textual Practice*, *Gay Times*, *Pink Paper*, *Modern Drama*, and *European Journal of English Studies*, and in Andy Medhurst and Sally Munt, eds., *Lesbian and Gay Studies* (Cassell, 1997) and Lynne Segal, ed., *New Sexual Agendas* (Macmillan, 1997).

Brighton, 1997

1 The post-gay

Millennial visions

Whatever next! Now these gays are trying to claim their own millennium. Actually, the anniversary of the start of the period when Christians began to impose their calendar, and so much else, on a large part of the world, has more significance for sexual dissidents than for many people today.

Michelangelo knew this (let's have the big names on at the start). His picture *The Holy Family* (*Doni Tondo*, in the Uffizi, Florence) centres upon Mary, the infant Jesus, and Joseph. Jesus seems to be clambering earnestly between his parents; Joseph offers anxious support, while Mary looks and strains up over her shoulder to steady the child. In the background, to either side, are naked, somewhat androgynous, young men: they have been exercising, and their postures are notably relaxed; their bodies touch, but it seems unremarkable. These pagans are thoughtlessly besporting themselves, but a strenuous, family-structured Christianity is on the point of displacing them. For 0000 BC/AD marks the point where the pagan accommodation between sex-for-reproduction and sex-for-pleasure began to be displaced in Europe and much of the world by the Judaeo–Christian idea of sex-for-reproduction and guilt-if-you-try-anything-else.

If les/bi/gay people have some reason to take a long view of their situation, we know also that, in our current modes, we are a recent and ongoing creation. For we did not *come out*, in the wake of the Stonewall Riot of 1969, in the sense of emerging, already formed, as if from behind a curtain. Rather, we have been making our history and hence our selves – though not, of course, in conditions of our own choosing. Now, it seems, we may be growing out of 'gay'. Suddenly, improbably, we are in a position to envisage a new refocussing of sexual dissidence for the next millennium. It is a point at which to reassess our situation and the cultural resources through which we comprehend it.

Going west

The record 'Go West' was made by the Village People in 1979.
David Drake, in his play *The Night Larry Kramer Kissed Me*
(1992), gives a sense of what the Village People were like, as
perceived by the eight-year-old David when he bought Mommy
their record 'YMCA' for Christmas. 'They're fairies!' his sister
exclaims.

> But they don't look like fairies on the record cover. They look
> really tough – really cool. There's a Cowboy and an Indian and
> a Policeman and an Army Guy and a Motorcycle Guy – and he
> looks really tough . . . So, why are they called Village People?
> Do they all like live in the same small town or something? . . .
> Boy, if I was big and tough like the Village People, Cliffy sure
> wouldn't mess with me. He'd be the one getting chased through
> the woods.[1]

The joke is that David, in his perplexed eagerness to accommodate
himself to conventional manliness, reads the Village People
straight (so to speak). He doesn't see that their excessively butch
manner is pastiche, in the tradition of camp self-mockery (at least
we know we are silly), depending on the thought that even manly
gay men are not all that manly. Their novelty was to display, to
gays and the general public, a comic version of the macho style
that was being cultivated by gay men in 1979.

That macho style and 'Go West' allude, quite specifically, to
the nineteenth-century 'American' drive to dominate the sub-
continent. 'Go west, this is our destiny', the song runs, using a
typical imperial motif; 'Together, we'll find a place / To settle
where there's so much space' (it was supposed that no one was
living there – anyway, no one worth bothering about). The
trappings of 'manly' pioneering had become part of the fantasy
paraphernalia of the gay leatherman.

Yet, at the same time, it was 'coming true', for gay men were
redefining the idea of going west: they were making a subcultural
colony in the Castro district. 'Now if we make a stand, / We'll
find our promised land' ('Go West'). 'The West in the end meant

only one thing', the narrator declares in Andrew Holleran's novel
Nights in Aruba (1983): 'San Francisco. Everyone in the little
band went to San Francisco.'[2] 'There where the air is free, / We'll
be what we want to be'. The Village People celebrated an
attainment of gay citizenship even while recognising, through
camp self-mockery, that gay men could not achieve more than a
hybrid, self-cancelling, pastiche relation to the pioneer values that
are supposed to constitute 'America'. If this was not a real
colonisation of manliness, it did indicate that some gay men were
having a lot of fun.

The Pet Shop Boys' remake of 'Go West', released in the entirely
different circumstances of 1993, is fraught with nostalgia. There
is a manly, *Oklahoma*, male chorus, but it is exaggerated only in
the way that such choruses generally are, and it alternates with
Neil Tennant's plangent tones. Suddenly, if you listen, the words
all mean differently. 'Go West, sun in winter time, / Go west, we
will feel just fine'. We went west and behaved in ways that
asserted our freedom, we believed, but it went terribly wrong.
Our friends fell ill and died, and an entirely new phase of
stigmatisation was legitimated. 'Together, we will fly so high, /
Together, tell all our friends goodbye'. In the two voices – the
manly chorus and Tennant – the aspirations of the 1970s
encounter the distress of the AIDS emergency. This is not my
reading alone; it's what Neil Tennant said on television in an
interview with Andi Peters.[3]

Even so, HIV and AIDS in gay districts of San Francisco and
other cities have called forth resources beyond what we had
believed ourselves capable of. 'Together, we will work and strive'.
The chorus builds in purposefulness, claiming eventually the
heroic dimension that in 1979 had seemed merely pastiche.
'Together, your hand in my hand'.

I have started with 'Go West' because, as a model instance of
how subculture may work, it enables me to announce some of my
preoccupations. There is an element of gay affirmation and a
good rhythm to dance to, but the Pet Shop Boys' remake gives us
a good deal more than that. It invites us to review our history, not
in the abstract but as a song that once we sung; it revises camp as

a gay manner; it memorialises our loss. To be sure, little of this is heard by mainstream record-buyers, but why should that matter? They may listen if they wish, but they have plenty of records of their own. At the same time, this instance illustrates also some of the problems that we encounter.

As with another Pet Shop Boys' song, 'Being Boring', I recall precisely when and where I first heard the remake of 'Go West'. So you can imagine how angry and betrayed I felt when I saw the video. This is set outside the Kremlin, with a lot of men marching around in vaguely kinky 'uniforms', encouraging some listeners to hear in the music an allusion to the Russian national anthem. In this setting, going west appears to refer to the incorporation of the Eastern Bloc into capitalism. What I had appreciated as a specifically gay intervention is abruptly redirected. Peters challenged Tennant on this in the interview: the video 'changes the meaning', doesn't it? Tennant's response – that Russia is trying to move in a Western direction – did not address the suggestion that the video backs away from the gay meaning.

Am I being sentimental? Naturally, the Pet Shop Boys want their records to chart and relatively few potential buyers are interested in gay men and AIDS; the effect I have been admiring is expensive to produce, and there is not a gay cultural apparatus capable of circulating it. Those are the real conditions of cultural production.

Probably it was not so different for Michelangelo. If, as art critics generally suppose, his *Holy Family* is about the world redeemed from sin by the triumphant arrival of Christ, with the naked athletes figuring the world of sinners before redemption, then why (as Robert S. Liebert asks) do the sinners appear so happy and why are they represented with such sensual vividness?[4] Giorgio Vasari in his *Lives of the Painters, Sculptors and Architects* (1550) says the 'reclining nude figures in the background' were included by Michelangelo because the holy family 'did not suffice to display his powers'; but that sounds a bit thin. Was the artist drawn to the pagan ideal of male sensual beauty but masking it to please his patron? Or was it perhaps the patron who wanted the sexually dissident implication? The painting was done for Agnolo Doni, a 'lover of all beautiful works whether ancient or modern', Vasari records; could there be a hint there?[5]

If we find both Michelangelo and the Pet Shop Boys responding to the conditions in which they were having to work, that is hardly surprising. Very many of the materials available to lesbian and gay subcultures are located ambivalently between sexual dissidence and a more conventional stance; we are practised at drawing imaginative and intellectual sustenance out of such work. From Plato, through Shakespeare, Wilde, Proust and Tennessee Williams, to Donna Summer and Freddie Mercury, we have learnt to insinuate our own readings, alongside and in violation of the mainstream.

One of the leading ideas of this book is that les/bi/gay people would do well to recognise the processes of the *subcultural work* through which we become who we are. I expound in chapters 4 and 5 the idea of subcultural myth, maintaining that we need to regard such myths critically; I focus upon ideas and images of AIDS, gay history, and women, as they are broached in the work of Bill T. Jones and Marlon Riggs, Stephen Spender and David Leavitt, Alan Hollinghurst and Harvey Fierstein. Chapters 6 and 7 explore the conservative and transgressive projects of Bruce Bawer and Leo Bersani, as they argue them through mythic texts by Mary Renault, Andrew Holleran and Jean Genet. In these discussions, fiction, film and song are regarded not as documentary evidence or as vehicles for transcendent truths, but as reservoirs of significant and complex representations through which we think ourselves. Chapter 8 seeks to formalise a more sustained and intricate theory of gay cultural production, and of the role of the sexually dissident intellectual.

At the same time, a second leading idea is that we have to entertain the thought that 'gay' as we have produced it and lived it, and perhaps 'lesbian' also, are historical phenomena and may now be hindering us more than they help us. The remainder of this chapter presents reasons for believing this, and several chapters explore its implications. I discuss in chapter 2 whether we have the stability often associated with an ethnic group, and how we should regard the hybridity that seems inevitable in our subcultures (Derek Jarman's reworking of Christopher Marlowe's *Edward II* is taken as a case in point). I consider in chapter 3 what we may learn by comparing non-metropolitan concepts of same-sex passion, 'femininity', 'masculinity' and 'family', as they occur in Latin America and Taiwan. In chapter 9, following up some of the comments here on 'Go West', I assess the political potential of current marketing attention to gay men and lesbians.

The reader may notice that I have produced a difficulty for myself. One of my leading ideas calls for more determined subcultural work; the other calls for a recognition that the kinds of subcultural cohesion that we have developed since Stonewall are losing effectiveness. These two projects are pulling in different directions: it will not be easy to fortify a subculture whose bases are disintegrating. Nevertheless, the fact that a task is difficult does not make it unnecessary to attempt it – rather the opposite. If we – whoever we are – are to make sense out of the provisionality and indeterminacy that haunt les/bi/gay cultures at the present time, we need subcultural work that is purposeful, informed and critical.

Post-gay

In North America and North-western Europe, the years since Stonewall have afforded good opportunity to those who have wanted to be what we have come to recognise as gay or lesbian. We have developed significant institutions and the beginnings of a climate where we may express ourselves without too many restraints. This has been a phenomenon mainly of cities in the West; also, business and tourist travel have spread 'gay' and 'lesbian' through the cities of the globe. With all this in view, I will be calling our post-Stonewall lesbian and gay identities *metropolitan* and placing them within the metropolitan sex–gender system. This word referred initially to principal cities, but lately in postcolonial contexts it means the global centres of capital. I intend to exploit this ambiguity: metropolitan lesbian and gay identities have been emerging in the capitalist heartlands of the West, but are found also in large cities around the world, generally alongside older, local kinds of relations.

But every identity is an exclusion as well as an inclusion. For those who have felt themselves to be interested in same-sex passion but somewhat to one side of the metropolitan identities, *gay has been a constraint*. Increasingly, people have been saying this. Here I will discuss, briefly as a way of opening up the topic, four current challenges to the metropolitan model: racial minorities, the Queer movement, bisexuals, and men who have sex with men/women who have sex with women.

The emergence of metropolitan gay identities has coincided with and depended on a weakening of family ties. Partly as a consequence of education, many younger people do not share, or expect to share, the outlook of their parents. Capitalism requires us to learn work-skills that our elders do not comprehend, and to move around the country and the globe. In such a context, to disaffiliate from family and acquire a different identity – a different class identity, for instance – is common. If our parents don't understand our sexualities, then, that is not too surprising and we can probably cope with it. We hope that, when we come upon hard times, friendship networks, pension schemes and social services will sustain us.

But this metropolitan disaffiliation from family does not suit members of racial minorities. For Black and Asian gays in Britain, Sunil Gupta observes, 'the family was the source of both material and communal well-being. In a hostile white environment, for the first generation the community was their only hope of comfort and security. To turn your backs on it was to cut yourself off from both this security in real terms and from a sense of identity that was/is separate from the whites.'[6] Cherríe Moraga indicates that the relation of American Chicana lesbians to their families is both necessary and impossible:

> It seems my life has always been a kind of Catch 22. For any way you look at it, Chicanas are denied one another's fidelity. If women betray one another through heterosexism, then lesbianism is a kind of visible statement of our faithfulness to one another. But if lesbianism is white, then the women I am

faithful to can never be my own. And we are forced to move
away from our people. As Gloria Anzaldúa once said to me, 'If
I stayed in Hargill, I would never have been able to be myself.
I had to leave to come out as the person I really was.' And if I
had stayed in the San Gabriel Valley, I would have been found
for dead, at least the walking dead.[7]

The writing of people such as Moraga and Anzaldúa will
gradually reorient ideas of what Chicana women may do; they
will help Chicana lesbians to take same-sex passion back to their
families and communities. Thus they may produce new modes of
relating that will be valuable for many in those communities, and
instructive for the rest of us.

The Queer movement of the early 1990s had three principal
targets. One was the feeble establishment response to AIDS (this
was the target of ACT UP in particular); another was the notion
that dissident sexuality can be simply compatible with bourgeois
society today (that sexual dissidence is potentially revolutionary
was not a new idea, but the new queers didn't know very much
about 1960s gurus such as Herbert Marcuse or Wilhelm Reich,
or about the initial phase of Gay Lib); a third target was the
complacency of lesbians and gay men who have found convenient
niches for themselves and who believe that keeping quiet may
lead to social acceptance. The use of the terms of our stigma in
the anonymous London leaflet 'Queer Power Now' (1991) is
intended as much to confront the metropolitan models of lesbians
and gay men as to seize a language from the straight system:

> Queers, start speaking for yourself! Queers, Dykes, Fags,
> Fairies, Arse Bandits, Drag Queens, Trannies, Clubbers, Sluts
> . . . Call yourself what you want. Reject all labels. Be all labels.
> Liberate yourself from the lie that we're all lesbians and gay
> men. Free yourself from the lie that we're all the same . . .
> Liberate your minds. Queer is not about gay or lesbian – it's
> about sex![8]

That may sound inclusive, but the tone is calculated to repel the
cautious.

Also, in that quotation, Queer reinforces a tendency of lesbians and gay men to split into more particular groups. SMers have developed specialised subcultural facilities, and new anger through the Spanner case (in which, between 1987 and 1997, the right to private, consensual SM relations was fought and lost through the courts of England and Europe). Transvestites also, partly through a resurgence in drag artistry, have come into focus in their own right. We are reminded that they are not necessarily gay; nor are they necessarily male – drag kings have appeared in London. Transsexuals also have claimed attention, though at the cost of falling into the hands of surgeons and psychiatrists. Lately we have television programmes about people undergoing sex-change operations, and books with such titles as *Gender Dysphoria*; *Gender Outlaw*; *Changing Sex*; *Male Femaling*.[9] Thinking again about Radclyffe Hall's commitment to the 'sexual inversion' theory of Havelock Ellis, and the stress Stephen places upon her masculine attributes, it occurs to me that *The Well of Loneliness* might be regarded as a classic of transgenderism, as much as a classic of lesbianism; or, better perhaps, that the two may not then have been so distinct as we have assumed lately.[10] All these groups have found the current metropolitan gay and lesbian identities more constraining than enabling.

Bisexuals became more assertive at about the same time as, and partly through, the Queer movement. Once, Gay Liberation sought to challenge all categories but since the 1970s, the Off-Pink Collective complains,

> a progressive narrowing of the term 'gay' took place ... first with a split between gay men and lesbian feminists, and then more recently, over the last ten to fifteen years [since the 70s], with homosexual identity taking on an 'ethnic' meaning. Whereas before it was enough to love members of your own sex to be considered gay, now it is necessary never to have loved or experienced attraction to members of the opposite sex, or to repudiate such feelings if you ever had them.[11]

It is one of the oddities of the present political conjuncture that bisexuals should regard other sexual dissidents as the obstacle in the way of progress; I suspect that when they have persuaded sufficient lesbians and gay men they will be startled at the further hostility that awaits them. Nonetheless, it is true that lesbians and gay men in the metropolitan model have tended to suppose, with insufficient thought, that self-proclaimed bisexuals merely lack the courage to relinquish a protective stake in heterosexuality. This is not surprising: in the 1970s and 1980s, to declare yourself gay or lesbian was such a strenuous project that to blur the effect by adding that sometimes you were a bit straight after all seemed just too complicated, and scarcely plausible. Now, in the mid-1990s, some young people are not daunted by such pressures. And some noted lesbian and gay activists, who can hardly be accused of running scared, have been venturing beyond customary identities. A sensitive account of these changes among women in San Francisco, by Arlene Stein, has just been published.[12] I have the impression that the push for recognition of bisexuality is coming more from women; perhaps they will succeed in establishing a new 'right to choose'.

In fact, in the days of the queer gent and his bit of rough, it was likely that the latter would marry: part of his attraction was the thought that he was substantially straight. One of the achievements of post-Stonewall metropolitan gayness has been to find a way out of the dilemma marked by Quentin Crisp: 'they set out to win the love of a "real" man. If they succeed, they fail. A man who "goes with" other men is not what they would call a real man.'[13] Now we are proud enough to want to go with other gays. Now we may become able to allow, also, that some of us may want to be straight(ish) some of the time; after all, most of the movement is still in the other direction (straights becoming gay or bisexual).

Looking beyond the gay/straight binary allows some intriguing thoughts. One is that, although SMers, transvestites and transsexuals and bisexuals have appeared marginal to lesbian and gay subcultures, it is equally plausible to regard their purposeful revisions of gender imagery as central to any project of sexual dissidence. Another thought is that some male and female SMers, transsexuals and bisexuals may have more in common with each other – as SMers, transsexuals and bisexuals respectively – than with other male and female gays respectively. If this is the case, it will tend to undermine the dominant pattern – shared by gays and straights – whereby the gender of one's partner (same/ different) is the overwhelming factor.

People belonging to racial minorities, queers and people who term themselves 'bisexual' are still, for the most part, declaring some kind of relation to current lesbian and gay concepts and institutions. Indeed, if 'les/bi/gay' turns out to be a satisfactory term for the time being (in my view the task is not to discover the 'right' word but to deploy, tactically, terms that will be effective at the moment), bisexuals may have contributed the missing conceptual link between lesbian and gay. A fourth disturbance in metropolitan lesbian and gay images comes from people who scarcely see themselves in relation to prevailing modes of sexual dissidence: men who have sex with men, and women who have sex with women, while living generally as heterosexuals and regarding themselves as basically 'normal'.

In his book *Coming Out*, back in 1977, Jeffrey Weeks observed in nineteenth-century Britain, alongside precursors of our current gay identity, three other kinds of same-sex experience. One is 'the casual encounter, which rarely touches the self-concept'; another is a deeply emotional bonding between two individuals; a third is 'situational: activity which may be regarded as legitimate in certain circumstances, for example in schools or the army and navy or prisons'.[14] It was altogether possible to have same-sex experience without regarding oneself as 'homosexual', 'queer' or 'gay'. However, since Stonewall our societies (gay people and straight people) have been preoccupied with the self-identified gay man and lesbian, to the point where the kinds of relations located by Weeks have been widely regarded as 'latently homosexual' or 'closet cases'. Indeed, if men who have sex with men are now on the agenda, it is because they are difficult to reach with guidance about safer sex (they don't read the gay press or pick up condoms as they leave the pub; they may not have discrete/discreet space in which such matters may be conveniently negotiated; they may even think that HIV is what gays get, and therefore not relevant to them).

But neither Weeks' categories nor those modern glosses upon them adequately describe what now seems to be happening. Once, we supposed that the opportunity to be more or less openly gay would attract many spouses away from their marriages and save younger people from making such a 'mistake'; the straights and the gays would separate out, and married homosexuals would disappear as a breed. But today some gay men of my acquaintance are meeting married men on a casual basis, and others are having ongoing, usually secret, affairs with them. Some of these husbands enjoy family life, love their spouses, and see no inevitable contradiction between occasional or secondary gay experience and a heterosexual self-image and lifestyle.

Comparable adjustments are probably occurring among women although, as usual, there are fewer studies. Jeanette Winterson's novel *Written on the Body* (1992) is noted specially for the ambiguity as to whether the narrator, an enthusiastic lover of women, is female or male. One effect of this ambiguity is to license representation of a woman who has the predatory disposition conventionally associated with men (for she might, after all, be a man); it allows her lesbian seductions – if that is what they are – of married women to appear almost as common-place as the adulterous liaisons of heterosexuals, undoing any assumption that Lothario must be a man. 'I've been through a lot of marriages. Not down the aisle but always up the stairs', the narrator says.[15] Most of these women enjoy love-making with the narrator, but remain committed to their marriages. In fact, the narrator does not altogether dislike this – 'I'm addicted to the first six months', s/he says (p. 76). Perhaps women having sex with women who maintain a heterosexual identity and lifestyle, if that is what is happening here, suits all parties rather well. When the narrator settles down with Jacqueline, who has never been married, s/he is soon bored.

Then the narrator and Louise fall in love, such that the narrator feels obliged to abandon Jacqueline, and Louise to leave her husband. 'I love you and my love for you makes any other life a lie', Louise says (p. 19); the casual relationship is not good enough. As the story develops (I won't give it away), true love auto-destructs under patriarchal pressure, but the answer, readers are probably meant to infer, is even more commitment. Yet while the compromise of women who have sex with women (if it is that) is found wanting in *Written on the Body*, the novel does put it on the map, on a par with conventional adultery.

What has occurred, I suspect, is that while many people who once would have been married and/or covert are now leading an openly gay or lesbian life, a further cohort that would once have scarcely allowed themselves fantasies is now having covert same-sex experience. And, beyond that, almost certainly, there are people who are thinking about it, but as yet hardly doing anything. The relative legitimation that the lesbian and gay movement has achieved has allowed everyone to move one space across.

If this is the case, the proportion of people likely to engage in same-sex experience is larger than we have supposed – probably far larger than the proportion of people who will ever identify as gay or lesbian (as those terms are currently conceived). A stronger availability of bisexuality as a positive condition may afford them a dissident identity if they want it. Even so, the drawing of these people into a les/bi/gay consciousness will never be complete: for as we incorporate one cohort, the further legitimation thereby produced will enable another cohort to feel they can have sex with persons of their own gender, while not taking the further step of identifying as other-than-straight.

In an article on Joe Orton, written in the late 1980s, I argued that, so far from being subversive, Orton was bent on scandalising a fuddy-duddy theatre public which was, in fact, already on the run in the face of the 1960s radicalism that was to sponsor the Women's Movement and Gay Liberation (*What the Butler Saw* was produced in 1969). With this analysis in view, I complained that Orton had insisted that none of his characters should appear to be a homosexual. This insistence 'seems radical; it is against stereotypes', I observed; 'On the other hand, "we're all bisexual really" is the commonest evasion.' Orton would have been more

radical, I argued, if he had contributed to the assertion of a
modern gay identity: 'male homosexuals were struggling to be
gay, not to be indifferent to sexual orientation'.[16]

While I stand by my historical account of Orton, I think
Marjorie Garber is right to suggest that I was writing from a
particular time and hence a particular gay identity (she calls it
'the Sinfield moment' but the stance was integral to the metropolitan lesbian and gay models).[17] I think that current changes in
perceptions of bisexuals, along with the other developments I
have mentioned, indicate that we may now be entering the period
of *the post-gay* – a period when it will not seem so necessary to
define, and hence to limit, our sexualities.

To be sure, proclaiming that whatever most of us thought we
were doing is passé because it's 'post-' is an easy way for the
trend-setter to make a mark. And I don't want to devalue the
continuing struggle of many people, in Britain and elsewhere, to
become lesbian and gay. In South Africa, while I am keen to learn
about the distinctive sexual identities of *moffies* and *skesanas*, an
activist such as Zackie Achmat of the National Coalition for
Lesbian and Gay Equality is telling me that a stronger presence
of metropolitan lesbian and gay models offers the best way
forward for sexual dissidents there – for instance for the woman
who because of her relationship with another woman is being
imprisoned and beaten by her husband.[18]

Nevertheless, the four groups I have been considering require a
reconsideration of our post-Stonewall identities. People in ethnic
minorities who are determined to remain in negotiation with their
families may have something to teach us all; Queer had a point;
it is not adequate to regard bisexuals as in bad faith; and men
who have sex with men/women who have sex with women are a
significant development. Lesbians and gay men need to recognise
that, for all our anti-essentialist theory, we have imagined
sexuality to be less diverse and less mobile than, for many people,
it is. Our current identities will never account for more than a
proportion of the same-sex passion in our society, let alone in
other parts of the world. It is out of respect for both our diversity
and our potential for sharing that I write sometimes of sexual

dissidents or les/bi/gay people, sometimes of lesbians and gay men together, sometimes just of gay men. These variations are purposeful: my policy is to welcome common interests where they occur, but otherwise to avoid pronouncing upon people beyond my own constituency: (still) gay men.

Identity and politics

In my advocacy of the post-gay, and my call for a more intelligent and critical gay culture, I am not intending to reinforce the position taken by Mark Simpson and Toby Manning in the recent collection of essays, *Anti-Gay*. In 'Gay Dream Believer: Inside the Underwear Cult', Simpson takes young men dancing in their underwear on sponsored floats at the annual Pride celebration as an index of our general triviality. He objects to what he sees as the born-again intensity of coming out, the self-congratulation and silliness of Pride, and the vaunting of disco as a magical realm of ultimate pleasure. Manning excoriates 'the mindless uniformity of gay culture'; it 'must be kept bland, middle-brow and mainstream'; 'gay offers a culture of official mediocrity'.[19]

The trouble is that *Anti-Gay* takes as its notion of *gay* the candyfloss of *Boyz* and *Attitude*, and the half-baked attempts of other papers to keep up with that. (When I made that reference to 'other papers' in a review for *Gay Times*, a sub-editor changed it to 'some other papers'. Sensitive.) But what if you are a gay opera buff, Christian, sporty type, or Tory? For Simpson and Manning, none of that is to do with being gay. Nor if you meet with the Outdoor Club, the Humanist Association, or a Black or Asian group. Nor if you are a PWA, or buddying. Ignoring all this diversity might be all right as a way of making a point, but it's then a bit much when Manning says gay culture is 'a monolith' marked by 'mindless uniformity' (pp. 94, 107). He says we have a lot to learn from such writers as Genet, Burroughs, Tennessee Williams and Dennis Cooper, but since they are 'transgressive' they are, by definition, not gay.

Simpson says we have arranged the world so that 'wherever you go you can pick up a gay publication which is full of people just like you' (p. 7). Would it were true. Gay papers are full of someone quite different from me: a youngster who drinks spirits, wears designer clothes, goes to new clubs, takes out life insurance, goes abroad for his holidays, and does a lot of phone sex. He is conjured up not because he represents us, any more than colour supplements represent people who read newspapers on Sunday, but because he may have some money to spend. It is bad enough reading about this fantasy figure; now I am accused of being him.

Actually, gay subculture is shaped broadly by the patterns of gender, class, race, age and education that shape straight culture. There are mindless bits and thoughtful bits; some of us find Genet hard going, others don't. Gay discos are like straight discos, except that you can chat up someone without fear of getting punched. Complaining about the club scene being boring has been a standard part of the scene since the New Curtain Club was new. Of course it's not a big deal if gay men dance to Erasure; who said it was? True, we do make a fuss about coming out, but that's because we have reason to be afraid that our families and friends will disown us. And sometimes we get carried away by second-rate artistes when they make gay-positive gestures. But then, everyone gets sentimental now and then; at funerals I find myself perversely moved by 'Abide with Me'.

If it is just a question of terminology – alternative versions of what counts as 'gay' – then does it matter? I think it does, because if we are to get a more intelligent and critical subculture, which I agree we need, a good deal will depend on journalists such as Mark Simpson and Toby Manning. And they are not going to be much help if they begin by dismissing the ordinary pleasures of people who have not yet arrived at their stage of urbane world-weariness. Gay was a response to a situation which we have transformed. If it is time to negotiate the post-gay, we need to build on what we have done so far, and to take as many people with us as possible.

Relinquishing our strenuously forged identities for the post-gay threatens new difficulties and dangers. As feminists and commentators from racial and ethnic groups have remarked, it is ironic that just at the moment when subordinated peoples strive to centre themselves as agents in their own lives, anti-essentialist criticism tells us that the centred subject is a delusion. Straight WASP men abandon the game and take their ball away. And how are we to found an effective political movement on dispersed subjectivities?

Many lesbians and gay men believe that asserting essential, coherent sexual identities as natural – in our genes, perhaps – will strengthen our case against homophobia. Like an ethnic group (I consider this in the next chapter). However, essentialist assumptions have not protected Jews, or Blacks, or innumerable native peoples from oppression and exploitation. They have not protected women. Conversely, religious faith is not generally reckoned to be innate, and that has not discouraged believers from asserting rights. Despite the difficulties, which I hope will eventually prove productive, I mean to argue that current metropolitan lesbian and gay identities are products of our place and time, deriving from social process in our subcultures and in interaction with the mainstream. Indeed, we might think it more dignified to assert that we have chosen who we want to be. Women who identify as lesbian, Vera Whisman finds, are more likely to believe that they have made a choice.[20] I will be looking not at sexuality as deeply implanted in the individual, like some secular version of the soul, but at the place of same-sex passion in the sex–gender system.

One inference from anti-essentialist theory should be that we cannot simply throw off our current constructions. We are consequences of our histories – those that have been forced upon us and those that we have made ourselves – and we have to start from there. At the same time, it is because we believe that culture constructs the scope for our identities that we may believe those identities to be contingent and provisional, and therefore may strive to revise our own self-understanding and representation. The post-gay, if that is where we are, will demand more urgent and intelligent subcultural work, not less. I will be exploring some of the key issues, taking it as axiomatic that our movement will thrive best on a cultivation, not a simplification, of our potential.

'Together, we will learn and teach' – 'Go West'.

2 Ethnicity, diaspora, and hybridity

'It's as if we were an ethnic grouping' Peter Burton writes in *Gay Times* (April 1995). The idea goes back, at least, to *The Homosexualization of America* (1982), where Dennis Altman observes that gay men in the United States have since the 1970s adopted an 'ethnic' mode of identification: 'As gays are increasingly being perceived as a minority in the best American tradition, it is hardly surprising that they have come to claim a political role based on this fact.'[1]

Ethnicity is not the only framework through which we have envisaged same-sex passion. As Eve Sedgwick points out, we have operated, together and incoherently, two ideas: minoritising and universalising. In the former, lesbians and gay men constitute a fairly fixed minority, as an ethnic group is supposed to do; in the latter, virtually everyone has a potential for same-sex passion.[2] Hence the ongoing argy-bargy about how 'widespread' homosexuality is: it depends how the question is put. If 'it' is defined so as to require an acknowledged identity and a gay 'lifestyle' that you are prepared to disclose to a doorstep questioner, research will find relatively few instances (three to four per cent of the population in some surveys of males, fewer still of females). If 'it' is any intense same-sex bonding or the occasional occurrence of any same-sex act, then research will find hardly anyone to be immune.

Ethnicity-and-rights

Thinking of lesbians and/or gay men as an ethnic group is a minoritising move, and it runs counter to the constructed and decentred status of the subject as s/he is apprehended in current theory. Nonetheless, very many lesbians and gay men today feel, intuitively, that the ethnicity model best accounts for them. This is partly because, as Steven Epstein suggests, we have constituted ourselves in the period when ethnicity, following the precedent of the Black Civil Rights movement, has offered the dominant paradigm for political advancement. It has become 'the default model for all minority movements', Michael Warner remarks.[3] So we too claim our rights: that is what ethnic groups do. One culmination of this tendency is Simon LeVay's belief that he is doing us all a good turn by locating a part of the brain that is different in gay men, because this will enable US gays to claim recognition in the courts as a minority having immutable characteristics.[4] So lesbians and gays can get to be as well off as the Indian peoples.

In other quarters, the ethnic model is under new kinds of question. In a review of Marjorie Garber's book, *Vice Versa: Bisexuality and the Eroticism of Everyday Life*, Edmund White begins by remarking: 'In the United States, where so many political factions are linked to ethnic identity, homosexuals have been astute in presenting themselves as something very much like a racial or cultural identity.' But White concludes by wondering 'whether I myself might not have been bisexual had I lived in another era'. The post-Stonewall drive to *be gay* limited him: 'I denied the authenticity of my earlier heterosexual feelings in the light of my later homosexual identity.'[5] We should not suppose that our post-Stonewall lesbian and gay identities, and their heterosexual corollaries, are the last word; as I argued in chapter 1, we may be entering the period of the 'post-gay'.

It is not, altogether, a matter of deciding how far we want to go with ethnicity-and-rights; the dominance of that model is not incidental. For it is not that existing categories of gay men and lesbians have come forward to claim their rights, but that we have become constituted *as gay* in the terms of a discourse of ethnicity-and-rights. This discourse was active, and apparently effective, elsewhere in the political formation, and afforded us opportunities to identify ourselves – to *become ourselves*. This has meant both adding to and subtracting from our potential subjectivities. As Didi Herman puts it, rights frameworks 'pull in "new" identities . . . people are forced to compartmentalise their complex subjectivities in order to "make a claim".'[6] 'The person who takes up a post-Stonewall gay identity feels compelled to act in a way that will constitute her or himself as a subject appropriate to civil rights discourse,' Cindy Patton observes.[7] Gay men and lesbians *are*: a group, or groups, claiming rights.

There are drawbacks with envisaging ourselves through a framework of ethnicity-and-rights. One is that it consolidates our constituency at the expense of limiting it. If you are lower-class, gay lobbying and lifestyle are less convenient and may seem alien. If you are young, or entertaining new practices and commitments, the call to declare a sexual identity imposes the anxiety that exploration of your gay potential may close your options for ever. And if you are a person of colour, the prominence of a mainly white model makes it more difficult for you to negotiate ways of thinking about sexualities that will be compatible with your cultures of family and neighbourhood, while dealing with the racism in white gay subculture.

Also, fixing our constituency on the ethnicity-and-rights model lets the sex–gender system off the hook. It encourages the inference that an out-group needs concessions, rather than the mainstream needing correction; so lesbians and gay men, Herman observes, may be 'granted legitimacy, not on the basis that there might be something problematic with gender roles and sexual hierarchies, but on the basis that they constitute a fixed group of "others" who need and deserve protection'.[8] Initially in Gay Liberation, we aspired to open out the scope of sexual expression for everyone, in the process displacing the oppressive ideologies that sexuality is used to police. By inviting us to perceive ourselves as settled in our sexuality, the ethnicity-and-rights model releases others from the invitation to re-envision theirs. 'At best, a minority group analysis and a civil rights strategy pertain to those of us who already are gay', John D'Emilio argues. 'Our movement may have begun as the struggle of a "minority", but what we should now be trying to "liberate" is an aspect of the personal lives of all people – sexual expression.'[9]

Widening the relevance of dissident sexuality was one goal of 'Queer Nation'. 'Queer', Michael Warner writes, 'rejects a minoritizing logic of toleration or simple political interest-representation in favor of a more thorough resistance to regimes of the normal.'[10] Henry Abelove reads 'nation', in 'Queer Nation', as an aspiration, in the tradition of Henry David Thoreau's *Walden* (a gayer book than is generally acknowledged) not to join, but to *become* 'America' – *the* nation.[11] The problem for Queer Nation was the scale of that aspiration: relatively few people were ready for it. In many small-town and rural circumstances, being gay is quite a struggle; the last thing you want is someone from a city telling you that you don't measure up because you can't handle 'queer'. In fact, a problem for Queer as a movement was that its programme entailed rejecting most of its potential constituency at the start. Hence the movement was composed almost entirely of vanguard, and the exhaustion that afflicts activists set in quite rapidly.

The Castro and the White House

The ethnicity-and-rights model encourages us to imagine a process whereby, win some/lose some, we all advance gradually towards full, democratic, national citizenship. However, as Hans Mayer and Homi Bhabha point out, the development of the European nation-state since the eighteenth century coincides with mass migration within the West and colonial aggrandisement elsewhere. In our Enlightenment inheritance, the nation is an unstable construct, and ideas of citizenship are deployed, typically, in a hegemonic process whereby outsiders are stigmatised and potential deviants jostled into place.[12] 'Citizen' is a defensive construct, therefore; it has never meant 'inhabitant'. It always counterposes some others who are present but not full citizens – at best, visitors, but usually also racial, ethnic and sexual minorities, slaves, children, criminals, the lower classes, women, the elderly. The corollary of the 'Citizens' Charter', propagated by the UK Conservative Government in the early 1990s, is the harassing of people who try to live outside a narrow norm – travellers, ravers, SMers, lone parents.

Discussion of citizenship in the United Kingdom usually invokes T. H. Marshall, who in 1947 analysed modern constitutional history as a broad progress – from class hierarchy, towards equal rights of citizenship. Civil rights – of property, speech and religion, justice before the law – developed in the eighteenth century, Marshall says; political rights (mainly the franchise) were achieved during the nineteenth and early twentieth centuries; and, lately, in the 1940s, social rights were being added – 'the components of a civilised and cultured life, formerly the monopoly of a few, were brought progressively within the reach of the many'.[13] Marshall's analysis reflects the optimistic, egalitarian climate at the end of World War II, when an apparatus of welfare benefits was installed to ameliorate the worst consequences of capitalism, effectively relegitimating the British state through an ideology of fairness and consensus. In this framework, even homosexuals became a 'social problem' requiring a benign state solution; the Wolfenden Report was commissioned in 1954 to find one, and in 1967 its proposals became the basis of the current law.[14]

The UK version of citizenship positions out-groups as petitioning for concessions, which appear analagous to the welfare granted to the unfortunate. In the USA, where a constitution professes to guarantee rights to all citizens, it is more a matter of asserting a claim. 'Each time there is a major defeat of gay rights in the voting polls of middle America, gays take to the streets of San Francisco chanting "Civil Rights or Civil War" ', Manuel Castells notes.[15] This threatens, metaphorically, a repeat of the founding revolt of the United States, or perhaps of the war that freed Black slaves. Either way, it wouldn't work in England because our civil war means differently – probably the dominant connotations are upper-class incompetence (cavaliers) versus vulgar fanaticism (roundheads); this is echoed, still, in perceptions of the Conservative and Labour parties today. Nevertheless, gay activism in Britain often adopts an 'American' rhetoric, because it seems more determined and dignified. In fact, I think, British images of male gayness are generally dependent on North American examples – to a far larger extent than British people realise (I return to this in chapters 4 and 5).

The US ideology of rights, as Epstein says, 'functions typically through appeals to the professed beliefs of the dominant culture, emphasizing traditional American values such as equality, fairness, and freedom from persecution'; it implies the goal of 'gaining entry into the system'; it appeals to 'the rules of the modern American pluralist myth, which portrays a harmonious competition among distinct social groups'.[16] How far that myth is to be trusted is a question far wider than les/bi/gay politics: it is about how much we expect from the institutions through which capitalism and hetero-patriarchy are reproduced.

The ethnicity-and-rights model aspires to two main spheres of political effectivity. One is a claim for space within which the minority may legitimately express itself. For gay men, classically, this was the Castro district of San Francisco. Manuel Castells, in a moment of exuberance in the early 1980s, saw there a recovery of the merchant citizenship of the Italian Renaissance: 'We are almost in the world of the Renaissance city where political freedom, economic exchange, and cultural innovation, as well as open sexuality, developed together in a self-reinforcing process on the basis of a common space won by citizens struggling for their freedom.' Castro gay leaders spoke of a 'liberated zone'.[17]

However, if it is hard to achieve socialism in one country, as Trotsky insisted against Stalin, it is even less likely that sexual liberation can work in one sector of one, capitalist, city. Castells observes how inter-communal hostility developed in and around the Castro, as gentrification (also known as 'gay sensibility') raised property values and squeezed out other, mainly Black and Latino, minorities.

The clashing of competing interests is endemic to the ethnicity-and-rights model. When ACT UP intruded on the Roman Catholic service of Cardinal O'Connor in New York, Douglas Crimp reports, it was said that they had 'denied Catholic parishioners their freedom of religion'. Similarly in Britain, Rachel Thomson notes, Department of Education and Science circular 11/87 declares: 'It must also be recognised that for many people, including members of religious faiths, homosexual practice is not morally acceptable.'[18] One interest group is used against another. Castells observes: 'each player defines him/herself as having to

pursue his/her own interests in a remarkable mirror image of the
ideal model of the free market'.[19] However, the free market, we
should know, does not generally present itself in 'ideal' form.
Generally, it sets us all at each other's throats.

The second sphere where the ethnicity-and-rights model aspires
to political effectivity is through the organs of the state. In *Close
to the Knives* David Wojnarowicz propounds an urgent critique
of US political, religious and judicial systems (that aspect of his
book is left out of Steve McLean's 1994 film, *Postcards from
America*). However, alongside that Wojnarowicz manifests an
underlying vein of surprise that gay rights have not been
acknowledged; he is shocked to read of a Supreme Court ruling
(presumably *Bowers vs. Hardwick*), that 'only people who are
heterosexual or married or who have families can expect these
constitutional rights'.[20] Lamenting the suicide of his friend
Dakota, Wojnarowicz asks: 'Man, why did you do it? Why didn't
you wait for the possibilities to reveal themselves in this shit
country, on this planet?' (p. 241). Despite his indictment,
Wojnarowicz still expects Uncle Sam to come up trumps eventually. A leitmotiv in *Close to the Knives* is that if only President
Reagan would pay attention to AIDS, we would begin to get
somewhere with it. Wojnarowicz writes:

> I imagine what it would be like if, each time a lover, friend or
> stranger died of this disease, their friends, lovers or neighbors
> would take the dead body and drive with it in a car a hundred
> miles an hour to washington d.c. and blast through the gates of
> the white house and come to a screeching halt before the
> entrance and dump their lifeless form on the front steps. (p. 122)

It is as if recognition in official quarters would not only help
resource a campaign to alert gay men to HIV and AIDS; not only
legitimate the campaign; but somehow magic away the epidemic.
Reagan's silence on AIDS preoccupies Randy Shilts in *And the
Band Played On*, culminating in the prophecy that Reagan would
go down in history as 'the man who had let AIDS rage through
America'.[21]

In comparable mode, Larry Kramer's persona in *The Normal Heart* (1985) throws his large energies into getting the attention of city hall, the mayor, the *New York Times* newspaper. As late as 1995, Kramer says in an interview with Lisa Power that he has been 'accepting and facing ... that all these myths I have swallowed about humanity and America and "one voice can make a difference" – these things that we're all taught, that democracy works and all – turn out to be bullshit when you're gay or you have AIDS or are a member of a minority or whatever the reason'. 'That was a surprise?' Power asks, 'curiously'.[22]

Is homosexuality intolerable? – that is the ultimate question. One answer is that actually lesbians and gay men are pretty much like other people but we got off on the wrong foot somewhere around St Paul; it just needs a few more of us to come out, so that the nervous among our compatriots can see we really aren't so dreadful, and then everyone will live and let live; sexuality will become unimportant. That scenario is offered by Bruce Bawer, who calls himself a conservative, in his book *A Place at the Table*. He believes US gay men can rely upon 'democracy' to gain 'acceptance', because 'to attempt to place restrictions on individual liberty and the right of others to pursue happiness is, quite simply, un-American'.[23] What Bawer calls 'subculture-oriented gays' impede this process by appearing radical and bohemian.

The other answer is that homophobia contributes crucially to structures of capital and patriarchy, and that lesbian and gay people offer, willy-nilly, a profound resistance to prevailing values in our kinds of society. The point may be figured through a distinction which Shane Phelan draws, between ethnicity and race. While ethnicity has enabled a discourse of rights and incorporation, race (despite the formative moment of Black Civil Rights) has proved less pliable. People deriving from Europe, Phelan observes, have been assimilated, but 'Race in the United States has been the mark of the unassimilable, the "truly different".'[24] Racial difference is doing more ideological work, and hence is more – perhaps ultimately – resistant. Which is closer to the situations of lesbians and gay men?

We cannot expect to settle this question. However, it would be rash to suppose that the criminalising and stigmatising of same-sex practices and lifestyles is an incidental kink in an otherwise reasonable structure; that the present system could, without cost, relinquish its prohibitions and legitimations. Consider: parents will repudiate their offspring because of gayness. Something very powerful is operating there.

In my view, the pluralist myth which legitimates the ethnicity-and-rights model affords useful tactical opportunities, but it is optimistic to suppose that it will get us very far. Nevertheless, I will argue eventually that we cannot afford entirely to abandon a minoritising model because we cannot afford to abandon subculture and political organisation.

Diaspora, hybridity, and the doorstep Christian

Meanwhile, in another part of the wood, theorists of 'race' and 'ethnicity' have been questioning how far those constructs offer a secure base for self-understanding and political action. Stuart Hall traces two phases in self-awareness among British Black people. In the first, 'Black' is the organising principle: instead of colluding with hegemonic versions of themselves, Blacks seek to make their own images, to represent themselves. In the second phase (which Hall says does not displace the first) it is recognised that representation is formative – active, constitutive – rather than mimetic. ' "Black" is essentially a politically and culturally *constructed* category,' Hall writes, 'one which cannot be grounded in a set of fixed transcultural or transcendental racial categories and which therefore has no guarantees in Nature.'[25]

Henry Louis Gates, Jr., makes a similar point: in the language of Derridean deconstruction, he calls for a 'thorough critique of blackness as a presence, which is merely another transcendent signified'.[26]

In respect of European and American – *diasporic* – Black peoples, this may seem merely a necessary move: after forced migration, forced miscegenation and all kinds of economic and cultural oppression it must be hard to isolate an uncontaminated

Africanness. 'Our task is not to reinvent our traditions as if they bore no relation to that tradition created and borne, in the main, by white men', Gates declares (p. xxiii). 'Diaspora' (a Greek, biblical term, denoting the captivity of the Hebrews in Babylon and, latterly, the worldwide dispersal of Jewry) usually invokes a true point of origin, and an authentic line – hereditary and/or historical – back to that. However, diasporic Black culture, Hall says, is defined 'not by essence or purity, but by the recognition of a necessary heterogeneity and diversity; by a conception of "identity" which lives with and through, not despite, difference; by *hybridity*'. Alluding to the improvisatory virtuosity of Black jazz musicians, blues singers, rappers, dubbers and samplers, Hall writes of 'the process of unsettling, recombination, hybridization and "cut-and-mix" ' arising out of '*diaspora* experience'.[27]

Hall is inclined to celebrate hybridity; I mean to question that. But two immediate qualifications are appropriate. First, many non-white cultures are neither diasporic nor notably hybrid; those of many Africans born and living in Africa, for instance. Second, it is quite hard to envisage a culture that is not hybrid; Lévi-Strauss specifies *bricolage* as the vital process through which cultures extend themselves, and Hall deployed the concept a while ago, with white youth cultures mainly in view.[28]

With these provisos, it still makes intuitive sense to regard diasporic Black cultures as distinctively hybrid. Paul Gilroy in his book *The Black Atlantic* offers the image of a ship, situated in mid-Atlantic – in continuous negotiation between Africa, the Americas and Western Europe. 'Because of the experience of diaspora', says Gates, 'the fragments that contain the traces of a coherent system of order must be reassembled.'[29] He discusses myths of the trickster, myths which embody a self-reflexive attitude to Black traditions, prizing agility and cunning at adaptation and insinuation in African-American culture, rather than an authentic African heritage.

Such arguments for hybridity have not gone unchallenged. G. N. Devy, in his book *After Amnesia* (1992) and various essays, invokes an Indian tradition that preceded what he regards as a relatively slight Western imperial intrusion and continues through

and beyond it. However, there are reactionary connotations in
such an assertion as this: 'In order that a literature becomes a
great literature it should develop from a language that is rooted
in the soil, that grows organically from peoples' experiences piled
together for generations.'[30] Comparably, Molefi Kete Asente in
his book *Afrocentricity* acknowledges that African genes have
been mixed with others, but

> it is also a fact that the core of our collective being is African,
> that is, our awareness of separateness from the Anglo-American
> experience is a function of our historical memory, the memory
> we have frequently denied or distorted. Such experiences are
> rooted in our ancestral home and defined by social and legal
> sanctions of four hundred years in America.[31]

These commentators tend to be hostile to homosexuality. Asente
says it 'cannot be condoned or accepted as good for the national
development of a strong people'; it comes from 'European
decadence' and must be corrected by 'the redemptive power of
Afrocentricity'. Devy criticises Indian English literature for
'androgynous disab[i]lity'.[32] There are dangers in assertive
essentialism.

Of course, constructionist commentators do not mean to
abandon Black and Asian traditions. 'The past continues to speak
to us. But it no longer addresses us as a simple, factual "past" ',
Hall declares. bell hooks writes: 'There is a radical difference
between a repudiation of the idea that there is a black "essence"
and recognition of the way black identity has been specifically
constituted in the experience of exile and struggle.'[33] In practice,
however, it is not easy to keep tradition and hybridity together in
the same frame.

Gates, for instance, sounds *just a bit* essentialist when he argues
that a distinctively Black pattern can be uncovered in the hybrid
history that we know: 'The Black tradition has inscribed within it
the very principles by which it can be read.' To be sure, these
principles cannot be securely discerned – 'To reassemble fragments,
of course, is to engage in an act of speculation, to attempt to weave

a fiction of origins and subgeneration.' Nonetheless, Gates believes he can 'render the implicit as explicit' and 'imagine the whole from the part'.[34] He needs to do this partly because the idea of hybridity implies *at least some* identifiable element of Blackness in the mix, and partly because the thought that African-Americans may have nothing that they can call their own is intolerable.

Recognition that race and ethnicity might be constructed, hybrid and insecure, but yet necessary, has obvious resonances for lesbian and gay cultural politics, and may help us to think about ourselves. For gay subculture, certainly, is hybrid, to the point where it is difficult to locate anything that is crucially gay – either at the core of gayness, or having gayness at its core. What about drag, then? Mostly – from pantomime and music hall to working men's clubs and film and television comedy – it is consumed by straight audiences. Drag plays at the borders of those fraught and insecure categories, male and female, masculine and feminine, and all sorts of people are interested in that. The disco scene, perhaps? Well yes, except that a standard feature is the latest diva calling down God's punishment on people with AIDS. The ancient Greeks, maybe? Well, the organising principle of their sexual regime seems to have been that a citizen (male) may fuck any inferior – women, slaves, boys. That is the stuff heroes are made of, but hardly sexual liberation. Camp then? Since Susan Sontag's defining essay of 1964, it has appeared to be anybody's, and now it is co-opted into 'the postmodern'. There is art and literature: surely gay men are justly famed for our achievement there? Yes, but we have been allowed to produce quality culture on condition that we are discreet – thereby confirming our unspeakableness. Opera too: since 'The Three Tenors' were offered as a curtain-raiser for the World Cup Final in 1994 it correlates with soccer rather than, in Wayne Koestenbaum's title, *The Queen's Throat*. Even our pin-ups are not our own. John Weir wonders how to explain 'what makes Marky Mark a gay icon, except that he looks like the guy from high school gym class who spent half his time exciting your ashamed desire, and the other half shutting your head in his locker'.[35]

When Frank Mort writes of 'a well-established homosexual diaspora, crossing nation-states and linking individuals and social constituencies', we know what he means. However, as Warner remarks, there is no remote place or time, not even in myth and fantasy, from which lesbians and gay men have dispersed.[36] Our hybridity is constituted differently. Indeed, while ethnicity is transmitted usually through family and lineage, most of us are born and/or socialised into (presumptively) heterosexual families. We have to move away from them, at least to some degree; and *into*, if we are lucky, the culture of a minority community. 'Home is the place you get to, not the place you came from', it says at the end of Paul Monette's novel, *Half-way Home*.[37] In fact, for lesbians and gay men the diasporic sense of separation and loss, so far from affording a principle of coherence for our subcultures, may actually attach to aspects of the (heterosexual) culture of our childhood, where we are no longer 'at home'. Instead of dispersing, we assemble.

The hybridity of our subcultures derives not from the loss of even a mythical unity, but from the difficulty we experience in envisioning ourselves beyond the framework of normative heterosexism – the *straightgeist* – as Nicholson Baker calls it, on the model of *zeitgeist*.[38] If diasporic Africans are poised between alternative homelands – in mid-Atlantic, Gilroy suggests – then lesbians and gay men are stuck at the moment of emergence. For coming out is not once-and-for-all; like the Africans, we never quite arrive. Let's be clear: I am not proposing any equivalence between the oppressions of race and sexuality – anyway, there is not one oppression of either race or sexuality, there are many. But, while in some instances race and ethnicity are not manifest, for lesbians and gay men passing is almost unavoidable.[39] And passing rehearses continually our moment of enforced but imperfect separation from the straightgeist. You can try to be up-front all the time – wearing a queer badge or T-shirt, perhaps – but you still get the telephone salesperson who wants to speak to the man of the house or to his lady wife. Or the doorstep Christian who catches you in only your bathtowel, bereft of signifiers. The phrase 'coming out', even, is not special to us. It is a hybrid appropriation, alluding parodically to what debutantes do; the joke is that they emerge, through balls, garden parties, and the court pages of *The Times*, into centrality, whereas we come out into the marginal spaces of discos, cruising grounds and Lesbian and Gay Studies.

This entanglement in heterosexism does have advantages. It allows us to know what people say when they think we aren't around. And at least we can't be told to go back to where we came from, as happens to racial minorities in Britain. Conversely though, it makes us the perfect subversive implants, the quintessential enemy within. We instance what Jonathan Dollimore calls a 'perverse dynamic': we emanate from within the dominant, exciting a particular insecurity – 'that fearful interconnectedness whereby the antithetical inheres within, and is partly produced by, what it opposes'.[40] The lesbian or gay person is poised at the brink of a perpetual emergence, troubling the straightgeist with a separation that cannot be completed, a distinction that cannot be confirmed. It makes it hard for us to know, even to recognise, ourselves. It is a kind of reverse diaspora that makes our subcultures hybrid.

Hybridity and dissidence

I was set on to this phase of work by a passage in Philip Roth's novel *Operation Shylock* (1993), where it is remarked how Irving Berlin, a Jew, wrote 'Easter Parade' and 'White Christmas':

> The two holidays that celebrate the divinity of Christ – the divinity that's the very heart of the Jewish rejection of Christianity ... Easter he turns into a fashion show and Christmas into a holiday about snow. Gone is the gore and the murder of Christ – down with the crucifix and up with the bonnet! *He turns their religion into schlock*. But nicely! Nicely! So nicely the goyim don't even know what hit 'em.[41]

Hybrid, diasporic Jewish culture is preferred to the arrogance that typifies the ethnically-authorised state of Israel. Jews belong in central Europe, it is suggested, and the brief dominance of the Nazis should not be allowed to wipe out centuries of Jewish-European, hybrid civilisation: 'The time has come to return to the Europe that was for centuries, and remains to this day, the most authentic Jewish homeland there has ever been, the birthplace of rabbinic Judaism, Hasidic Judaism, Jewish secularism, socialism – on and on' (pp. 31–2). The boldness of this conception challenges other subcultural formations to review their own traditions and their relations with other cultures. However, I believe hybridity is, so to speak, a mixed blessing.

Because the prime strategy of ideology is to naturalise itself, it has been tempting to suppose that virtually any disruption of symbolic categories or levels is dissident. This can lead to the inference that hybridity is, in its general nature and effects, progressive. Homi Bhabha puts the case that has to be considered:

> hybridity to me is the 'third space' which enables other positions to emerge. This third space displaces the histories that constitute it, and sets up new structures of authority, new political initiatives, which are inadequately understood through received wisdom . . . The process of cultural hybridity gives rise to something different, something new and unrecognisable, a new area of meaning and representation.[42]

This is compelling and salutary, but runs the risk of suggesting that virtually *any* instability will be progressive. The problem, Bhabha suggests, lies with left politics 'not being able to cope with certain forms of uncertainty and fixity in the construction of political identity and its programmatic, policy implications'. We should be welcoming opportunities for 'negotiation' – to 'translate your principles, rethink them, extend them'. In fact, since Bhabha has just said that 'all forms of culture are continually in a process of hybridity', it would seem that everything that happens is potentially progressive, and only the dreary old/new left is holding us all back.[43] Well, we have to work, of course, with the situations that global capitalism and its local conditions visit upon us, but this sounds indiscriminately stoic.

Bhabha's case for hybridity is related to his argument that the 'mimicry' of the colonial subject hovers, indeterminately, between respect and mockery; that it menaces, through 'its *double* vision which in disclosing the ambivalence of colonial discourse, also disrupts its authority'. Judith Butler makes a compatible case for cross-dressing, suggesting that it 'implicitly reveals the imitative structure of gender itself – as well as its contingency'.[44] Bhabha and Butler are proposing that the subtle imperfection in subaltern imitation of colonial discourse, or in the drag artist's mimicking of gender norms, plays back the dominant manner in a way that discloses the precariousness of its authority.

Now, symbolic disjunction may indeed disturb settled categories and demand new alignments. But the components of hybrid cultures rarely stand in positions of unequal power. I fear that imperialists cope all too conveniently with the subaltern mimic: simply, he or she cannot be the genuine article because of an intrinsic inferiority. And gay pastiche and its excesses may easily be pigeon-holed as illustrating all too well that lesbians and gay men can only play at true manliness and womanliness. To say this is not to deny resistance; only to doubt how far it may be advanced by cultural hybridity. The Stonewall queens instigated Gay Liberation not because they were camp or wore drag – there was nothing new about that; but because they fought the police.

We have supposed too readily that to demonstrate indeterminacy in a dominant construct is to demonstrate its weakness and its vulnerability to subversion. That is optimistic. To be sure, the ideologies of many nation-states exhort us to credit the stabilising virtues of established political institutions and cultural heritages. However, as Robert Young points out, English and British have never been secure concepts, for instance as they manifest in 'the English novel'. Nor is this necessarily a disadvantage. In actuality, as Marx tells us, capitalism thrives on instability: 'Constant revolutionizing of production, uninterrupted disturbance of all social conditions, everlasting uncertainty and agitation distinguish the bourgeois epoch from all earlier ones. All fixed, fast-frozen relations, with their train of ancient and venerable prejudices and opinions, are swept away, all new-formed ones become antiquated before they can ossify.'[45] Capital ruthlessly transforms the conditions of life: industries are introduced and abandoned; people are trained for skills that become useless, employed and made redundant, shifted from town to town, from country to country.

It is easier than we once imagined to dislocate language and ideology; and harder to get such dislocations to make a practical difference. Hybridity has to be addressed not in the abstract, but as social practice. Kobena Mercer posits a dialectic between dissidence and incorporation. He takes a difficult instance – the straightened hairstyle favoured by African-Americans in the 1940s:

> On the one hand, the conk was conceived in a subaltern culture, dominated and hedged in by a capitalist master culture, yet operating in an 'underground' manner to subvert given elements by creolizing stylization. Style encoded political 'messages' to those in the know which were otherwise unintelligible to white society by virtue of their ambiguous accentuation and intonation. But, on the other hand, that dominant commodity culture appropriated bits and pieces from the otherness of ethnic differentiation in order to reproduce the 'new' and so, in turn, to strengthen its dominance and revalorize its own symbolic capital.[46]

Hybridity, this instance says, is both an imposition and an opportunity. Which of these will win out depends on the forces against us in that context, and on our resourcefulness. 'Once "camp" is commodified by the culture industry, how do we continue to camp it up?' Danae Clark asks. 'The only assurance we have in the shadow of colonization is that lesbians *as lesbians* have developed strategies of selection, (re)appropriation, resistance, and subversion.'[47]

Jarman's *Edward II*

Consider Derek Jarman's film, *Edward II* (1991). When it was shown on television (BBC2), *Radio Times* presented it as something of a surprise, coming from the director of *Sebastiane* and *Jubilee*: 'Jarman's latest film is a portrait of an English monarch – a project funded, in part, by the BBC.'[48] They have a point: this is not a likely theme or source of funding for radical gay work. Equally unpromising, the main plot and almost all the dialogue for the film are adopted by Jarman from a classic of English Literature on the next rung down from Shakespeare's *Richard II*, Christopher Marlowe's *Edward II* (1592). The outcome has to be hybrid.

Intimations of same-sex passion in Marlowe's play have been handled hostilely by traditional literary critics. M. M. Mahood, in 1950, found only a negative correlation between Edward and her idea of Christian humanism: 'weak possessiveness makes Edward an easy prey to jealousy and thus estranges him from the Queen. She understands his nature less perfectly than does Gaveston, who plays deftly upon the king's craving for admiration and approval, deflecting it to a perverted and barren affection for himself.' Edward's gay sensibility (as we might term it today) is a sign of weakness: he is 'a sharp contrast to the earlier heroes in his taste for the histrionic and the tawdry'.[49] In 1986, still, Judith Cook found it easy to explain why *Edward II* is not much performed: 'We have to accept in Marlowe's world that the Edward who has been shown as so unsympathetic in the first half of the play becomes sympathetic to us in the second in spite of his proclivities and his weaknesses, but there is no logical link to show us how this comes about.'[50] Once you have these 'proclivities and weaknesses' you are pretty unredeemable.

For gay scholar-critics, Marlowe's play is a welcome but complicated text. Its interest in same-sex love is welcome; the complication lurks around the term 'tragedy', which the play seems to invite. Paul Hammond sums this up in terms of dominant Elizabethan beliefs: 'The play is remarkable for its sympathetic evocation of a homosexual relationship, but its conception of tragedy is common to Renaissance representations of the fall of princes, in that it shows the dire consequences which follow from the misgovernment of the passions by those entrusted with the government of the realm.'[51] Insofar as Edward and Gaveston challenge the social order, which is perceived as a divine order, they are shown to be duly punished. That *Edward II* exhibits such containment of potential dissidence is not surprising. Whatever Marlowe thought personally, his plays were written for the tightly policed Elizabethan theatre, under a regime where torture and death might follow conviction for sodomy – or, indeed, for anything that might threaten the stability of the State, the ruling elite and the religious establishment.

Jarman is surely on the right track, then, when he sets out to hybridise, and thereby appropriate, the Marlovian text. 'I've definitely improved it', he says; 'Marlowe should be really pleased with me. I think the original ending [Edward's torture and death] was a bit of propaganda, just as Shakespeare's *Richard III* was.'[52] In Jarman's version a main strut of tragedy is abrogated: Edward survives. Lightborn has a change of heart about his mission, flings the spit into the pool, and kisses Edward lightly on the lips. Sexual dissidence is not punished.

Yet Jarman plays the original ending as well, at length and with conviction. The dungeon scene (Act V, scene v) – the maudlin alternation of lament and acquiescence which the Marlovian text supplies for Edward – is cut in all the way through Jarman's film. Repeatedly we see Lightborn heating up the spit which, everyone knows, is destined for Edward's rectum. And the murder duly follows, gruesomely enough. Edward's fate seems bound up with his dissident passion and ('tragically') inevitable. Only subsequently, at the end, does it transpire that the murder is to be viewed as Edward's nightmare.

In principle, Jarman's revision seems on the right lines: we are led into the traditional 'tragic' framework of fate and retribution, but then challenged to envisage an alternative outcome. 'It doesn't have to be like this' is the key proposition for any radical representation; that much was established by Bertolt Brecht. Unfortunately, in Jarman's film we get no hint of how Edward's reprieve may come about, in the face of the extreme ideological and physical coercion that has prevailed in all parts of the action. Edward has a troupe of queer activist supporters, but they are shown sitting idly. Is the point supposed to be that some individual villains may experience a change of heart if you talk poetically to them? That won't get us very far – someone else would be sent to kill Edward.

Worse still, despite Edward's reprieve, Jarman closes the film with a reassertion of the 'tragic' note, quite purposefully drawing lines from three points in Marlowe's murder scene:

> But what are kings, when regiment is gone,
> But perfect shadows in a sunshine day?
> I know not; but of this am I assur'd,
> That death ends all, and I can die but once.
> Come death, and with thy fingers close my eyes,
> Or if I live, let me forget myself.[53]

This is very touching, but why are kings such a big deal, why is death made the measure of everything, why is death to be desired, and why, unless he is the disgusting creature of homophobia, should Edward want to forget himself? These lines do little for Jarman's declared project of improving the story.

This may happen partly because the film is also about something else: Jarman's AIDS-related illness. The part of Lightborn is taken by Jarman's lover, Kevin Collins; if the subtext is Collins saving the life of the apparently-doomed Jarman (Edward), then its articulation is necessarily thwarted because Collins was sadly unable to accomplish this.[54]

This unofficial personal scenario apart, my case is that deference toward Marlowe's text, perhaps encouraged by the backers of the film, drags Jarman back into reactionary attitudes. Hybridisation may be a necessary tactic, but it has to be pursued with determination and suspicion (of straightgeist influence). Certainly its political impetus cannot be taken for granted, as some theorists seem to be saying.

To be sure, Jarman is able to supply dialogue and action that

will prompt a gay-friendly interpretation. Thus he augments the
emotional pitch of Marlowe's distinctly low-key dialogue at the
parting of Gaveston and Edward by having Annie Lennox sing
'Every Time We Say Goodbye'. That works very well, I think. So
does the treatment of Edward III, the son of Isabella and Edward.
At first, noting the ways of his parents, the boy becomes fascinated
with violence, but by the end he is sporting earrings, make-up
and a hairstyle like his mother's, and conducting to the tune of
Tchaikovsky's 'Dance of the Sugar Plum Fairy'. The queer
succession to the throne of England seems assured.

So far so good. Jarman should intervene more along such lines
– lots more. But he allows himself to be constrained by the
Marlovian text. In fact, in my view, he is generally too deferent
towards the artworks which he uses; compare his versions of
Shakespeare, *The Tempest* and *The Angelic Conversation* (I
discuss in chapters 4 and 8 ideas of art and literature and how
les/bi/gay subcultures might regard them).

Again, Jarman seems to be on good lines when he links
Edward's fall to a confrontation between riot police and an
OutRage demonstration against violence against lesbians. However, placing any monarch at the head of a demonstration for
queer rights is troubling; the Marlovian slogan the demonstrators
chant – 'St George for England, and Edward's right' – is not one
that would occur spontaneously to an OutRage activist. Indeed,
Jarman makes Edward behave with the same brutality, selfishness
and irresponsibility as the rest of the ruling elite. That is plausible
enough (it is anticipated by Marlowe), and it does effect a
repudiation of the liberal notion that we should try to gain
straightgeist tolerance by being nice; as Jarman remarks, 'you
don't have to like somebody to accept their right to have a love
affair'.[55] Even so, having had a love affair is not sufficient to set
somebody at the head of Queer politics. The barons and Edward
bathe the country in blood in pursuit of their quarrel: that is how
the ruling elite behaves – in the play, in the film, and in history.
None of those people should be accorded an unchallenged priority
in a radical les/bi/gay movement.

The awkwardness in deploying OutRage alongside the monarch

is compounded by the fact that the scenario allows no further role for the demonstrators. As Edward moves into his final 'what are kings' speech (quoted above), they appear to be waiting, as if disempowered by Edward's imprisonment – as if our protest required prompting from the ruling elite. The attempt to hybridise and hence appropriate straightgeist cultural icons may draw us into regressive identifications, rather than strengthening and illuminating our subculture.

There are other difficulties with Jarman's *Edward II*, especially in the representation of Queen Isabella. However, while it might be convenient to ascribe misogynist aspects to poor old Marlowe, I don't think that would be a fair reading: both Marlowe and Jarman are misogynist.[56] Misogyny does not derive from hybridity here, therefore, so I am not pursuing it; I discuss it in chapter 5.

Edward II affords a good instance for a consideration of hybridity because we have a classic text against which we may measure Jarman's treatment. Usually, it is less easy to see how the negotiation between deference and appropriation has worked. And even here we cannot expect to discover how far Jarman was seduced by the ideology of tragedy, and how far he felt he had to avoid alienating the organisations that put up the money (little as it was) for the film, and that would distribute it. The same question arises in relation to the Pet Shop Boys' 'Go West' (discussed in chapter 1): the shift of emphasis in the video may represent a belief that global politics is as interesting as the impact of AIDS on gay communities, or an understanding that the music business had to be accommodated.

Subculture in the post-gay

Hybridity may or may not disconcert the system. My case is that being always-already tangled up with it, institutionally as well as conceptually, makes it hard for les/bi/gay people to clear a space where we may talk among ourselves. We used to say that we were silenced, invisible, secret. Now, though our subcultures are still censored, there is intense mainstream investment in everything that we do, or are imagined as doing. We are spoken of, written of, and filmed everywhere, though rarely in terms that we can entirely welcome. Gayatri Spivak advises a 'strategic essentialism', and Jeffrey Weeks writes of identities as 'necessary fictions', but lesbians and gay men find even an artificial coherence hard to sustain.[57] In the face of such pressures and opportunities, we need various but purposeful subcultural work – with a view neither to disturbing nor pleasing the straightgeist, but to meeting our own, diverse needs.

The dominant ideology constitutes subjectivities that will find 'natural' its view of the world: hence its dominance (that is an Althusserian axiom). Within that framework, lesbians and gay men are, ineluctably, marginal. However, subcultures constitute *partially alternative subjectivities*. In that bit of the world where the subculture runs, you may feel, as we used to say, that Black is beautiful, gay is good. It is through such sharing – through interaction with others who are engaged with compatible preoccupations – that one may cultivate a workable alternative subject position.

The nearest equivalent to a queer diasporic experience, Simon Watney remarks, is 'the sense of relief and safety which a gay man or lesbian finds in a gay bar or a dyke bar in a strange city in a foreign country'.[58] Considered as a model for the good society, a gay bar lacks quite a lot, but for a gay man it is a place where he is in the majority, where some of his values and assumptions run. Of course, it is an artificial security, as he knows all too well from the risk of street aggression as he enters and leaves. But, by so much, it is a place of reassurance and sharing – and this holds for all the trivia of our culture.

Subculture is not just good for morale, though; it does not, particularly, require positive images; and it doesn't occur only, or specially, in bars and the like. Lesbian and gay subcultures are the aggregate of what lesbians and gay men do, and that includes music, fiction, poetry, plays, film and video, cultural commentary. They are where we may address, in terms that make sense to us, the problems that confront us. We may work on our confusions, conflicts and griefs – matters of class, racial and inter-generational exploitation; of misogyny, bisexuality and sado-masochism; of

HIV and AIDS. For it is dangerous to leave these matters within the control of people who, we know, do not like us.

Wojnarowicz and Kramer wanted to catch the attention of the president and the mayor, but they themselves, through their work, have done vastly more than the city or the State in helping us to think about safer sex. At a poignant moment in Oscar Moore's novel, *A Matter of Life and Sex*, the protagonist proclaims his 'contempt for having to die of a gay disease when he had stood so firmly outside the gay scene, standing on the touchline with his back turned' (he prefers to imagine that being a call-boy is not a part of 'the gay scene').[59] He has it precisely the wrong way around; as Weeks puts it, 'it was the existence of strong lesbian and gay communities and identities which provided the essential context for combating the virus: in providing social networks for support and campaigning, in developing a grammar for safer sex, in promoting a language of resistance and survival'.[60] Watney links the fact that the French have the worst HIV epidemic in Western Europe to the fact that they have no gay institutions. Interestingly in the present context, Edmund White and Larys Frogier trace this absence to a distinctive ideology of rights, which regards the French citizen as an abstract, universal individual, enjoying a tradition of tolerance and assimilation within an impartial State. In this ideology, calls for attention to minority groups appear unseemly.[61]

Straightgeist culture often manifests consternation that we might be gaining our own resources. When *Longtime Companion* was shown on television, film guru Barry Norman commended it because, while it is about the deaths of middle-class gay men in New York through the 1980s, it 'deals with important topics that should concern us all no matter what our sexual proclivities – such things as love and caring, friendship, loyalty and fidelity'. Norman doesn't like movies that 'are simply about being gay – as if the condition of homosexuality were in itself drama enough'. Or, perhaps it is all right 'if you are gay', he grants, but 'it doesn't help to increase general understanding'. Norman doesn't entertain the thought that we might have just a few films for gay people, and even be able to see them on TV now and then. He believes that *Philadelphia* was successful because it incorporated 'a tense courtroom drama', whereas *Jeffrey*, 'though an amiable enough comedy, was merely about being gay in New York'.[62] Well, to me, the courtroom drama in *Philadelphia* was an offensive intrusion, whereas *Jeffrey*, though I quarrel with it in chapter 5, raises disturbing questions about how HIV-negative men are to handle the AIDS emergency. Perhaps there should have been a car chase. That's pretty universal – men being macho.

Richard Rorty has tried to distinguish a wrong and a right kind of multiculturalism. It is admirable that Black children should learn about Frederick Douglass, Harriet Tubman and W. E. B. Du Bois, he says, but this may lead to 'the dubious recommendation that a black child should be brought up in a special culture, one peculiar to blacks'. Rorty doesn't want Black children to feel that 'their culture is not that of their white schoolmates: that they have no share in the mythic America imagined by the Founders and by Emerson and Whitman, the America partially realised by Lincoln and by King'.[63] Like Wojnarowicz, he is waiting 'for the possibilities to reveal themselves in this shit country'. The consequence of thus crediting the prevailing ideology is that Rorty makes subculture sound like an optional extra. Rather, it is an indispensable resource, for the alternative is the continuing dominance of straightgeist accounts of ourselves. 'They had the power to make us see and experience *ourselves* as "Other" ', Hall remarks of colonial regimes.[64] In Roth's *Operation Shylock*, despite the sharp look at the state of Israel and the arguments about hybridity, the (somewhat unexpected) conclusion, as I read it, is that Jewish people cannot risk abandoning the last-ditch refuge which Israel represents.

Am I proposing a 'gay ghetto', then, in which we must all think the same? There is no question, in practice, of this. First, it is subordinated groups that have to be bilingual and mainstream groups that need not bother. 'Marginal people know how they live and they know how the dominant culture lives. Dominant culture people only know how they live', Sarah Schulman remarks.[65] Gays need to be able to read the language of straights so we can take evasive action when they get vicious. Second, working through our differences will produce an enhanced awareness of diversity. For instance, Native American gays may be drawing their own thoughts from 'Go West'.

And third, there is no new, allegedly-empty world in which to 'settle where there's so much space' (the phrase in 'Go West'). When I was involved in a television programme about Oscar Wilde, well-meaning strangers stopped me at work and in the street to tell me that while they have nothing against gays, they do object to the way we have co-opted Wilde. The response, of course, is that it is not we who got at Wilde; he was just doing his thing, and the system moved in and victimised him. In the trials of 1895, and still in reactions to my programme a century later, the straightgeist has innumerable strategies for reappropriating our interventions. Increasingly in a global system, subcultures are not a way of side-stepping hybridity, but of maintaining any space at all that is not entirely incorporated, in which we may pursue our own conversations.

The problem, rather, is this: I have been writing 'we'. Insofar as 'we' address 'our' problems today and work through 'our' history and 'our' culture, in the face of inevitable hybridising pressures, 'we' suppose a minority awareness. Despite all the arguments I assembled initially about the damaging consequences of the ethnicity-and-rights model, a project of subcultural work leads us back towards a version of that model. For, as bell hooks writes, it is with reason that subordinated peoples hold on to ideas of genetic innateness, cultural purity, and other essentialist notions: 'The unwillingness to critique essentialism on the part of many African-Americans is rooted in the fear that it will cause folks to lose sight of the specific history and experience of African-Americans and the unique sensibilities and culture that arise from that experience.'[66] It is to protect my argument from the disadvantages of the ethnicity model that I have been insisting on 'subculture', as opposed to 'identity' or 'community': I envisage it as retaining a strong sense of diversity, of provisionality, of constructedness.

If we cannot afford to abandon minority awareness, then, our subcultural task will have to include a reappraisal of its nature and scope. We have to develop a theory and a politics that will enable us to recognise that our identities (like those of hetero-sexuals) are constituted through cultural interactions, and are provisional and permeable. We need to draw upon the experience of elderly gays. We have to maximise opportunities for lesbian and gay alliances, and to explore sexualities that the gay movement has treated as marginal – bisexuality, transvestism, transsexuality. We need to speak with people who proclaim themselves to be 'straight-acting' and who demand and promise discretion in contact ads. We must be ready to learn from the different kinds of 'gayness' that are occurring in other parts of the world, and among ethnic and racial minorities in Western societies.

For it would be arrogant to suppose that the ways we have 'developed' in parts of North America and Northern Europe of being lesbian and gay constitute the necessary, proper, or ultimate potential for our sexualities. Thus we may make the diversity of our constituency into a source of strength. Subcultural work is our opportunity to support each other in our present conditions, and to work towards transforming those conditions.

3 Effeminacy and reproduction in different cultures

> Transvestite prostitute groups in Argentina are planning a
> demonstration at a Buenos Aires police station to
> highlight police brutality against them following the
> murder of a well-known street worker ... Mocha had
> been shot twice in the penis.
>
> (*Gay Times*, October 1996, p. 55.)

Towards the end of the previous chapter I said we should be ready
to reappraise the nature and scope of our subcultures. It seems
sensible to suppose that this book will be read for the most part
by people whose expectations fall largely within the metropolitan
sex–gender system.[1] Therefore, in order to unsettle and refocus
such expectations, I mean to consider fictions from Latin America
and Taiwan. I do not suppose that these novels will yield merely
documentary evidence of non-metropolitan sex–gender systems;
to the contrary, it will appear that their authors had larger
intentions. Nor will I be attempting to convey the full complexity
of (to me) remote cultures; that is quite beyond my power. This
will be a self-confessed exercise in metropolitan self-referentiality,
though with the aim of prising apart some customary assumptions
and pointing to the cultural specificity of same-sex practices
everywhere. The question I will be asking of other cultures is, not
how far they seem to approve of gayness as we understand it, but
what part same-sex passion plays in their lives. For we are not
going to understand our local situations without addressing the
wider ensemble of sexual practices in its historical specificity.

Kiss of the Spider Woman

In Manuel Puig's novel *Kiss of the Spider Woman* (1979), Molina
speaks of himself consistently as a woman, identifying with strong
but doomed women in the movies which he recounts to Valentin

(a political prisoner) in their prison cell. In respect of transvestites and transsexuals in the metropolitan sex–gender system, it is often pointed out that an individual may be gay, straight or anything. But Molina's 'femininity' is organised uncompromisingly around his yearning for a real man – 'Listen, I'm sorry, but when it comes to him [the waiter Gabriel] I can't talk about myself like a man, because I don't feel like one.'[2] Moreover, Molina has an old-fashioned and oppressive idea of proper womanly behaviour, as Valentin points out: 'Yes, always impeccable. Perfect. She has her servants, she exploits people who can't do anything but serve her, for a few pennies. And clearly, she felt very happy with her husband, who in turn exploited her, forced her to do whatever he wanted, keeping her cooped up in a house like a slave, waiting for him –' (p. 16). Even though Molina wants to be a woman, Valentin insists, he doesn't have to 'submit', to be 'a martyr'. Molina replies: 'But if a man is . . . my husband, he has to give the orders, so that he will feel right. That's the natural thing, because that makes him the . . . the man of the house' (pp. 243–4).

However, it is impossible for Molina to attain such an ideal partnership because he loves 'real men' and they, by definition, go with women. Relationships with other queens don't count: 'We don't put too much faith in one another, because of the way we are . . . so easy to scare, so wishy-washy. And what we're always waiting for . . . is like a friendship or something, with a more serious person . . . with a man, of course. And that can't happen, because a man . . . what he wants is a woman.' Only Molina's mother, to whom he is devoted, accepts him as he is (p. 203).

Commentators whose expectations are framed within the metropolitan sex–gender system tend to disapprove of this representation of (what we are likely to perceive as) a gay man. For Rebecca Bell-Metereau, William Hurt's portrayal of Molina in the film version (Hector Babenco, 1985) is 'problematic'. He 'applies make-up, wraps his hair in a towel, simpers and bats his eyelashes in imitation of his favorite movie star', and it all 'serves to reinforce many stereotypes about homosexuals'.[3]

Kiss of the Spider Woman makes best sense if we place it

geographically: it is set in 1975, in a country which is in some aspects Argentina, in others Brazil; in effect, it is 'somewhere in Latin America'.[4] There, *machismo* and the family count for everything, and homosocial bonding is often intense. Single males normally live with their parents until they marry, unless their work makes this impractical. Maintaining the honour of the family is an inalienable obligation. Women, Juanita Ramos observes, 'are supposed to grow up submissive, virtuous, respect-ful of elders and helpful to our mothers, long suffering, deferring to men, industrious and devoted'.[5]

These gender norms correlate with a clear distinction between sexual roles: men are 'active' (inserters) and women are 'passive' (insertees). The priority of this dichotomy has large consequences for the perception of male same-sex passion. According to the anthropologist Joseph Carrier, who has carried out lengthy studies in Mexico,

> The ideal male must be tough, invulnerable, and penetrating, whereas the ideal female must exhibit the opposite of these qualities. It follows then that only the receptive, anally passive male is identified culturally as effeminate and homosexual. The active male, the insertor, retains his masculinity and therefore cannot be considered homosexual.[6]

Most of the current words for same-sex practices in Mexico refer to the insertee, and invoke his despised 'effeminacy', for he is perceived as a kind of woman (Molina uses the words *puto* and *loca*). If two 'effeminate' homosexual males sleep together, they are jokingly termed *locas manfloras* – 'crazy lesbians'.[7]

The traditional sex–gender system in Latin American countries is less preoccupied with same-sex passion, then, than is the case in the metropolitan system. The key distinction is between the masculine (active) inserter and the feminine (passive) insertee. So long as a man maintains a *macho* stance, he may get away with quite a lot – even, so long as he is discreet, with same-sex practices (probably this is how it was in Shakespearean England).[8] There are 'feminine' men, but they are regarded as freakish. In this framework, it is hard to conceive the gay man as he has been constituted in the metropolis.

It is equally hard for a person to envisage herself a lesbian. In her introduction to *Compañeras*, a collection of oral and written testimonies, Mariana Romo-Carmona writes: 'We also know that any deviation from these expectations [of women] constitutes an act of rebellion, and there is great pressure to conform. Independence is discouraged, and we learn early that women who think for themselves are branded "putas" or "marimaches". Being a lesbian is by definition an act of treason against our cultural values.'[9] In fact, the Latina family depends totally upon the strength and combined commitment of mothers, grandmothers, sisters and daughters. But that makes it the more necessary to police the line where devotion becomes independent, for instance in sexual commitment, and seems to challenge male power. Again, there are rebels; the reports in *Compañeras* show women conceiving and living something like a metropolitan lesbian identity, but with great difficulty.

A few provisos. Of course, we are talking here about cultural norms, and these are not evenly distributed. First, Mexico is not the same as Argentina and Brazil, and, indeed, these large countries are internally diverse. Second, middle-class people are more likely to be oriented towards the United States, and hence aware of the metropolitan idea of a gay man; he is usually called *moderno*, *internacional*, or *gay*, indicating an imported concept.[10] Third, there will always be faultlines and opportunities for dissident practice and self-understanding – on the one hand, for instance, Valentin holds feminist views about women; on the other, it transpires that he himself is attracted by submissive women.

Nonetheless, it does seem that we are looking at a general Iberian and Latin American sex–gender formation. Federico Garcia Lorca in his 'Ode to Walt Whitman', written in 1930, lists urban street 'effeminates' from a string of Latin communities:

> *Fairies* of North America,
> *Pájaros* of Havana,
> *Jotos* of Mexico,

Sarasas of Cadiz,
Apios of Seville,
Cancos of Madrid,
Floras of Alicante,
Adelaidas of Portugal.[11]

Lorca condemns these 'pansies [*maricas*] of the cities' (Whitman, on the other hand, was satisfactorily *macho*).

From this point I cease putting quote marks round 'active', 'passive', 'masculine', 'feminine', 'effeminate', 'real men', and so on. However, it must be remembered that these are ideological constructs, not natural attributes, and that their primary function is sustaining the prevailing pattern of heterosexual relations. As I argue in *The Wilde Century*, very many heterosexuals are not respectively masculine and feminine, or not in certain aspects, or not all of the time. That is why we find heterosexuality plunged into inconsistency and anxiety. For lesbians and gay men, the situation is indeed perverse: a model of how heterosexual men and women are supposed to be, which is tendentious, inadequate and oppressive in the first place, is twisted into bizarre contortions in order to purport to describe us. Who is active, who passive, in fellatio?[12]

A normative account of the Latin American sex–gender system helps us to comprehend one of the principal turns in *Kiss of the Spider Woman*: the two men become affectionate to the point where Valentin fucks Molina. This is not (just) the resort of a heterosexual man in prison, and still less is it a revelation of Valentin's latent homosexuality, or even his essential bisexuality; he just adapts his manly role slightly. For casual same-sex practice may be regarded in Latin America with a certain indulgence, on a par, almost, with the other non-marital outlets which the real man is expected to pursue – so long as he is *activo*, seen to be going with women as well, and constrained by circumstances (e.g. money or opportunity). Andrea Cornwall makes the same point about Brazil.[13] In the last episode of the novel, under the influence of morphine and (presumably) dying, Valentin is sad about Molina's death (in a shoot-out between the revolutionaries and the security forces), misses him and credits him with helping him. But Valentin's reference point in his dream is Marta, the woman revolutionary, and his erotic fantasy is of a native girl. He has learnt from Molina how to feel – he speaks Molina's language of sentiment with confidence and commitment – but his heterosexual preference is not modified. Conversely, and it is the central triumph of a distinctly gloomy book, Molina has actually succeeded in getting fucked by a real man.

It may seem that the Latin American sex–gender system has a distinctively firm grip on gender roles, but there are faultlines in any ideology. Valentin asks Molina why he never takes the active role: 'you, physically you're a man as much as I am ... Sure, you're not in any way inferior. Then why doesn't it occur to you to ever be ... to ever act like a man? I don't say with women, if they don't attract you. But with another man' (*Kiss*, pp. 243–4). Note the hesitation there between 'to ever be' and 'to ever act like'. On the one hand, as Valentin points out, Molina is 'physically' a man already. On the other, Molina is so determined to be a woman that perhaps, even in a manly role, he would only be 'acting'.

Valentin's questioning indicates that he is entertaining the idea of being fucked by Molina: 'If it weren't for the fact that it must hurt a hell of a lot, I'd tell you to do it to me, to demonstrate that this business of being a man, it doesn't give special rights to anyone.' However, Molina will not even talk about this, so contrary is it to his self-definition (p. 244). Nevertheless, Valentin obtains an acknowledgement that there are 'homosexuals' who think and behave differently. There is 'the other kind who fall in love with one another', Molina says. 'But as for my friends and myself, we're a hundred percent female. We don't go in for those little games – that's strictly for homos. We're normal women; we sleep with men' (p. 203; see also p. 243). No further explication is given to these 'homos'; they seem to represent an intrusion of the metropolitan gay concept. Commentators agree that this concept is making little headway, however; and the action of *Kiss of the Spider Woman* is set back in 1975. Puig is claiming space for new thought on gender and sexuality. While the relationship of Valentin and Molina makes best sense in terms of traditional Latin American sex–gender ideology, the book is not contained by that ideology.

Of course, Puig is under no obligation to document Latin American mores. After all, he settled in New York in 1963, twelve years before the action of the book. Indeed, the reader is prompted to probe further beyond convention by the commentary on Molina's and Valentin's attitudes in a sequence of long footnotes reporting metropolitan theories about homosexuality.

The footnotes are inspired only loosely by the text. They begin when Valentin remarks: 'If we're going to be in this cell together like this, we ought to understand one another better, and I know very little about people with your type of inclination' (p. 59). Molina responds by talking earnestly about his 'womanly' passion for Gabriel, who is so straight that 'Nothing at all happened. Ever!' (p. 66). But two lengthy footnotes supply another kind of understanding: accounts and refutations of physical and popular theories about homosexuality drawn from D. J. West's book, *Homosexuality* (1955). Twenty pages later, Molina's care for Valentin prompts a note about Anna Freud's idea of how people relate; this leads into Freud's *Three Essays on the Theory of Sexuality*, and further psychoanalytic explications and discussions. While Valentin and the reader are finding out about 'people with your type of inclination' from Molina's experience, therefore, the reader gains a further perspective from the theoretical footnotes. However, insofar as these theories are founded in conventional assumptions about gender (for instance the notion attributed here to Freud, that 'the male homosexual would begin with a temporary maternal fixation, only to finally identify himself as a woman'), they scarcely encroach upon Molina's idea that he is some kind of woman.[14]

When the warden warns Molina about the 'proficiency' of the people who interrogate political prisoners such as Valentin, a footnote makes a timely shift to the topic of repression (p. 151). Freud's view is set against arguments associated with Wilhelm Reich, Herbert Marcuse and Norman O. Brown: that sexual repression is specially developed in Judaeo–Christian tradition and capitalism, and that it might be (substantially) eliminated. The introduction of these ideas decisively shifts the terrain of *Kiss of the Spider Woman*. In the main text, Valentin is a Marxist and concerned only secondarily with gender and sexual liberation, while Molina sees no virtue in political action – to the point where he endorses a Nazi propaganda film because he is moved by the plight of the female lead. The footnotes invite readers to regard Molina's situation not in terms of his individual, distorted adaptation to normal sexuality and hence to society, but as 'surplus repression' (Marcuse) – 'that part of sexual repression created to maintain the power of the dominant class' (p. 164). Insofar as the warden is attempting to use Molina's vulnerability as a sexual dissident to gain information about Valentin's revolutionary project, Marcuse's theory receives a literal illustration.

Latin America afforded Puig an apposite setting for a discussion of how what are often regarded in the metropolitan sex–gender system as individual matters may be relevant to the power of the State. Diverse regimes engaged in fascistic repression of deviant, minority and progressive tendencies. In 1977 a member of the Argentinian junta declared that the ills of Western society could be traced to three intellectuals: Marx, Freud and Einstein. Martin Edwin Andersen glosses: 'Marx, the admiral said, was guilty of questioning conventional attitudes about private property, Freud of "attacking the sacred internal being of the human person", and Einstein of challenging existing ideas about space and time. He did not mention the fact – he didn't need to – that all three were Jews.'[15] Marcuse might have been grimly satisfied by the admiral's pronouncement.

While the main action of *Kiss of the Spider Woman* focusses upon right-wing regimes, Puig's investigation of the revolutionary significance of sexuality in the footnotes intervenes most effectively within leftist attitudes. Notoriously, homosexuals were persecuted systematically in Fidel Castro's socialist regime, until very recently. The Cuban revolution had been energised partly by resistance to United States exploitation, including sex tourism, and Stalinist dogma found fertile ground in traditional Latin American prejudices against *maricones*.[16]

The last authority in the footnotes is 'the Danish doctor Anneli Taube' – according to Pamela Bacarisse, an expert invented by Puig.[17] Taube says that, in refusing the oppressive masculinity of the father, the sensitive boy 'is actually exercising a free and revolutionary choice inasmuch as he is rejecting the role of the stronger, the exploitative one' (*Kiss*, p. 207). The problem is that the available alternative model is the boy's mother, and her world is marked by submission. Hence 'the imitative attitude practised, until very recently, by a high percentage of homosexuals, an attitude imitative, above all, of the defects of heterosexuality. What has been characteristic of male homosexuals is a submissive spirit, a conservative attitude, a love of peace at any cost, even at the cost of perpetuating their own marginality' (pp. 211–12). Hence, Taube adds, the customary mistrust of gays in socialist milieux. But that was 'until very recently'. Now change is occurring, because the emergence of the women's liberation movement is discrediting 'those unattainable but tenaciously imitated roles of "strong male" and "weak female". The subsequent formation of homosexual liberation fronts is one proof of that' (p. 214). In other words, Molina's stance is being superseded as a progressive, metropolitan politics of gender and sexualities emerges.

Such a change is partially adumbrated in Molina's development towards the end of *Kiss of the Spider Woman*. Valentin makes him promise not to let himself be kicked around; he takes a more independent stance towards his mother and Gabriel. The report on his death indicates that he had expected to be killed and perhaps courted it. Marta, in Valentin's final dream, wonders whether Molina died happily for a just cause, or in order to be like a tragic movie heroine. Both may be true, but above all, I think, he dies for love of Valentin (he agrees to work for the guerillas while Valentin is fucking him, and after his release looks repeatedly from his window toward the prison). This may be regarded either as a continuation of the pattern of feminine martyrdom (which, it could then be argued, Valentin exploits for the ends of his movement even while he criticises it), or as a manifestation of a nobler commitment, to love and hence to revolutionary change. The manner of Molina's death corresponds to the new gay mode identified by doctor Taube – he repudiates 'a submissive spirit, a conservative attitude, a love of peace at any cost' (p. 212). But he does it in a paradoxical adaptation of the Latin American style: first, he is responding to Valentin's demand that he act like a man; second, he is still (partly) like a heroine from one of his movies.

Furthermore, Molina contributes thereby to a programme not of personal sexual liberation, in the manner construed in Western social democracies, but of general political liberation. For although he contrives to protect Valentin from torture and thus gains his protective affection, eventually Valentin is tortured and Molina is killed. Individual liberation gets you only so far. Like Marcuse, *Kiss of the Spider Woman* finally situates sexual oppression within the general oppression of the State. In this light, Valentin's wariness of what both he and Molina perceive as womanly sentiment represents neither personal sterility nor conventional masculine gender construction, but a pragmatic assessment of the dangerous conditions within which opponents of the State must function.

Paradoxically, as Valentin points out, it is the prison cell that frees Molina and himself from customary constraints: 'In a sense we're perfectly free to behave however we choose with respect to one another, am I making myself clear? It's as if we were on some desert island . . . Because, well, outside of this cell we may have our oppressors, yes, but not inside' (pp. 201–2). Yet, we see, even this space is in fact subject to State interference – the interaction between the two men is partly determined by the contrivances pressed upon Molina by the warder.

While Puig slants his narrative towards the metropolitan sex–gender system, therefore, he also questions its emphasis on merely individual fulfilment. If such an insight is specially provoked by fascistic regimes in Latin America, we should not imagine that is irrelevant in the West – which has done much to sustain those regimes.

Becoming a man

I have been trying to use traditional Latin American sex–gender assumptions to expose the construction of metropolitan assumptions. The crucial difference (to recapitulate) is that the Latin American sex–gender system makes the gender of one's partner less important, so long as a man maintains the dominant, masculine role, and hence a conventional gender hierarchy. Nevertheless, gender hierarchy and the notion that dissident sexuality should be interpreted in terms of freakish gender abnormality are not foreign to the metropolitan sex–gender system. The notion of the female soul in the male body and the male soul in the female body was propounded by the sexologists at the turn of the century and only partly qualified by Freud. When Quentin Crisp, who was born in 1908, writes in the 1960s that male homosexuals 'must, with every breath they draw, with every step they take, demonstrate that they are feminine', he sounds like Molina.[18]

This idea of queerness fed into the idea that leisure-class men were effeminate – idle and dissolute – anyway, and the notoriety of Oscar Wilde confirmed that they might well be homosexual. In the model which resulted, the effeminate queer gent looked for a partner who was masculine because lower-class; this latter did not need to regard himself as other than normal, and would very likely marry.

For many mid-twentieth-century would-be gay men this emphasis on effeminacy was perplexing and distressing. One says: 'There was one particular guy who was the very first extremely effeminate gay I'd ever met – and he was my worst fear. I kept thinking, "I think I know I'm homosexual, but that's what homosexuals are – and I'm not like that".'[19] The central project in the self-assertion of metropolitan gay men, since the riot at the Stonewall Inn in New York in 1969, has been the attempt to rehandle gender assignment and gender hierarchy, and hence to repel the stigma of effeminacy. This has involved (i) claiming masculinity for gay men, (ii) declaring that gay femininity is all right, and (iii) various combinations of (i) and (ii). The story is

further complicated by the fact that we have been pursuing
divergent modes of validation. Some of us want to say that our
gender attributes (whatever they are) don't make us very different
from other people and homophobia is just a misunderstanding;
others want to say that les/bi/gay versions of gender attributes
are fundamentally dissident and subversive of hetero-patriarchy,
and hence are indeed, and properly, disturbing to other people.
Gay Liberation has been broadly egalitarian in tone, and has
tended to disavow or evade other hierarchies as well – of class,
age and race. But the masculine/feminine boundary has produced
the most urgent defensive work.

Overall, I locate six tendencies in gender management among
gay-identified men in the metropolitan model, as exemplified
centrally in North America and North-western Europe today:

(a) any gay man may wear masculine jeans and T-shirts (and
    perhaps boots and a moustache), regardless of his preferred
    role in bed;
(b) any gay man may wear feminine or androgynous clothes,
    regardless of his preferred role in bed;
(c) a gay man may do almost anything in bed, without regard
    to conventional gendered roles;
(d) even if two men maintain gendered roles in appearance
    and/or in bed, this does not thereby constitute a hierarchy
    (it does not bear a particular relation to who does the
    housework or drives the car);
(e) any gay cultivation of gendered roles may be either parodic
    or in earnest, and sometimes both at once;
(f) above all, there are few distinct terms for gendered roles:
    in the dominant gay perception, *all these men are gay*.[20]

Mapping the influences upon this metropolitan gay identity – in
its diverse manifestations – would be a substantial task. We would
have to consider the initial radical influence of the Gay Liberation
Front, the countervailing pressure to conform, and the persistence
of both into the present time; the (partial) decline in class and
familial deference; how the women's movement has interacted

with changing patterns of employment and family to redefine femininity, and to some extent masculinity; the development of the notion that citizenship is mainly a matter of consuming; and the hegemony of the United States (for 'pioneer' notions of maleness are deeply inscribed in US ideology and the metropolitan male gay image is very 'American').

These influences have affected lesbians also. However, because women are likely to be perceived as aspiring to masculine prestige, rather than declining into feminine indignity, their situation is not symmetrical with that of men. They are coping with the subordination of women, as well as the stigma of 'wrong' gender assignment, but still the rehandling of gender hierarchy has been important. Sue-Ellen Case describes how the butch/femme pattern was suppressed during the heyday of radical feminism, but is now reasserted both as a notable historical formation (for instance by Joan Nestle) and as productive in the current situation.[21]

However, the dominant sex–gender ideology is hardly to be overthrown, nor even notably reoriented, by some gay men, or for that matter some lesbians, growing moustaches. The fact that we have been following divergent strategies – trying to collude with gender norms and trying to subvert them – indicates the extent to which we have been thrashing around in a system that allows us few good options. It is doubtful whether, without a huge change in hetero-normative patterns, the system could afford to concede masculinity to gays. For however manly a gay man appears, he unsettles the principle that men fuck women; indeed, the more manly he appears, the more he may unsettle it. And, conversely (for when you are coming from the subordinate position you generally lose both ways round), the *macho* gay man is likely to appear excessive and, anyway, will never be as masculine as a heterosexual male.

In practice, we all know, the stigma of effeminacy is fully available today to the press, in the playground, and in male-bonding contexts of all kinds. As Cornwall remarks, 'Attributing passivity as an essential attribute of a particular category is, then, an act of power that serves to legitimize inequalities rather than define them.'[22] Enveloped in this hostile ideology, many gay men themselves still believe, though perhaps residually, that the insertee is feminine and hence inferior. Stephen O. Murray asked a sample of gay men in San Francisco whether gay men tend to be effeminate and got very dusty answers.[23] But the sample doth protest too much; effeminacy remains crucial in our subculture. In a study of gay and straight consumer preferences, Nancy A. Rudd got divergent readings on scent: 'floral, sweet fragrance categories and oriental, spicy categories' were preferred by homosexual men, while 'heterosexual men preferred woody, green fragrance categories'.[24] Notice how the feminine correlates with the oriental, the masculine with the (pioneer) woodman.

For Andrew Holleran, Latin Americans have a truth that needs to be outed. He accepts the question: 'What is your take on the gay man's obsession with the straight man?' Gay men, Holleran replies, are

> trying to complete themselves, trying to get masculinity out of this other person because they don't feel they have it . . . the logical conclusion of that value system would be a straight man. And when you read Latin American writers like Manuel Puig, Reinaldo Arenas, they've even said in interviews they can't even understand gay bars or homosexuals going to be with each other. Then they say, 'Well, who's the man then?'[25]

As I have suggested, this is too simple as an account of Puig, and it hardly begins to measure the complexity of gay lives today.

But it does help us to see that, in the last analysis, all this is less to do with gayness than with the dominance of men over women. That is what gender hierarchy is about. It is perhaps obvious that perceptions of lesbians are dependent on perceptions of women. But for gay men also, I believe, there can be no ultimately positive prospects while the 'feminine' is inferior or secondary. Noting how mainstream films clean up representations of gay men, Michael Cunningham adds:

> at certain angles and in certain lights hatred of gay men can be hard to distinguish from hatred of women. We gay men are sometimes reviled, I believe, because there are straight people

who associate our lives and habits with the lives and habits of women. I worry that a certain equation is developing. The less like a woman a gay man is, the more eagerly movie-goers will embrace him.[26]

So long as women are regarded as feminine and inferior, lesbians and gay men will be in difficulty. Sexual liberation requires a shift in the entire sex–gender system, and that will not occur without women's liberation.

Crystal Boys/Evil Sons

Pai Hsien-yung's novel, translated in 1990 from the revised edition of 1984 as *Crystal Boys*, illuminates a further set of issues. It is set in Taipei (Taiwan) in 1970, and focusses upon a group of runaway boy prostitutes, exploring their interactions and their relations with their families, clients and backers. The title of the translation by Howard Goldblatt, *Crystal Boys*, renders the term used in the novel for homosexuals. However, the Chinese title of the novel is *Neih-Tzu*, which means 'evil sons'. This seems to me such an important change that I intend to use the Chinese title of the novel, even though I am quoting from Goldblatt's translation and have no acquaintance with Chinese languages (however, I do have some help from friends).[27] For the crucial factor is the relation of these boys to the concept of family. Their homo-sexuality is an affront to their fathers' expectations: that is the motor of the novel.

The story begins with the expulsion of the central character, A-qing, from home and school for being 'caught in an immoral act with the lab supervisor':

> Father was running after me, his large, husky frame swaying as he ran. He was brandishing the pistol he'd carried as a brigade commander back on the Mainland . . . He was screaming in a trembling, hoarse voice filled with anguish and fury:
> YOU SCUM! YOU FILTHY SCUM![28]

A-qing's father had been a regimental commander, decorated in the war against Japan, but subsequently disgraced by being captured; he was relying on A-qing to restore the family's reputation by following in his footsteps. Becoming a crystal boy – an evil son – is the absolute negation of such aspirations.

In *Nieh-Tzu* the demand to please and emulate the father dominates the social structure, and gayness is constituted primarily in its terms. In the concluding episode A-qing picks up a new runaway: why isn't he at home? 'He lowered his head and didn't answer' (p. 327). Like A-qing, he has been thrown out of his home by the father, the reader probably infers. Wang Kuilong (Dragon Prince), who was so deeply in love with Phoenix Boy that he killed him because he couldn't accept his infidelities, was expelled from the country by his father and did not return until after his father's death (this story has mythic significance for the crystal boys). 'It's the Wang family's misfortune to have had an evil son like me. Father's reputation was ruined because of it', Dragon Prince says (p. 255). Little Jade cultivates sugar daddies as a way of searching for his emigré father – to the point where A-qing thinks him a little crazy. 'What do you know? People like you, who've got fathers, don't know shit! I won't rest, dead or alive, until I've found that goddam father of mine!' (p. 131). Conversely, Lin *san* cannot take Little Jade to Tokyo, as he would like, because of his son. Not his wife, notice (pp. 130–1); women hardly come into it – any independent action by them appears disreputable in this novel.

The authoritative figure in the novel is Fu Chongshan, a former military commander and successful businessman. He is 'not part of the gay community' (p. 196), but he protects the boys (they call him 'Papa'): he pays their medical bills, gets them released when they are arrested, supports the Cozy Nest venture (an attempt to create an alternative home for the boys in a café-bar). Fu Chongshan does all this because his son shot himself after his military career was destroyed when he was discovered in homosexual relations and Fu Chongshan rejected him, and because he subsequently met and talked with Phoenix Boy – on the night, as it turned out, of his death.

Despite his commitment to the boys, Fu Chongshan declares

plainly and repeatedly that it is the plight of the fathers that is important. 'How could A-wei, whom I'd raised to adulthood by myself, the son I loved and revered, a young man perfectly suited to the military, do something so shameful, so despicable, and with one of his own soldiers?' he asks A-qing (p. 260). He says Little Jade's obsessive search for his father is 'a good thing' (p. 292). The persistent image of the father as military hero raises the stakes; A-qing's favourite reading is a martial arts novel in which the warrior father has to kill his son for the sake of honour.[29]

Towards the end of the novel A-qing is made to realise the offence he has committed against his father: 'my knowledge of the terrible agony he was enduring pressed down more and more heavily on my heart. That unbearable agony was probably what I was trying to hide from.' However, there is no going back: 'I had to keep away from Father because I knew I couldn't bear to see the look of anguish on his devastated face' (p. 265). There is no opportunity for reconciliation; no resolution. A-qing can only live with the knowledge that he is not the son his father wanted.

Such respect for family, defined as the honour of the father, is central to the Confucian ideology that has traditionally informed Chinese societies. Harmony and moral stability are secured when individuals are situated as superior and inferior on the basis of age, social position and moral cultivation. Bret Hinsch sums up the consequences for same-sex relations:

> Whereas Westerners generally disparage homosexuality for religious and ethical reasons, to most Chinese homosexuality seems evil because it disrupts the accepted life cycle. They see the self-identified homosexual, who foregoes heterosexual marriage and the raising of children, as a grave enemy of the family structure, which still forms the foundation of Chinese society. And they are correct in asserting that the homosexual who refuses to marry is alien to the Chinese tradition.[30]

This may mean, as in Latin America, that the man who marries but goes with boys may not be greatly disapproved of. (I consider shortly how far this tradition informs the scope for same-sex passion in Taiwan today; as I have noted, *Neih-Tzu* is set in 1970.)

The gay world in *Neih-Tzu* is organised through a mirror version of the patriarchal-paternal-patronal structure. Fu Chongshan is called 'Papa' and said to be 'family'; Yang Jinhai, the boys' well-connected leader, is called 'Chief'; even 'Dada', the gardener at the park where the boys gather, is Grandpa Guo. Chief Yang arranges or approves new punters for the boys; he says the relation is one of master and disciple. Lin *san* understands this: when he wants to put Little Jade into conventional work he undertakes an elaborate negotiation with the Chief to gain his permission (pp. 93–4). The dependence of the boys on these men corresponds to the hierarchy of the wider, legitimate world.

Patriarchal-paternal-patronal relations form the fantasy base for the boys' sexuality as well. Little Jade makes this clear: 'I'm going to search every inch of Japan, and if Papa Fu was right when he said that Heaven will have mercy on me, one day I'll track down my father. You know the first thing I'm going to do when I find him? I'm going to take a bite out of that bastard's dick and ask him why he had to bring a bastard like me into the world to suffer like this' (p. 319). Little Jade takes it for granted that he will become aware of the identity of his father during a sexual encounter. Little Jade is not the only boy seeking to reconstitute a lost family. Wu Min is confident that he is wanted only when he is being abused by an older man, and A-qing is looking to create a relationship like that which he had with his deceased brother.

Of course, the father–son scenario is perfectly recognisable in the West. It is, if you like, the story of *Hamlet*. However, Westerners are likely to regard it as a hang-up with which the boy has to come to terms. Richard Isay in his book *Being Homosexual* comes surprisingly close to the Taiwanese model. He refuses the Freudian notion that a dysfunctional family pattern produces gay boys: rather, we are born that way, and therefore likely to have adaptational problems – deriving, above all, from a longing for the father who has withdrawn himself, probably because he doesn't like having a sissy son. Isay proposes a therapy that will help gay men overcome the consequent sense of worthlessness, and urges a reevaluation of gay – feminine –

qualities: placing the same value 'upon sensitivity, compassion, nurturing, and loving as on aggressivity, competition, and productivity'.[31] To my mind, Isay is trying to re-use too many of the oppressive constructs of the prevailing gender hierarchy. But whether or not we share his precise analysis, most Westerners will share his assumption that it is the effects on the psychological make-up of the boy that are important. In *Neih-Tzu* the opposite assumption prevails. It is the disappointed fathers who are entitled to sympathy and respect. Hence, I think, Goldblatt's 'mistranslation' of the title: he has westernized it by shifting the emphasis from the filial relation to the boys.

To me, as a Western reader, it seems that these boys are coerced, psychically as well as physically, into a fantasy attempt to retrieve the ideal, or anyway the necessary, family. With their (feminised) bodies they are trying to win the love of a surrogate for the father who has rejected them. However, since it is their femininity that has caused the problem, the project must be futile. The men who will love them are men they will have difficulty respecting, and when A-qing meets a worthwhile potential partner he is too ashamed to allow a relationship to develop. 'I couldn't tell him about all those dark nights in low-class hotels behind the train station, or about the filth that was left on my body by those faceless men in the foul-smelling public toilets' (p. 271).

The attempt to recover the lost ideal family falls the more oddly (on Western ears) because the families in *Neih-Tzu* are all violent and unsatisfactory. The fathers abscond or are in prison; they physically abuse their wives and children, but succeed in controlling neither. Their vaunted military ethos is scarcely relevant to their present situation; A-qing's father 'didn't know how to do anything else' and can manage only a sinecure job; another boy's father used to fly bomber planes but now raises chickens (pp. 49, 63). If the father is absent, the older brother is brutal instead. A-qing finds the gay world incompatible with positive relationships: 'We were all reaching out hungrily, desperately, violently, to clutch, scratch, tear, rend each other, trying to retrieve something from other's bodies that we'd lost in our own' (p. 102). This is presented as a consequence of gayness, but might, as plausibly, be regarded as a consequence of the family.

There is one point where A-qing entertains the idea of purposeful rebellion: Fu Chongshan's son, he thinks, must have resented his father hugely to kill himself on Fu Chongshan's birthday. However, even that thought has already been placed, earlier on the same page, by Fu Chongshan: 'All you kids know how to do is be resentful of your fathers, but have you ever thought about how much your fathers have suffered because of you, or how deeply?' (p. 264). Rebellion is not validated. Rather, the boys all embark upon a process of reform and relative respectability as *Neih-Tzu* draws to a close. Also, they are approved insofar as they take on more militaristic attributes. 'Chief Yang was like a drill instructor calling out the names of his troops'; in the last episode A-qing, thinking of his days as platoon leader at school, shouts 'Left right', as he and a boy he has picked up run down the road together (pp. 324, 328).

A pertinent interface with the metropolitan sex–gender system occurs in Ang Lee's film *The Wedding Banquet* (Taiwan, 1992). Wai-Tung and Simon look like the usual perfect Manhattan couple of the US gay-affirmative movie, but Wai-Tung is under pressure to marry from his Taiwanese parents (the father, again, an ex-general). So he and Wei-Wei, who likes Wai-Tung and wants a work permit, decide to marry and Mr and Mrs Gao come to celebrate. The intrusion of the parents on the New Yorkers increases hugely when it is pointed out that they deserve a wedding banquet – 'If you refuse your father that, you are an ungrateful son.' This (to my Western eyes) tiresome event further complicates matters, by making Mr Gao ill so that he and Mrs Gao cannot return home, and Wei-Wei, in a drunken moment, pregnant. Everyone becomes uncomfortable, angry, and very unhappy. Eventually Wai-Tung tells his incredulous mother that he is gay – 'If Papa hadn't wanted a grandchild so much, I'd have been very happy with my life as it is.'

In *The Wedding Banquet*, as in the Japanese films *Okoge* (1992) and *Twinkle* (1992), Chris Berry observes, there is no question of 'coming out' in the sense of becoming separated from blood relatives: 'the possibility of a satisfactory life outside the family is not even considered; instead, the problem is how to reconcile gay identity with a position inside the Confucian family'.[32] At each crisis in *The Wedding Banquet* it is agreed: they mustn't tell father, it would kill him. Eventually, however, Mr Gao tells Simon that he knows anyway – he understands English. But, he demands, the others are not to know he knows: appearances must be maintained. Reflecting on this moment in the film, I realise how Western (anti-Confucian) my reading of it is. I hate old Mr Gao for this: everybody's life is being ruined so that his feelings will not be hurt, but he knows anyway; and yet still he will not acknowledge his son for who he is. In fact, though, the film is quite even-handed: the deceit has been reciprocal and everyone's feelings are fragile. My assumption (I realise) is that it is all right to deceive parents, who come second to one's intimate-partner relations and cannot expect to be taken seriously unless they accommodate themselves to contemporary values. Conversely, I am disappointed that there is very little in the film of the 'alternative' family of the New York gay community.

Wei-Wei eventually pleases everyone by deciding to keep the baby, but there is no true reconciliation. Mr and Mrs Gao can maintain contact with their son (unlike the parents in *Neih-Tzu*) because he will be in New York and not bringing scandal upon them; and Wei-Wei, Wai-Tung and Simon will rear the child in a metropolitan-style neo-family, but only because the grandparents are leaving; in Taipei, on its own ground, the Confucian family would overwhelm them.

The emphasis upon fathers in these Taiwanese contexts may suggest that we might regard homosexuality there as organised around age hierarchy (boys and men), whereas in Latin America it is organised around gender hierarchy (feminine men and real men). David Greenberg starts with this distinction in his survey of homosexualities in kinship-structured societies, and Randolph Trumbach uses it in his discussion of the emergence of the homosexual role in the West.[33] What is striking, however, is that, time and again, when we think we see a model based on age we find that the boys are positioned as feminine, and when we think we have a model based on gender we find that the feminised partners are younger. In *Neih-Tzu* the femininity of the boys is established at the start when Yang Jinhai, their leader, calls them 'You bunch of shit-eating fairies' (p. 20). Boys who might seem masculine are nonetheless feminised: one who is 'husky as an ox' is called 'Little Fairy', and one with 'a wonderful physique' – 'broad shoulders, and a muscular chest' – is called 'the Butch Queen' (pp. 27, 100). A newspaper exposé of their bar, the Cozy Nest, reports: 'here you will find only a group of pretty-faced, scarlet-lipped, giggling "fairies" ' (p. 282).

What we are seeing, I think, here and elsewhere, is a *conflation of subordinations*: since both boys and women figure subordination in these cultures, they can be blurred together. In fact, an attraction of same-sex relations may reside partly in their potential to invoke, simultaneously, two principal social hierarchies. Further, the elaborate social structures of modernity offer equally potent hierarchies of class and race, and they too may be conflated with subordinations of age and gender.

When Little Jade is told that having his hair cut short for work in an office will diminish his sexual attractiveness (*Neih-Tzu*, p. 117), we may wonder what is happening: if clients want someone like a woman, why do they not hire a woman? However, as I remark in chapter 2, it is a mistake to suppose that demonstrating incoherence in a dominant construct exposes its weakness. It appears, rather, that hegemony thrives upon incoherence. The crystal boy may be exploited, alternately and simultaneously, both as a youngster and as a kind of displaced woman; if they can't get you one way, they get you the other. Indeed, it may be a mistake to suppose an original menu of discrete subordinations, wherein everything was simply itself. If the crucial point is the exercise of power difference, then the social categories through which it is articulated may well be secondary.

The young men in *The Wedding Banquet* are another matter again. It is hard to discern any markers of age, gender or even racial hierarchy between them. If you had been supposing that Wai-Tung is sexually passive because Asian, you would be surprised when he conceives a child with Wei-Wei. As in Hanif Kureishi's film *My Beautiful Launderette* (1985), racial difference is the most obvious challenge in the representation of a gay relationship, but the characters appear strangely indifferent to it. The consequence is an apparent triumph over contemporary racism; but since this occurs only magically, it has little purchase upon the world (in fact if it were a heterosexual mixed-race couple running the launderette, the problems for British Asian culture might be greater). In *The Wedding Banquet* this evasion of race occurs probably because Ang Lee is far more interested in the Taiwanese family than in the US gay couple, and therefore takes the line of least resistance with the latter – that is, he follows the post-Stonewall metropolitan gay project, as I have described it, whereby we have tried to disavow gender, and other, hierarchies.

The subversive, almost-silenced undercurrent in *Neih-Tzu* – the point at which it offers a local alternative to the oppressive family – is the relationship among the boys: they experience love, humour, generosity and strength together. In fact, they are said to manifest an egalitarian vision: 'In this kingdom of ours there are no distinctions of social rank, eminence, age, or strength.' However, the positive implication in that sentence is withdrawn as A-qing continues: 'What we share in common are bodies filled with aching, irrepressible desire and hearts filled with insane loneliness' (p. 30).[34] The tone of moral doom pervades the accounts of the boys and strives to disallow any egalitarian social vision. Nonetheless, once an idea is released in a text, it cannot be altogether controlled. The novel permits us to think that the boys' camaraderie deserves to survive the oppressive demands of the wider society.

Such a subversive thought looks forward to a change in Taiwan. *Neith-Tzu* is set in 1970, when the prospect of national military operations was by no means theoretical. As the country of the remnant who did not submit to the Maoist forces, recently freed from Japanese occupation, Taiwan was subjected to the military regime of Chiang Kai Shek, and was a focal point of the Cold War. However, with the presidential election of 1996 it completed a transition to liberal democracy, and at the time of writing there is a small but vigorous gay movement. *Neih-Tzu* begins: 'There are no days in our kingdom, only nights. As the sun comes up, our kingdom goes into hiding, for it is an unlawful nation; we have no government and no constitution, we are neither recognized nor respected by anyone, our citizenry is little more than rabble' (p. 17). A recent pamphlet takes up and revises that picture:

> In our kingdom, we are no longer afraid of daylight, are not forced to remain invisible, for it is no longer an unlawful nation:
> we have reasonable distribution of resources from the government,
> we are fully protected by the laws of the country,
> we are recognized and blessed by the multitude,
> we are being respected by History, which also inscribes us.[35]

The world of the crystal boys is no more, it seems. However, my information is that such campaigning is conducted mainly by people who are not identified (explicitly at least) as lesbian or gay. Coming out, as understood in the metropolitan model, is still scarcely in prospect – one would care too much about the reputation of one's family. But then, it would be facile to assume that Taiwan will follow the same path as Western societies.

Global and local

The temptation, upon encountering these alternative ways of regarding same-sex passion, as Murray observes, is to suppose a 'developmental' model: Third World countries should 'catch up' by producing lesbians and gay men like those in the metropole – just as, at one time, the economies of Third World countries were envisaged as 'underdeveloped', then as 'developing', in the direction marked out by the West.[36] As I have remarked, in some ways that is happening, but it would be arrogant to suppose that metropolitan ideas of sexuality will simply sweep aside indigenous modes, or that they offer the optimum scope for human sexualities. For, as Arjun Appadurai observes, 'the new global economy has to be understood as a complex, overlapping, disjunctive order, which cannot any longer be understood in terms of the existing center-periphery models'.[37] We know only too well that metropolitan gay, lesbian and bisexual identities are not coherent; they are conflicted in themselves and in their interfaces with other aspects of the sex–gender system. So how could they be simply planted, like a flag on a pole, in other countries? 'At least as rapidly as forces from various metropolises are brought into new societies they tend to become indigenized in one or other way', Appadurai says (p. 295).

The power relations in the idea that gayness may simply be internationalised are exposed by Martin F. Manalansan IV, who shows the cultural imperialism in the assumption that the New York Stonewall anniversary march of 1994 should start at the United Nations building, and in the pursuit of 'a universalised and formulaic picture of the future of all gay and lesbian political and cultural efforts' by the International Lesbian and Gay Association.[38] Such an attempt to globalise gayness obscures differences between the metropolis and the places it renders peripheral, and is likely to involve the co-opting of subaltern peoples for the ideological purposes of the expansionist capitalist centre. Manalansan juxtaposes the current uneven adoption of metropolitan constructs in the Philippines and the unease of New York Filipinos with these constructs – including their indifference to the Stonewall anniversary. In particular, the closet and coming out do not seem relevant to them, because in their culture the relation between public and private is differently constituted. Filipinos see public declarations, US-style, as inappropriate, unnecessary and shaming; one informant says: 'I know who I am and most people, including my family, know about me – without any declaration' (p. 434). (Do they get Oprah Winfrey?) Manalansan concludes that we should attend to voices from the margins, and hence gain a better perspective upon the interactions between global and local.

As I have said, I can hope to give only sketches of non-metropolitan systems, hoping to use differences and similarities to raise awareness. But I am interested in the advantages that non-metropolitan arrangements may display. For instance, it does strike me that in comparison with Reaganite/Thatcherite societies, where no one is expected to take responsibility for anyone else, the Confucian family may claim some points. The crystal boys seem to have a better time than, from what I hear, prostitutes in Birmingham, England. At least someone is looking after them. And one of the reasons why education about HIV and AIDS seems not to be working very well in the West is that our young people tend to disdain the wisdom of their elders.

In Latin American countries also, the family is a crucial support; in Mexico, 'contact with parents, siblings, and other family members is, in the long run, [al]most always maintained and cherished', Carrier reports.[39] There are two ways of regarding this:

Taiwan/Latin America	the metropolis
(1) conformity	individuality
(2) community	alienation

At first sight, (1), Taiwanese and Latin American cultures may strike North Americans and North-west Europeans as demanding conformity and failing to allow for individuality; at second sight, (2), they may suggest an idea of community that might ameliorate the alienation we experience in the West.

What is distinctive about the metropolitan sex–gender system, both geographically and historically, is that the nuclear family, and above all the loving couple, have become the source of all meaning and truth. For what else is there? Most people have attenuated relations with wider family networks and neighbour-hoods; no religious or political beliefs worth speaking of; meaningless or positively harmful jobs with no commitment on either side and no real responsibility; few possessions that they have owned for more than a few years; art and literature dominated by market forces. The loving couple is the one place where we expect to find meaning and truth. Of course, only a few partnerships, gay or straight, can bear such a weight of significance – the entire social order is balanced upon them, like an inverted pyramid. No wonder couples crumble and split apart

– often to seek the same ultimate existential justification with another partner.

It is approximation to this pattern that has accorded lesbians and gay men some degree of acceptance in the metropolis. We too form loving couples and, for some at least in the straightgeist and for some of us, the relationship justifies the sexuality. Indeed, insofar as we are pushed out of, or to the edge of, conventional family relations and into the anonymity of cities, we may constitute paradigmatic instances of the pressure toward the exclusive loving-couple pattern. For the post-Stonewall consolidation of our identities has correlated, plainly, with urbanisation and the weakening of traditional family and neighbourhood ties. The *Manifesto* of the London Gay Liberation Front formalised the opposition in 1971: 'The oppression of gay people starts in the basic unit of society, the family, consisting of the man in charge, a slave as his wife, and their children on whom they force themselves as the ideal models. The very form of the family works against homosexuality.'[40]

But can we not do something more creative with all this? – after all, very many les/bi/gay people have parents and children and some of us are trying to look after them in the face of official and other hostility. And cannot other, more various kinds of intimate relations be significant as well? Consider: gays who focus their political energies upon the right to marry are invoking almost the same ideal as 'pro-family' conservatives: two people in an exclusive relationship, with kids if you can get them, cats and dogs if you can't. What needs to be cultivated, perhaps alongside that, is the opportunity to experiment with other kinds of relationship – as, of course, many les/bi/gay people are doing (see Kath Weston's study, *Families We Choose*).[41] We have to develop new structures, not just for pair-bonding but for looking after children, elderly people, and our friends when they are ill or lonely, and for accommodating a range of emotional needs as they change through time.

Simon Edge, in an opinion-piece in *Gay Times*, declares that we pay taxes so that other people can parent, and demands that 'heterosexuals get their act together and learn to bring up their children as responsible members of society. Strong families could well be in our interest'.[42] This is not on.

First, straight or gay, people in the West are not going back to the mythic family of the closed-down 1950s, where once you were married you stayed married (unless you were wealthy) until one of you died from exhaustion. People just won't put up with that. And, speaking practically, the system doesn't want it either: businesses need employees to work unsocial hours and move around, women to work, children to consume. Above all, mothers don't want it. When they are lone parenting it is mostly because the man has made himself objectionable – more of a hindrance than a help. This is generally because of the dominant, 'strong family' idea of what a heterosexual man should be like. Gays know more than enough about that. Should we suppose that queer-bashers suddenly become nice men when they get home and resume their fatherly role? The way forward is to support lone parents, not vilify them. They are bearing, for the rest of us, the overwhelming burden of caring for the next generation. This must be recognised and endorsed: we must exhort the State to fund it, and everyone else must help as best they can.

Second, we do care for children. Many lesbians, bisexuals and gay men have children of their own, and many of us are involved in medical, social, nursery, educational and therapeutic services. The rest of us should be looking for opportunities to help out as 'uncles' and 'aunts'. Because of our distinctive experiences, we tend to know things about children that others may not. Our influence upon them may be a good deal more humane and progressive than what politicians mean by 'the family'.

The Mexican film *Doña Herlinda and Her Son* (directed by Jaime Humberto Hermosillo, 1985) is fun in this context. Ramón, a music student, is in love with Rodolfo, a doctor who returns his passion but feels obliged to go along with the plans of his mother, Doña Herlinda, for his marriage. She is more or less aware of the situation, and invites Ramón into the house as part of the family. She even draws Ramón's suspicious mother into complicity.

Ramón is very distressed by the marriage, but Olga, the wife, explains to him that she has married to free herself from her conservative family. She is independent, capable, politically active, and intends to study abroad for a year; evidently she knows the score and doesn't wish to keep Rodolfo to herself. She gives Ramón food for thought when she points out that Rodolfo is a male chauvinist, and they become close. Mother and daughter-in-law go shopping, making it clear that there is plenty of time for Ramón and Rodolfo to make love. Doña Herlinda announces that she is developing the property so that they will each have private living space. The film ends with Ramón helping Olga look after the baby at the christening party.

For a gay viewer socialised into the metropolitan sex–gender system, the effect is puzzling as well as pleasing. The manipulative skill of the mother is awesome, the priority accorded to marriage is disappointing, and Ramón, who is truly in love, seems to be giving most. But *Doña Herlinda and Her Son* has a different, non-metropolitan starting point, and hence is able to achieve a distinctive conservative and radical ideological blend. Conservative elements are that Doña Herlinda needs a grandson at any cost; Olga can't escape her family without marrying; and Rodolfo is allowed to have sex with anyone he chooses so long as he appears *macho* and doesn't make a statement out of it. Radical elements are Olga's feminism, Ramón's dignity and commitment, and Ramón's involvement in childcare. The outcome is that no one is excluded, or even marginalised, including the widowed Doña Herlinda and her grandson. Compare *The Wedding Banquet*, where the parents have to be sent home and the wife relegated for the metropolitan-style gay relationship to have a happy ending. Or the fate of Rose in *The Lost Language of Cranes* by David Leavitt, and so many real-life comings out, where the wife has to be ditched in the interests of the husband's expression of gayness.

If *Doña Herlinda and Her Son* presents a utopian version of the scope of the Latin American family, it also promotes a critique – of Rodolfo, the son. The pampered *macho* male, the object of everybody's passionate attention, is pleasant, but lazy, vain, self-regarding and rather boring. He is entirely amiable, but then he has no reason not to be. It is not so nice for a boy to be the only child, Ramón says, as Olga embarks upon perpetuating the process with the infant Rodolfo. This critique allows us to recognise the importance of the relationships which do not require masculinity – between the women, between them and Ramón, between Ramón and the baby. True, these relationships revolve around the *macho* head of the family, but they are not contained by him. Indeed, a bedroom shot towards the end indicates that Ramón (to use the terms of the Latin American system) takes the part of the man with Rodolfo. The film shows how the family may open out into diverse spaces for alternative kinds of relating.

Reproduction and recreation

'Well, we all know what we mean by the family' (Tony Blair, Radio 4, October 1996)

If many of these variations upon the themes of gender hierarchy and family, in the metropolis and elsewhere, hinge upon new negotiations of family patterns, the ultimate issue still has traditional ideas of family at its core. It is the distinction between reproductive or procreative sex on the one hand, and recreative or pleasure-oriented sex on the other. In the Judaeo-Christian tradition, and on into sociobiology, psychoanalysis and psychiatry, sexual behaviour that cannot result in legitimate procreation is derogated as at best secondary ('foreplay'), at worst, inferior, perverse. It is this ideology that requires gender hierarchy: men have to penetrate women, who have to submit. Guilt and stigma attach to all other sexual practices. As Michèle Barrett and Mary McIntosh remark, this division does not operate evenly, for 'women's sexual pleasure has no procreative function whereas the man's orgasm in intercourse is necessary to conception'.[43]

In some measure, the demand that sexual activity be reproductive, at least in its potential outcome, is being displaced by the notion – which has partially licensed lesbian and gay relationships – that whatever a stable, loving couple does is more-or-less-all-right. However, that emergent notion, insofar as it proposes a monogamous couple, has an underlying correlation with the procreative model, and it is under persisting challenge from pro-family lobbies, religious fundamentalists of various kinds, and strangely resurgent socio-biological theories. Some gay men, even, are taking this line. Holleran says: 'Men look at women physically because they're looking for fertile young vessels for their sperm, who can give them children.' He seems to think this explains why gay men 'don't care about the content of the mind or the character' of the men they are attracted to – as if a preference for 'fertile young vessels' would guarantee rewarding personal relationships to straight men. What women might be looking for doesn't get mentioned.[44] And Mark Simpson, as part of his 'anti-gay' agenda, accuses gays of perversely vaunting their independence of procreation: 'Nature and heterosexuality have no claim on you anymore as you become a godlike creature of culture. By heroically refusing to allow contact between penis and vagina the gay man refuses to accept his mortality.'[45] But has social constructionism been making people feel godlike? And should heterosexual passion (more than any other) be reminding us of death?

Simpson complains that gay men who come out feel that 'There are no longer any conflicts to be told, any mysteries to unravel or any dreams to be interpreted', and that they can 'leave psycho-analysis behind' (p. 8). The Freud to whom he would return us is, I suppose, the one who records a breakthrough in the 'Wolfman' analysis at the point where the boy 'discovered the vagina and the biological significance of masculine and feminine. He understood now that active was the same as masculine, while passive was the same as feminine.'[46] This will be the Freud who asks himself 'how does a girl pass from her mother to an attachment to her father? or, in other words, how does she pass from her masculine phase to the feminine one to which she is biologically destined?'[47]

HIV and AIDS, Christopher Robinson observes, have rein-forced 'a public mythology which gives a moral basis to the procreational sex/recreational sex opposition by setting the equation heterosexuality=monogamy=procreation=life against the equation homosexuality = promiscuity = disease = death'.[48] The virulence of the hostility toward gay men that the AIDS pandemic has released, it occurs to me, is proportionate to the idea, which was getting into general circulation around 1980, that gays were doing better with the sex-and-love questions. We seemed to have learned a few tricks that straights had yet to develop. Gay men had organised genial ways of meeting for casual sex, and also loving couples that might manage, even, to evade gendered roles. They knew how to see other men without falling out with their partners; how to go to bed with friends, how to remain on close terms with former lovers, how to make a virtue of age and class differences. They were at ease experimenting with kinky games; they were getting the fun back into sex. In other words, we were promoting not just homosexuality, but recreative sex – alongside other tendencies towards sexual and gender liberation.

For the right-wing bigot, therefore, AIDS was a godsend (so to speak): it proves that sex is for reproduction, within 'the family'. The gross irony here is that the only sex act that cannot be protected from HIV infection – the only one where some kind of barrier, latex or whatever, cannot be interposed – is that designed to be procreative. Yet heterosexual AIDS is always somewhere else and the mode of transmission somehow illicit or obscure. You *never* hear procreative sex discussed as, intrinsically, a high-risk activity.

For Camille Paglia, AIDS is the price of sexual adventure. 'We asked: why should I obey this law? and why shouldn't I act on every sexual impulse? The result was a descent into barbarism. We painfully discovered that a just society cannot, in fact, function if everyone does his own thing. And out of the pagan promiscuity of the Sixties came AIDS.' Like the markets, you can't buck nature. Hence, according to Paglia, the death of Foucault: he 'was struck down by the elemental force he repressed and edited out of his system'.[49] When Paglia declares that 'homosexuality is not "normal" ', she does not mean statistically, but humanly:

> Queer theorists – that wizened crew of flimflamming free-loaders – have tried to take the poststructuralist tack of claiming

that there is no norm, since everything is relative and contingent
... [But] in nature, procreation is the single, relentless rule.
That is the norm. Our sexual bodies were designed for
reproduction. Penis fits vagina: no fancy linguistic game playing
can change that biologic fact.[50]

Paglia says she is anti-Christian, so the *design* – 'our sexual bodies
were designed for reproduction' – must be that encoded by
evolution over millions of years, during which only those peoples
who reproduced effectively survived. The problem with this is
that rape and pillage were probably also very effective for survival.
Hence, I daresay, Paglia's admiration for 'strong' people: 'It is in
the best interests of the human race, and of women themselves,
for men to be strong. Inspired by my Italian heritage, with its
blazingly assertive personae, I call for strong men and strong
women, not strong women and castrated men' (pp. 85–6). This
leads her to declare that homophobic bullying by 'fractious young
boys' is good for the race because it enables such boys to establish
a proper masculinity (pp. 85–6).

In my view the error in socio-biology has nothing to do with
poststructuralism, or 'everything' being 'relative and contingent'.
More simply, it is just not so easy to say what is good for the
human race. A society composed of Paglia's powerful Italians –
Vittoria Accoramboni and Mussolini, perhaps – would not work
very well. Human welfare and survival may depend, just as
plausibly, upon the adaptability and variability of organs as upon
their alleged original function. We might, for instance, regard
homosexuality as a valuable way of limiting population growth,
alternative to the main strategy that has featured hitherto – war.
But then, war does give men opportunity to stamp around feeling
masterful.

Again, the initial vogue for socio-biology, in the late-nineteenth
and early-twentieth century, was linked to maintaining a supposed
racial purity, facilitating ideologically the pogroms and world
wars that accompanied the consolidation and expansion of the
nation-state.[51] But it is at least as plausible that further racial
mixing is to humankind's general advantage, and even to the

advantage of the current phase of global capitalism – witness the collapse of the apartheid regime in South Africa.

To be sure, people, including lesbians and gay men, should have reproductive sex when they want to and when it is socially responsible; if they did not, the race would die out. However, at the moment there is not a shortage of human beings. Our sex organs are no more *for* reproduction, in the world today, than our noses are for sniffing out predators.

Two things are superficially attractive about Paglia's line. One is that she calls upon lesbians and gays to reconsider fashionable positions; but, unfortunately, she merely ushers us back into the ones that were fashionable before (eg. gay men are sensitive and artistic). The other is that she does make male homosexuality appear significant: she declares it 'revolutionary' – a revolt against nature (pp. 70–1). However, such a revolt would, of course, have to be doomed, so gay men are 'aliens, cursed and gifted, the shamans of our time' (p. 86). Again, Paglia is drawing us back – into a vein of tragi-romantic posturing that we have been trying to grow out of. Her mode is precisely reactionary: everything that we have traditionally been said to be doing is identified as the way the world has to be.

If recreational sex is revolutionary (and Marcuse for one thought that it was), it is because the privileging of reproduction as the proper context for sexual expression has been connected profoundly with the distribution of wealth, the subordination of women, the socialisation of children, the maintenance of labour and other power relations, the pursuit of fantasies of racial purity, and the establishment of nationhood. That is why such frantic ideological work occurs around it. Judge Geoffrey Jones was faced with an eighteen-year-old man who had admitted sexually assaulting 9–10 year-olds – two boys, and then a girl. His barrister claimed he had been 'experimenting' to discover whether he was heterosexual or homosexual. Judge Jones noted that he had been moving in the right direction, and hence judged that a custodial sentence would be inappropriate for this 'normal young man': 'He is, after all, heterosexual. It is a sort of breath of fresh air, isn't it? The indecent assault is an expression of his sexuality.'[53]

We need to find ways beyond the procreative/recreative framework of thought. Because reproductive sex has held the monopoly of seriousness for two thousand years in the West, not a lot of consideration has been given to how alternatives may best be managed. Willy nilly, Westerners place recreational sex as frivolous, naughty, transient, self-indulgent; to do with pleasure and choice, and therefore – in our culture – not with responsibility and obligation. Walt Odets, even, in his splendid book *In the Shadow of the Epidemic*, uses 'recreational' as interchangeable with 'anonymous', in contrast with 'ongoing relationships'.[52] That is a mistake, but we do still have to find an accommodation that will enable us to repudiate the gender hierarchy, sexism and homophobia of the ideology of reproduction while sustaining love relationships, friendships, nurturing of children, care of the sick, appreciation of the elderly, and something partly like our families, pretended and otherwise.

4 AIDS, art, and subcultural myth

Art and the undiscussable

The renowned dance critic of the *New Yorker*, Arlene Croce, caused a stir in December 1994 with an essay entitled 'Discussing the Undiscussable'. She explained that she was refusing to visit the ballet/performance piece *Still/Here* by Bill T. Jones, because it included videotape of people with AIDS talking about themselves. In Croce's view this intrusion of personal material made the work unavailable to her as a critic of dance. 'For me, Jones is undiscussable', she says, 'because he has taken sanctuary among the unwell.'[1] Croce wants 'disinterested art' (p. 56), whereas Jones has created 'a kind of messianic travelling show, designed to do some good for sufferers of fatal illnesses, both those in the cast and those thousands more who may be in the audience' (p. 54). She makes *Still/Here* the ground for a general attack on 'victim art' and on public funding bodies in the United States that seek to justify themselves by supporting art that addresses minority communities (Jones is African-American, gay and HIV-positive; the photographs of Robert Mapplethorpe also, Croce believes, 'effectively disarmed criticism'; p. 58).

Unsurprisingly, Croce found supporters. Hilton Kramer, editor of *The New Criterion*, for instance, was keen to join the attack on 'philistine incomprehension of the nature of art and a blatant attempt to impose political standards on the creation of art'. But Croce's *opponents* – anyway, the ones who got printed in the *New Yorker* correspondence – did not repudiate her idea of art. She should at least have seen the work, they said; she was trying to censor free expression; she confused the dancer and the dance; art is born out of human reality; artists have always suffered from insensitive criticism.[2]

A radical response would say, rather, that PWAs (persons with

AIDS), with their lovers, friends, families and allies, do indeed constitute a distinct cultural and political constituency, and that our criteria for a rewarding artwork may not be those that will greatly move people located elsewhere. It would repudiate the implication that themes and techniques which move straightgeist critics are more real, more important and more appropriate for public representation. It would refuse the customary idea of 'art'.

The point is simple, and should be familiar: an allegedly universal culture, such as art is conventionally claimed to be, tends to subordinate other cultures: it is defined as *not* special to a locality, gender, sexual orientation, race. It 'rises above' such matters – and, in so doing, it pushes them down. As Gregory Woods puts it, 'The trouble with the universalising tendency – as others have said before me – is that, at worst, it is pandering to the requirement of WASP men that minorities deprive themselves of the right to a distinctive voice; at best, it becomes generalised and apolitical.'[3] The offence of Jones and his cast, in fact, is that they have *not* caved in like victims, but have maintained their viewpoints with independence and determination. They have not accepted the idea, which Douglas Crimp exposed back in 1987, that AIDS may be worthwhile, and gay people redeemed, if they play along with art and literature as conventionally understood.[4] They have contributed, I shall argue, to a *subcultural myth* – a collective, ongoing, lived scenario through which we create and recreate ourselves.

AIDS is affecting all kinds of people around the world, but because its transmission does have a distinctively gay aspect, because it has been labelled a gay plague in the West, and because many gay men – and lesbians – have embraced PWAs as our business, the story of HIV and AIDS has become inseparable from the story of gayness. As Simon Watney observes, AIDS 'threatens to corrode the most fundamental level of social "belonging" in most gay men's lives, namely those bonds of friendship and shared personal histories that constitute our sense of gay identity'.[5] It attacks us not just as individuals. We have been reconstituted, as a subculture, by AIDS.

We are mourning not just our friends, but the kinds of people that we had hoped to become. 'I never dreamt that I would get to be / The creature that I always meant to be' – so sang Neil Tennant in the Pet Shop Boys' 'Being Boring'. The song links the 1970s gay man to the 1920s bright young things; unlike intervening generations, we would not be intimidated by the straightgeist. Anyway, we thought, 'You could always rely on a friend'. The mourning is for the reliance as well as the friend. Thom Gunn, in his poem 'The Missing', feels bare, exposed, chilly – like a statue; whereas, before, he was surrounded by friends: 'The warmth investing me / Led outward through mind, limb, feeling, and more / In an involved increasing family'. One might suppose that the statue, as it emerges, becomes more clearly defined: but no, 'It was their pulsing presence made me clear'.[6] The subculture defined us. We have experienced a loss of this physically and emotionally expansive identity, and a requirement to replace it with one constituted around death. For Raymond J. Ricketts, who took part in the 'survival workshops' for *Still/Here*, a key line reorients the idea of friendly support: 'People who have died are / underneath me / holding me up'.[7]

Furthermore, this is not altogether new to us. From Rimbaud and Wilde, through T. E. Lawrence, Hart Crane and Lorca, to the tragic victim of mid-century fiction, and beyond to Harvey Milk, Pier Paulo Pasolini and Drew Griffiths, our prominent people, and thousands of others, have been killed or driven to their deaths. Suicide rates among gay youths are notoriously high. Just at the moment when AIDS arrived, Woods notes, we seemed to have some prospect of repudiating this link between homosexuality and death, but now, we have to come to terms with such imagery. Jeff Nunokawa remarks the uncanny prescience of the diseased portrait in Wilde's *Dorian Gray* as an image of our allegedly doomed condition. The question now, Nunokawa observes, 'is not how to expel the figure of the doomed homosexual when it appears in the midst of our own labors of mourning but, instead, how to confront it'.[8]

This massive task of collective self-reinterpretation is vastly more important than what Croce means by art. Edmund White writes: 'To have been oppressed in the 1950s, freed in the 1960s,

exalted in the 1970s, and wiped out in the 1980s is a quick
itinerary for a whole culture to follow. For we are witnessing not
just the death of individuals but a menace to an entire culture. All
the more reason to bear witness to the cultural moment.'[9]

All subcultures produce myths. Henry Murger records and
contributes to the self-understanding of Parisian bohemia in his
novel *Scènes de la Vie de Bohème* (1848). Several of the characters
die of tuberculosis because it was so common in that milieu;
Murger called himself a poet 'of the consumptive school'.[10]
Puccini's operetta *La Bohème* (1896) is based on the novel. And
lately Jonathan Larson's musical *Rent* has used *La Bohème* as a
model for a presentation of the impact of AIDS in New York's
East Village. We may think also of World War I writing; like
Wilfred Owen, the AIDS writer is likely to feel a responsibility to
tell the story on behalf of the group. David Wojnarowicz is one of
those who compare this compulsion to being a survivor of the
Nazi Holocaust: 'As a kid . . . I would only think of death when
I reached age eighty or ninety. To be losing one's friends at a
relatively young age leaves one with what I imagine a concentration camp survivor might feel – to be the repository of so many
voices and memories and gestures of those who haven't made
it.'[11] Wojnarowicz's voice is not just his own: he wants to
represent, to retrieve, the voices of his community. By so much as
the intensity and scope of this subcultural work exclude the
straightgeist critic, by that much they demand the involvement of
PWAs, their lovers, friends and allies.

'But is it really art?', Croce's *New Yorker* headline asks. She
complains that we have 'created an art with no power of
transcendence, no way of assuring us that the grandeur of the
individual spirit is more worth celebrating than the political clout
of the group'.[12] In her idea of art, the individual expresses him-
(or sometimes her-) self while aspiring to attain the universal by
transcending that self; so subcultural concerns are by definition
inappropriate. Whereas, she writes, 'the end of twentieth-century
collectivism is the AIDS quilt. The wistful desire to commemorate
is converted into a pathetic lumping together, the individual
absorbed by the group, the group by the disease' (p. 60).

Croce is right: the significance of AIDS art *is collective*; and that is precisely what the Quilt – the Names Project – is about. Each person is individually commemorated by his or her lover(s), family, friends in a cloth panel which they design and execute themselves, but the individual is subsumed into the myth as the panels are stitched into the whole. The obvious comparison is the list of names on a war memorial, but this one is made by the people involved, with no controlling interpretation by church or State. It is woven in cloth rather than carved in marble – a 'feminine' art. And war memorials are made when the war is over, but the Quilt continues to expand.[13] At the time of its Washington exhibition in October 1996, it had 70,000 panels. Overwhelmingly, these represent ordinary people whose ceasing-to-be, in the ordinary way of things, would be of note only to family and friends. But AIDS living and dying is not just a personal concern. It is part of a huge, continuing, subcultural event. Thom Gunn writes of 'the invitation list / To the largest gathering of the decade'.[14]

In fact, the list is one of our genres; in New York and San Francisco, weekly gay papers carry a page or two of obituaries in every issue; we light candles and read out lists of those who have died. Unlike the fully rounded artwork, the list is easily extended. At the start of Wojnarowicz's *Close to the Knives* the list of persons to be acknowledged is divided into the living and the dead. Each time he has picked up the phone in the last month, Wojnarowicz writes, another acquaintance has died; with each of them he feels 'more vulnerable, like I'm standing on a conveyor belt leading into an enormous killing machine'.[15] There is a reiterated list of personal losses in Derek Jarman's *Blue*: 'I am walking along the beach in a howling gale. Another year is passing. In the roaring waters I hear the voices of dead friends. Love is life, and lasts for ever. My heart's memory turns to you. David, Howard, Graham, Terry, Paul, David, Howard, Graham, Terry, Paul, David, Howard, Graham, Terry, Paul' (Channel Four, 19 September 1993).

Croce is right, also, to focus upon Jones' use of real-life material by PWAs. By just so much as this is an intrusion upon her idea of artistic sensibility, by that much it has real-life significance for people involved in the epidemic. It does make a difference, with writers such as Walter Rico Burrell, Cyril Collard, David Feinberg, Robert Ferro, Hervé Guibert, Essex Hemphill, Guy Hocquenghem, Derek Jarman, Paul Monette, Oscar Moore, John Preston, David Rees, Marlon Riggs, Randy Shilts, George Whitmore, David Wojnarowicz, that their semi-autobiographical writings have a point of closure beyond the end of the text – namely the illnesses and deaths associated with AIDS. (Another list; its length has doubled since I started working on this chapter.) Nor is it just that the author is known to have lived and died in the manner evoked in his or her book – the case, say, with Sylvia Plath. The point is that these writers are all on the one track, and AIDS is the story, positively and negatively, of the entire constituency.

That is why the theme will not stay inside the text. In William H. Hoffman's play *As Is*, one scene involves a sequence of names of people whose memorial services are said to have occurred; the names correspond to those of the forty people to whose memory the playtext is dedicated in the prefatory material.[16] At the back of *The Man with Night Sweats* Gunn adds a note, listing the men referred to in his poems: 'For the record – for *my* record if for no one else's, because they were not famous people – I wish to name them here' (p. 87). Because these people are not famous their names do not appear in the main text, but because AIDS and Gunn's writing have incorporated them into subcultural myth they belong in the book. The customary boundary between the individual and the general is reconstituted by the crisis, and this figures partly as the breakdown of the barrier between life and art.

Films by Marlon Riggs offer further African-American instances. In *Tongues Untied* (1989) he presents himself on screen as infected with the virus; the film was excerpted by US presidential candidate Pat Buchanan to illustrate how the National Endowment for the Arts was misusing resources.[17] The posthumous film *Black Is . . . Black Ain't* (1995) is a personal and documentary analysis of the vicissitudes of African-American identities (Bill T. Jones features as choreographer and dancer). At the start we see Riggs beginning to shoot the film, but information about his weight and T-cell count supervenes, and we are told straightaway that he died during production and the film was completed by others. Riggs does a lot of the voice-over, and at intervals we see him speaking from his hospital bed.

In Croce's aesthetic this must be a self-indulgent and manipulative bid for sympathy. But part of Riggs's project is to assert gayness as a proper kind of African-American identity, and his struggle against AIDS as continuous with other adversities that beset Black people. For people involved in the AIDS emergency Riggs's personal appearance in *Black Is ... Black Ain't* is a repudiation of stigma and an opportunity for identification. And for African-Americans it makes visible the presence of AIDS in that community. Again, the theme is bigger than the individual; too big for the discretions of art.

Actually, the collective orientation of AIDS art should not be so surprising; what we call art has very often been embedded, historically, in group structures and values (churches, ruling elites, powerful families, bohemias, political movements). Only lately (since 1750 or so) and in a small part of the world has the idea of art been narrowed to the supposed experience of 'the individual'. That tendency correlates with the rise of the mass market in printed books and the loss of a face-to-face underpinning for written culture among the middle and upper classes. Wordsworth had to educate his public to appreciate his writing, he says, because he was not sufficiently of that public. Obviously the situation was otherwise with the manuscript circulation of Sidney and Donne, or the playhouse argy-bargy of Shakespeare. Pope and Swift, still, met a significant proportion of their readers in private houses, the streets, coffee houses, theatres, pleasure gardens.

By the time of Dickens and Tennyson, books had become a commodity to be marketed. Yet at least those writers were of their culture in another sense: they were widely popular. The ballet customarily reviewed by Arlene Croce has not that privilege. Around the end of the nineteenth century the mass-marketing of popular culture provokes the bracketing off of art and literature, in contradistinction, as exalted discourses accessible mainly to those of cultivated taste. Writing splits into literature and journalism, art and kitsch, 'the novel' and popular genres such as romantic and detective fiction. The difference is produced in disputes between Henry James and Virginia Woolf on the one hand and Galsworthy, Wells and Bennett on the other; T. S. Eliot's writing on culture and society is mainly about this, and so is Leavisism. The artist makes a finely honed distillation of his experience, or in exceptional cases her experience; most people find it incomprehensible and perhaps abhorrent; the select few nurture it until it accrues classic status and gets taught in schools and universities. Meanwhile, the journalistic line continues through George Orwell and Norman Mailer (say). Their writing is, mostly, more immediate and casual; it doesn't hesitate to intervene in social and political change.

Today, what is usually presented as individual/transcendent art is in fact oriented towards the expectations of a particular group – the fraction of the professional and managerial middle class that feels at ease with big-C culture. Because that group is socially dominant, it tends to be unaware that it constitutes a special interest. Compare Sarah Schulman's remark: 'When a straight man says to me "I don't believe in groups, I'm not a group person", well, he belongs to the group that's not a group. He's unaware of the structure that he's living in.'[18]

It is an interesting complication, that the constituency for art overlaps considerably with gay subculture; since Oscar Wilde, perhaps, we have tended to regard ourselves as artistic.[19] Hence Bill T. Jones' supposition that dance is a proper form through which to explore the situation of PWAs. Croce's objection is, therefore, an attempt to expel gay men from one of their productive strongholds. She is offended because Jones has refused the discretion that was the condition, customarily, of gay art (I used to give a paper entitled 'How come they don't love us when we made all that art for them?'). But for people involved with HIV and AIDS, subcultural myth is not just a matter of a vivid evening in the theatre, or curling up with a good book. It is to do with survival. Schulman adds: 'You know there's this push for domestic partnership laws, for gay marriage. But if the gay community was divided up into privatized marriage family units, and wasn't a community, the response to AIDS would never have been what it has been.'[20]

Of course, subcultural writing is uneven. *Blue* is a seventy-minute film that offers to the viewer only a blue screen: the artist speaks but no longer makes images, he has gone blind. Is this deeply moving and productive of new insight, or is it avant-gardist, gestural and self-indulgent? That is a question for us to consider. Jarman's works and other AIDS writing are there for us, and to decide what we think about them is to decide what we think about ourselves. As Woods remarks, until recently our culture has been marred by interference, and, contrary to the straightgeist notion that we were more subtle and profound when suppressed, 'no censored book is as good as it might have been'.[21] What further qualities our work will attain is also a question for us.

A partly comparable case for a dedicated African-American theatre has been made recently by the dramatist August Wilson (to be fair, I should say that I read about it in the *New Yorker*). 'There are and have always been two distinct and parallel traditions in black art', Wilson argues. They are: 'art that is conceived and designed to entertain white society, and art that feeds the spirit and celebrates the life of black America'.[22] If we translate this into gay terms (for comparisons with other subordinated groups are always instructive), it is easy to think of the effort that we have put into entertaining straight society – from Rudolph Nureyev to Julian Clary – but most of the work for ourselves is still to come. Wilson particularly denounces 'color-blind' casting, which he believes turns Black people into 'mimics'. It is interesting, though, to envisage a gay equivalent – King Lear or Henry V dallying with male favourites, perhaps. And why not?

If we kick the dependence upon straightgeist approval, there will be costs. Without the endorsement of *New Yorker* columnists, we will have more difficulty getting funding. For the hegemonic position *is powerful* – always, by definition; that is why it is necessary not to let it pass without question. Perhaps, to get a share of resources, we sometimes have to frame our claims in Croce's terms. Even so, we should not accept the double indignity of *believing in* those terms. Indeed, we may find that when we are not playing the art game by conventional criteria then our work doesn't have to cost so much. Perhaps we don't need elaborately polished artefacts; perhaps, like 'disinterested art', that expectation is just local and temporary.

Living with AIDS

In 1996 I was shocked, at first glance, to read Simon Lovat's comment on Paul Monette's *Afterlife* (1990), which follows the various fortunes of three men whose lives are consumed by AIDS. Ultimately, Lovat says, the book 'is a dinosaur. Gay writing on Aids has evolved past the point where it can hold centre stage and be the single narrative topic. Weary readers have grown to expect more.' Again, Jonathan Hales, reviewing *American Studies* by Mark Merlis, comments: 'One hesitates to express the sentiment publically but it *is* refreshing to read a debut gay novel that does not deal with HIV/Aids.'[23]

These critics, writing in *Gay Times*, are certainly right to stir up this topic; we have to be prepared to re-view our subcultural myths, to reconsider the parts that feel comfortingly familiar but perhaps no longer take us forward. Probably novels complaining at the State, doctors and the drug companies are out of date; we have spent too much energy on attributing blame. Of course we must complain when resources are not properly allocated to us, but when we get treated unfairly we need a more complex response than indignation. For neither the State nor business has ever accepted as part of their responsibility that they should help gay men to fuck happily. I return in the next chapter to some of the principles involved in the production and critique of subcultural myth. Here I want to make some more comments on the story that we have been telling ourselves about AIDS.

What is troubling about AIDS in Britain is that we may seem to have passed *beyond* it, but actually we have not properly passed

through it. The reason for this is that the gay myth of AIDS is
mostly 'American' (I use quote marks because 'America', properly
speaking, is the name of the continent; its use to signify the United
States is an instance of US cultural hegemony). In this section I
want to propose some British, and probably North-west
European, distinctions.

In those US cities where gay men have gathered, around half
of them are reckoned to be HIV-positive at the present
time. Walt Odets has written an important book about survivor
guilt among those who test negative in San Francisco. Back in
1989, I was shaken and impressed to find there organisations
for people who test HIV-*negative* – to enable them to contribute,
to feel less guilty at being well. Odets's book is replete with
testimony such as this, from a man of twenty-eight: 'All my gay
relationships have been with people who have AIDS, who I knew
had AIDS ... You know, I've never thought about having a
relationship for more than a couple of years, because I've never
dated anyone who was going to live longer than that.'[24]
However, such experience derives, specifically, from those US
cities. Eric Rofes, in his analysis of how gay subculture has
experienced something akin to 'post-traumatic stress disorder',
indicates that he means mainly men aged thirty-five to fifty in
US 'epicenter cities'.[25] James Robert Baker's justly admired
novel, *Tim and Pete* (1995), set in Los Angeles, is still firmly
within this vision.

Europeans hear with horror of men attending a dozen funerals
in fewer months, and with fear of men nursing lovers and a
sequence of friends (how on earth would we cope?). But relatively
few of us have actually had such experiences – mainly those with
friends in the United States. Several British friends have remarked
to me, in a rather baffled manner, that they have suffered more
personal losses from cancers than from AIDS. This may be partly
to do with perceptions and the composition of different social
milieux. Britain is a very small place and therefore, although
lesbians and gay men move to cities, they do not get cut off from
other people to the degree that happens in the USA. Except for
those who work in it, gay subculture constitutes a thinner

network.[26] It is also to do with how old you are. But, above all, initial transmission of HIV was slower and later because Britons had not developed, or been allowed to have, bath-houses and back-rooms, so knowledge about safer sex arrived in time to hinder the rate of infection. Edward King has established this in his book, *Safety in Numbers.*[27]

Let's be clear. I have no intention of undervaluing the losses that many Europeans have suffered, or the commitment of many who are working here with AIDS issues. I am not saying that we should not be concerned with gay PWAs in the USA – or, for that matter, with 'heterosexual AIDS' elsewhere in the world. Least of all do I want to understate the new ways of thinking about living that are being created by Europeans who are HIV-positive; we need to hear more of their story. Nevertheless, *as a community*, North-west European gay men have not lived with AIDS in the way US people have lived with it – and represented it.

Yet, because a good deal of European gay identity derives from the United States, it is easy to suppose that we have been directly sharing the US epidemic. I remark in chapter 5 the extent to which the metropolitan imagery of gayness derives from the United States – how blue-jeans and T-shirts, short hair and moustaches have been adopted into British gay subculture, along with their 'American' significations. It is the same with candle-lit vigils, quilting, buddying and photo-obituaries, none of which has much historic resonance in Britain.

The danger in the uncritical European adoption of the US myth of the epidemic is that it allows those of us who are older and uninfected to feel that we have passed through it and survived, and those who are younger to regard it as history. Thus people may start to believe they will be all right whatever they do, or at least if they do it just a bit. Further, as a larger wave of full-blown AIDS reaches us – and it is arriving – we will have few relevant imaginative and intellectual resources to meet it. Meanwhile, bizarrely, campaigning is being wound down by the UK government on the pretext that figures show there was less risk than had been supposed; whereas, of course, it is far more likely that campaigning has been in some measure successful, and that to stop now is to expose young people, and the forgetful, to lethal danger.

As well as being out of sync with European experience, the US AIDS myth is involved in cultural attitudes, to do with individualism, psychotherapy and religion, that have relatively little purchase in Europe. Dennis Altman has remarked how the Americanisation of AIDS 'feeds into a particular moralistic view that depicts AIDS as a disease of modern decadence, for which both homosexuality and America itself can stand as convenient symbols', and how the vogue for up-front, Oprah Winfrey confession heightens the drama in any situation.[28]

In particular, the notion that one ought to be able to overcome anything if one gets into the right frame of mind and tries hard enough is relatively weak in Britain. We do think we should do our best and not give in. But the uplift rhetoric of 'we're not going to let this thing beat us' is 'American'. In *Blue* Jarman repudiates the term 'person living with AIDS', and the implicit demand to adopt the 'positive' attitude that says people are 'living', rather than, say, 'suffering'. He objects that the Quilt is made about, but not by, the dead:

> I shall not win the battle against the virus – in spite of the slogans like 'Living with AIDS'. The virus was appropriated by the well, so we have to live with AIDS while they spread the Quilt for the moths of Ithaca across the wine-dark sea. Awareness is heightened by this, but something else is lost; a sense of reality drowned in theatre.

Achieving individual fitness and success by getting your head right and refusing to contemplate failure is what US people are supposed to do generally. In all arenas the drawback is the same: those who don't get there seem to have only themselves to blame – they just didn't have what it takes. In my view this is a wicked idea: it is bad enough being poor, ill, or both, without being told it's your own fault for not trying hard enough. The ideological trick, of course, is that if the individual has only him- or herself to blame, then nothing needs to be done about the system – such as introduce public healthcare.

In Britain, gay subculture has to learn to work on the assumption that the main epidemic is not avoided but delayed, and that we still have to face the greater part of it. For even a very low rate of transmission, Rofes shows, will produce a large proportion of infected men in the urban epicentres where gay men congregate. 'If the infection rate among HIV-negative gay men somehow were to be reduced consistently to 1 percent a year, the population of gay men in American urban centers would continue to be half infected with HIV (the [infection] rate was about 2 percent in San Francisco in 1993).' We have 'to imagine vast numbers of men continuing to become infected in successive waves and HIV disease becoming integrated as a long-term feature of gay men's life cycles'.[29] The point is that even a low rate of infection will accumulate a large number of HIV-positive people over the years. And that, surely, is the likely future of London, Manchester, Birmingham, Glasgow, Bristol and Brighton.

Initially and through the 1980s, we hardly allowed ourselves to think that the virus might not be overcome, individually and overall. In 1997, we still cannot rely upon the prospect of a cure or even a vaccination; we will never return to the expansive way we lived before; the straightgeist will go on associating us with disease and death. Combination therapy, protease inhibitors and treatments for particular infections are raising hopes that HIV-positive people in wealthy countries will live longer and fitter lives. Probably there will not be fewer of us falling ill, but those who do will recover, and perhaps repeat this sequence many times; if anything, they will need more community support, not less. Adjustment to these conditions will not occur without new subcultural work; if some novels featuring AIDS seem to be old hat, we must try harder to write in ways that register the current situation.

The ultimate issue in our AIDS myth is still safer sex. We need to recognise that the gay community is not only the place where you will probably be cared for if you have AIDS, it is also the place, probably, where you caught it; as well as supporting each other, we have been infecting each other. Yet demonising people who have unsafe sex must be unproductive. Your first obligation, both to yourself and the community, is *always* to protect *yourself*. It is ridiculous to blame the person who infected you, or reinfected you, for failing to take care of you when you failed to take care of yourself.

Obviously we have to look with more subtlety at safer-sex messages and at the psychology of the condom. But, in the final analysis, if an informed person chooses to put him- or herself at risk – as with substance abuse, from saturated fats through alcohol and tobacco to heroin – we have to allow that he or she may have serious reasons. I write this with reluctance, because I belong to that cohort that picked up rumours of the 'gay plague' before the HIV virus was identified – before we knew how it is transmitted. We couldn't tell whether our current practices were inviting infection; whether we, or our partners, already had it. Every scratch or bruise – hard skin on your foot – might be the Kaposi's Sarcoma which we could barely pronounce or spell. Hospitalisation and ostracisation would immediately follow, we believed, and death within weeks. That is the moment of Larry Kramer's play *The Normal Heart*.

I am perplexed and distressed, therefore, when people question the inevitability of safer-sex practices. However, as King and Odets point out, while the myth says that unprotected sex occurs in anonymous encounters, more often it is the attempt of people in relationships to express closeness and commitment.[30] A person may feel that the quality of life she or he gains thereby makes up for a possible future loss in quantity. I can imagine circumstances in which I might feel that. After all, none of us lives forever, and who knows what further mischances await us down the line?

5   Reading gay myths

In the previous chapter I tried, mainly in respect of HIV and AIDS, to undermine the straightgeist concept of art and show the importance of subcultural myth for sexual dissidents. In this chapter I explore some of the implications of such an approach through two texts in particular: David Leavitt's novel *While England Sleeps* and Harvey Fierstein's plays, *Torch Song Trilogy*. We have both to strengthen and to challenge our own myths.

Stephen Spender's bit of rough

In November 1993 *While England Sleeps* was withdrawn from publication in England because Sir Stephen Spender recognised in it a reworking of his life and autobiographical writing. He objected that his copyright had been infringed and that his moral right not to have his work subjected to derogatory treatment had been violated.[1] The central dilemma in Leavitt's story is indeed from Spender's autobiographical work *World Within World* (1951). The middle-class writer takes up with a lower-class young man (Jimmy Younger in Spender, Edward Phelan in Leavitt), but gets drawn into a relationship with a marriageable young woman; Jimmy/Edward responds to this by joining the International Brigade; he attempts to desert and is imprisoned; the writer, stricken with guilt, goes to Spain to try to get him released, asserting his belief in the individual above the collective fight against Fascism.

Spender protested that Leavitt could 'lift incidents from my autobiography and describe them as having happened to a fictitious narrator in his novel'.[2] As with Bill T. Jones' *Still/Here* (chapter 4), queer art and life tangle in a questionable manner. But, as with the AIDS myth, this story is not just Spender's. The queer literary gent and his bit of rough were less an individual experience than a historical pattern of relating – one that remained prominent into the 1960s becoming, indeed, a subcultural myth.[3] Forster, we may now see, gives displaced versions of it in a couple

of novels before broaching it head-on in *Maurice*. It appears in
the personal writings of Jocelyn Brooke (*The Orchid Trilogy*,
1948–50) and Denton Welch (*Journals*, 1952); J. R. Ackerley's
veiled fiction *We Think the World of You* (1960) is centrally about
it; so are the autobiographies of Emlyn Williams (*George*, 1961),
Tom Driberg (*Ruling Passions*, 1978), and John Lehmann (*In a
Pagan Place*, 1985). In *The Swimming-Pool Library* (1988) Alan
Hollinghurst reviews both historical and contemporary manifestations of this myth.

More specifically, more intricately, members of the Auden-
Isherwood-Spender set have given their versions of Spender's
version. Christopher Isherwood in *Christopher and His Kind*
(1976) recounts quite briskly the story of Spender, his boyfriend
and his girlfriend.[4] Isherwood tells also the other story which
features in *While England Sleeps*: the nightmare attempt to get
for a semi-criminal and somewhat feckless German lover a
passport that will save him from Fascism – this happened to
Isherwood and Heinz. And T. C. (Cuthbert) Worsley, who actually
accompanied Spender on the mission to Spain, focusses in his
semi-fictional documentary novel *Fellow Travellers* (1971) upon
the relationship Leavitt represents – upon the Spender-kind-of-
person and an ex-guardsman, their circle in London, and their
experiences in Spain.

The self-conscious intertextual narrative devices deployed in
many of its versions help to establish this story's mythic dimension. An 'Introduction' to Worsley's *Fellow Travellers* says the
book is a sequence of notes and interviews towards a novel,
collected at the time and now edited only lightly by the narrator.
An 'Author's Note' frames that frame, claiming a different relation
between fact and fiction: 'This is not a novel, it is a memoir,
fictionalised only in the sense that I have fused people into my
characters; while the events and happenings, though they actually
occurred, have been arranged and reattributed to suit my pattern.'[5]
In *Christopher and His Kind* Isherwood repeatedly 'corrects' the
version of events given in his earlier novels, drawing on the
evidence of letters and journals. His earlier work, he says, 'is not
truly autobiographical . . . the Author conceals important facts

about himself. He over-dramatizes many episodes and gives his characters fictitious names . . . The book I am now going to write will be as frank and factual as I can make it' (p. 9). Forster wrote for *Maurice* a 'terminal note' explaining how it had been written, why it had not been published, and how it had been changed. *The Swimming-Pool Library* claims to reproduce parts of Lord Nantwich's memoirs. *While England Sleeps* has a double frame (I describe it in the next section).

Such intertextual devices, like Jones' framing of the videotaped testimony of PWAs, point towards authenticity and personal truth, while acknowledging also that reality is being mediated and arranged. These stories don't just occur naturally; their composition is shared by a number of people, partly in collaboration, taking particular forms in particular historical circumstances. Even the one storyteller gives different versions at different times. These devices effect and comment upon the transformation of experience, not just into writing but into subcultural myth. As we tell our story, it tells us.

Further, *World Within World* is not the only text in which Spender himself deals with these matters; his own writing is self-consciously intertextual. He prints parts of his journals and other fugitive writing from the 1930s in *The Thirties and After* (1978). And in 1988 he publishes *The Temple* which, he says in an 'Introduction', he wrote long ago as 'an autobiographical novel in which the author tries to report truthfully on his experiences in the summer of 1929'. It could not then be published because of censorship (Spender anticipates Leavitt here by acknowledging that there was more sex than he had initially admitted). He raided the manuscript, Spender says, for parts of *World Within World*; and now he has rewritten it. '*The Temple* is then a complex of memory, fiction and hindsight.' This confession of the mixed status of such a narrative is exactly to my point: Spender's work does not derive merely from an authentic moment in his own experience.

Indeed, he quotes a letter that he wrote to John Lehmann, about how he felt his experience to be that of his generation, and how he and his friends were, in a sense, working together:

'Whatever one of us does in writing or travelling or taking jobs, is a kind of exploration which may be taken up by the others.' There was a 'shared adventure'.[6] Precisely. As with AIDS writing, the story will not stay inside the text. That is why Sir Stephen was unwise to suppose that he could control it; it is as if Sophocles were to complain about Freud using the Oedipus story.

The gay justification for *While England Sleeps* transcends the bourgeois concept of individual intellectual property: it is a contribution to subcultural understanding. By recirculating this material for a later generation, extending it imaginatively so that its commitments and evasions may be explored, Leavitt offers to illuminate gay histories and our relations with them. Hardly any gay people today live quite like the queer gent and his bit of rough, but we may recognise the myth as part of where we have come from, and acknowledge traces of it in the class relations that persist in our subculture today. Indeed the Isherwood books, still, may be your best chance of finding out about homosexuality in an English provincial bookshop. In Helsinki in June 1996, according to *Gay Times*, *While England Sleeps* was the third best-selling gay/lesbian book.

It is ironic, therefore, and sad, that Leavitt says he dislikes subcultural writing. Gay literature should be 'literature first and gay second', he writes in his introduction to *The Penguin Book of Gay Short Stories* (1994); it should transform 'homosexual literature into human drama'.[7] He is pleased that E. M. Forster did not publish gay stories during his lifetime because that would have 'reduced the illustrious author of *A Passage to India*, at least in the eyes of the public, to a kind of literary sideshow freak – the male Radclyffe Hall' (p. xxvii). Leavitt does not actually discuss the merits of Forster's gay stories, though he publishes one of them, 'Arthur Snatchfold', in his collection. I think we should be proud if Forster had been as bold as Radclyffe Hall; Leavitt is too worried about 'the eyes of the public'.

Leavitt rejects the idea of homosexuals as (quoting Susan Sontag's words) 'something like an ethnic group, one whose distinctive folkloric custom was sexual voracity' (p. xxii). I register in chapter 2 some reasons for questioning the idea that lesbians and gay men are like an ethnic group. Leavitt's reasons are different: he fears that it risks 'forgetting that sexuality is an extremely individualistic business; that each gay man and lesbian is gay or lesbian in his or her own way' (p. xxvi). Leavitt wants 'a new level of liberation ... one that would allow gay men and lesbians to celebrate their identities without having to move into a gulag' (p. xxii). Yet he has to acknowledge the pressures that we currently experience: 'As long as the society we live in despises us as a group, we *are* a group, whether we like it or not' (p. xxvii).

The point, in my view, is not to celebrate our identities, but to investigate ways of living that we have pursued and might pursue. Actually, that is what Leavitt has done in *While England Sleeps*. Presumably he believes he has transformed 'homosexual literature into human drama'. Rather, from a position that is notably transient and local, he has contributed to a gay myth.

Critical positions

The counterpart of the subcultural myth is the subcultural reading formation. As Janice Radway shows in *Reading the Romance*,

> There are patterns or regularities to what viewers and readers bring to texts and media messages[,] in large part because they acquire specific cultural competencies as a result of their particular social location. Similar readings are produced, I argue, because similarly located readers learn a similar set of reading strategies and interpretive codes which they bring to bear upon the texts they encounter.[8]

Les/bi/gay people know how to read subcultural texts.

However, our relation to our myths should not be imagined as passive or simple. First, gay subculture is not an elementary monolith; it is fraught with the contradictions of its own history and of its crucial positioning in the prevailing sex–gender system; it is divided by the hierarchies of class, age, education, race and ethnicity that occur in society at large. That is why gay readers do not, and should not, all read the same; to the contrary, our readings are partly where we work through our differences.

Second, we don't, and shouldn't, believe everything we read – even when the writer is both gay and accomplished. Any writer is saying, implicitly, 'Look, it's like *this*, isn't it?' – he or she tries to make the representation plausible, persuasive. But this is potentially coercive; subculture is potentially coercive. In the US film *Jeffrey* (based on Paul Rudnick's play of 1992) Jeffrey's friends indicate, in no uncertain terms, that he is under an obligation – to gayness and humanity – to reorient himself and take a more affirmative attitude toward AIDS (initially he is too fearful to take as a lover a man who has tested positive). He becomes a 'good' member of the community when he is jostled into changing his stance. To me, however, this is a troubling effect: I feel that Jeffrey is subject to unreasonable coercion. Of course the relations between positive- and negative-testing men need cultural work, but the answer does not lie in shaming nervous people. In fact, apart from fancying each other in the gym, Jeffrey and the other man are scarcely acquainted; the demand to get the right line on HIV is so overwhelming that the need to set about building a relationship is overlooked. In a comparable way, the film seeks to persuade the audience; its exuberant closure incites rejoicing at Jeffrey's conversion.

Of course, Paul Rudnick must write his story in the way that makes best sense to him. But we don't have to accept it. It is there for us to experience, think about and use in our own ways. That is true of reading, and of other subcultural pressures also. Diana Fuss observes,

> In reading, for instance, we bring (old) subject-positions to the text at the same time the actual process of reading constructs (new) subject positions for us. Consequently we are always engaged in a 'double reading' ... in the sense that we are continually caught within and between *at least* two constantly shifting subject-positions (old and new, constructed and constructing) and these positions may often stand in complete contradiction to each other.[9]

Most gay men will be able to supply a reading position from

which to understand *While England Sleeps*, but this position will include a capacity to critique Leavitt's version. The stance Leavitt conveys in *While England Sleeps* jostles against other aspects of a gay reading formation, inviting challenge from within the subculture. It is there for us to dispute, as much as endorse, in its interpretation of history and in its implications for today. As I said in chapter 1, fiction, film and song are useful not as transcendent truths or documentary evidence, but as a reservoir of significant and complex representations through which we think ourselves.

Like Hollinghurst in *The Swimming-Pool Library*, Leavitt is interested in continuities between the 1930s and the 1980s. This is an entirely reasonable concern, but the work he does to attain continuity may make us aware also of discontinuities. He strives to make the cross-class relationship correspond better with today's relatively egalitarian gay ethos by building up Jimmy/Edward and giving him more status and independence (in *World Within World* Jimmy is *employed* by Spender!). Also, Jimmy, in Spender and Worsley, has a stomach ulcer and gets home safely, whereas Edward is made to contract typhoid and die on the boat back to England, in a way notably like that in which AIDS deaths are often represented today.

Without these changes, we might think the relationship with Jimmy/Edward quaint and exploitative. Above all, by making the Spender-like character appear to betray the kind of relationship that our culture considers 'good', Leavitt makes him appear more culpable. And this fits with his central reinterpretation of the story, which is to attribute failure of nerve and bad faith to the Spender-like protagonist, insofar as he undertakes heterosexual relations; the affair with Jimmy/Edward, he and we are made to realise, is the real one, the one that counts.

Marjorie Garber attacks this version of the Spender-like character: it manifests an inability or reluctance to entertain the potential of bisexuality. She quotes Leavitt's comment, that his protagonist 'ends up uninhibitedly and unapologetically gay'.[10] First, put as baldly as that, we may notice a divergence between Leavitt's sexual politics and his literary politics: for the former, he wants clear-cut gay men, for the latter he wants 'human drama'. Garber's point is that Leavitt's interpretation assimilates the historical material to the modern gay notion, namely that self-proclaimed bisexuals lack the courage to abandon a protective stake in heterosexuality. As I have acknowledged (for I shared it), this was a notion of the 1970s and 1980s; in the 1990s, it is being recognised that sexualities may be more various and more mobile.

Suppose, in the light of such changing patterns, we see Spender's movement between gay and straight relations not as a failure of nerve but (as with another figure from that milieu, John Maynard Keynes) as a pattern that made good enough sense in that generation? Suppose the 'uninhibitedly and unapologetically gay' (Leavitt's phrase) was hardly available as a self-concept – in effect, only at the price of becoming like Quentin Crisp? Leavitt's rejection of bisexuality may then appear over-strenuous, and we might call for a novel that will enable us to understand, rather than co-opt, that strange history. Such a thought does not destroy the subcultural significance of *While England Sleeps*: it discloses the historical construction of Spender's assumptions, of Leavitt's, and of those into which we may now be moving.

The points I have been raising are to do with a modernising tendency in *While England Sleeps*. Other features 'Americanise' what has been a notably English story. In the outer frame, set in 1978, the Spender-like character explains that his novel recalls 1937 from the vantage point of 1955, by which time the narrator has become a Hollywood screenwriter (as Isherwood did, of course). This situates the narrator in US terms, thereby mediating the story to North American readers. However, UK reviewers were quick to point out some errors in Leavitt's handling of this English story. There is talk of keeping Hitler out of power in Germany in 1936, and of 'Lord' Eden as foreign secretary; the narrator goes 'to wash up' (meaning 'wash').[11] And the London tube, despite the narrator's claim that he is studying it for his novel, is perceived through the eyes of a tourist. It is said that the trains smell of petrol and exhaust (pp. 11, 63), and Enfield West station is called by its later name of Oakwood (p. 64); unluckily, the UK publisher helps us to work this out by printing a 1930s Underground map as endpapers, but I know anyway because I grew up at that (for Leavitt, remote) end of the Piccadilly Line.

These could be the carefully planted lapses of the now-Americanised narrator. It doesn't much matter; whether by accident or design, *While England Sleeps* has helped me to see the extent to which European images of gayness now derive from the United States. When I find the style and self-understanding of the 1930s queer literary gent being reprocessed in an 'American' version, I notice also how blue-jeans and T-shirts, short hair and moustaches have been imported into British gay subculture (I remark this also in chapter 4, in relation to imagery of HIV and AIDS). Nick Walker comments: 'Walk down Old Compton Street and you see the American influence right down to the soles of the Timberland boots. The gay village is, after all, an American concept . . . London's status as the gay capital of Europe is partially an expression of the fact that England is an American cultural colony.'[12] This cultural interchange is registered also by Armistead Maupin in *Babycakes*, set in 1983. Michael visits the Coleherne (leather pub): 'there was something almost poignant about pasty-faced Britishers trying to pull off a butch biker routine. They were simply the wrong breed for it . . . Phrases like "Suck that big, fat cock" and "Yeah, you want it, don't you?" sounded just plain asinine when muttered with an Oxonian accent.'[13] Again, Maupin's is a tourist perception of Britain – the characters who don't have Oxonian accents are broad cockneys. Even so, he has a point.

It is not that this international bricolage is a bad thing; the modern metropolitan concept of gayness is something that we have been creating (like, say, pop music) through Anglo-American subcultural interaction. But we can better decide what to do next if we have a better idea of what we have been doing so far.

Misogyny and *Torch Song Trilogy*

Les/bi/gay subcultural myths, I have argued, are not simple; they are fraught with the contradictions of their own histories and of their crucial positioning in the prevailing sex–gender system. Like other people, we are subject to the common prejudices of our societies. Subcultural commentary has to engage with the awkward implications of all that.

In his book *No Respect*, Andrew Ross challenges progressive intellectuals to acknowledge that the popular culture which they like to champion is often marked by sexism, racism and militarism (and homophobia, we might add). These right-wing attitudes should not be overlooked or obscured, as if they were incidental embarrassments, Ross says. We need to consider why they are popular, and how they may actually be the vehicle for lower-class dissidence. They involve 'structures of feeling that draw upon hostility, resentment, and insubordination, as well as deference, consent, and respect'.[14] Progressive intellectuals have to work at such a juncture, because otherwise it is a gift to populist reactionaries.

One would not want, at this point, to slide into any assumption that popular culture is racist (for instance), whereas high culture is enlightened. Rather, as John McGrath says, the popular is 'the site of an ongoing struggle'; he regards himself as involved in 'the struggle for the "progressive" within popular culture'.[15] Les/bi/gay cultures also have their embarrassments, and they too may afford comparable scope for struggle.

It is worth noting, though, that the aggression born of class resentment, upon which Ross focusses, is rarely attractive to lesbians and gay men – we are too often its victims. It is probably true to say that the leading regressive temptations are different for different subcultural groups; for instance, Paul Gilroy has reactivated Richard Wright's call to acknowledge the danger of fascistic elements in Black 'nationalism'.[16] For les/bi/gay people, again, nationhood is not a plausible aspiration (though it may afford a polemical slogan). The challenging issue in gay subcultural myth is to do with women, femininity, and misogyny.

Of course, misogyny is central in male heterosexual cultures, but it is doing particular work for gay men. 'Do you like girls at all?' Will is asked by Lord Nantwich in Alan Hollinghurst's novel *The Swimming-Pool Library*. 'Yes, I like them quite a lot really', he replies. 'There are chaps who don't care for them, you know',

Nantwich observes. 'Simply can't abide them. Can't stand the sight of them, their titties and their big sit-upons, even the smell of them.'[17] With Nantwich's attitude, there is nothing to do but point out that it is phobic – precisely comparable to homophobia – and probably beyond the reach of reasonable discussion. However, Will himself spends no time with women during the action of the novel; he seems to know only two, his mother and sister; he sees far more of his nephew and brother-in-law. Later on he remarks: 'I think most men are happiest in a male world, with gangs and best friends and all that' (p. 242).

We have to entertain the thought, broached by Leo Bersani, that gay misogyny comes with the territory. He warns against 'a tendency among gay activists to ignore the connections between political sympathies and sexual fantasies'. 'Our feminist sympathies', he says, 'can't help being complicated by an inevitable narciss[is]tic investment in the objects of our desire . . . In his desires, the gay man always runs the risk of identifying with culturally dominant images of misogynist maleness.'[18] We desire men; men (in the culturally dominant mode) are misogynist; and hence we may identify with that and be misogynist ourselves, the argument runs. In my view those generalisations are rather insecure; for instance, some of us desire boys or 'feminine' men. Anyway, our fantasies don't have to determine our political, social or interpersonal behaviour, as Bersani readily concedes: 'Our fantasy investments are often countered by more consciously and more rationally elaborate modes of reaching out to others . . . In that tension lies an important moral dimension of our political engagement' (p. 64).

That is well said (and will inform the discussion in chapter 7) – though the argument seems to slip back a few notches when Bersani goes on to say that gay and lesbian community is 'something of a miracle', considering 'how remote lesbian desiring fantasies are, by definition, from gay male desiring fantasies' (p. 65; I believe he thinks this because of the distinctive genesis of male and female homosexuality in Freudian theory). It seems to me that there are actually various kinds of identifications between lesbians and gay men, including, perhaps, some interestingly complicated erotic ones. But I want to point to a structural dimension in the subcultural myths that link women and gay men, one not specially determined by fantasy and not easily to be evaded through individual political commitment.

The main theme of *The Swimming-Pool Library* is Will's discovery that he is deeply implicated in gay history and not, as he has supposed, free from responsibility and social process. Such a theme – an important one for gay men – does not involve fear and hatred of women, but it does tend to marginalise them. This is not quite 'misogyny', but who you write into your story and who just doesn't seem to count that much is nothing less than the infrastructure of routine gender-chauvinism. For what pushes women to the margins – as with other subordinated groups – is not just phobic prejudice or fantasy identification, but the narratives that we live through, in the world and in novels. These narratives are not individual inventions. They depend upon patterns of plausibility that are deeply encoded in culture; in fact, subculture *is* a bundle of more and less plausible narratives.

'You don't want to have written off half the human race at your time of life', Ralph tells Laurie in Mary Renault's *The Charioteer*.[19] However, insofar as that novel is about the possibility of two men leading a decent queer life together, it seems to produce and expel the women characters (nurses and matrons) as romantic or bossy. Again, Andrew Holleran's *Dancer from the Dance* is set in an entirely male milieu because it is about how some men contrived to live outside mainstream social arrangements. By definition, this leaves women out of the story. Their absence is the price of gay assertion (I discuss these novels in the next chapter).

In Leavitt's writing women are quite strongly included, but in order that they may be repudiated. A (communist) woman betrays Edward in *While England Sleeps*, and in *The Lost Language of Cranes* the wife and mother is notably closed-down as a personality. Dana Heller comments:

Leavitt's insistence on women's abject *presence* in a text that has no difficulty affirming homoerotic openness seems to indicate that no gay male character need assume a role analogous to woman's subordinate role so long as 'real' biological women remain formally positioned to absorb the fear, rage, victimization, loneliness, and rejection that homosexual men are, of course, also vulnerable to in homophobic culture.[20]

Leavitt is perhaps attempting to plug gay men into ancient homosocial feeling, and specifically into the pioneer fable through which the United States is supposed to have been established. Men are all right together, Leavitt and the myth declare; it's women that tie you down and wear you out because they can't cope. In fact, a family without women is even stronger, even more 'American'.[21] If gay men can hitch themselves onto this, perhaps they will be all right too.

Insofar as we expect writers to challenge as well as recycle our subcultural myths, we may want to ask Hollinghurst, Renault, Holleran and Leavitt to try harder to overthrow the assumption that the assertion of gay men must be at the expense of women. But we have all been accorded parts in this story, and it may not be easy for any of us to rewrite them.

Torch Song Trilogy by Harvey Fierstein was first produced at the La Mama Experimental Theatre Club between February 1978 and October 1979. It was presented on Broadway in 1982, and won Tony Awards for best play and best actor (Fierstein). It won awards in the West End of London in 1985; a film appeared in 1988. In all these productions Fierstein starred as Arnold Beckoff, a charismatic drag performer who wants little more than a partner to love and be loved by and to have great sex with. Things look promising with Ed, but Arnold finds himself making all the running because Ed is not prepared to be perceived as gay, and goes with women as well as men; this situation becomes clear in the first play. The second play explores the interactions within and between two couples – Arnold and Alan, and Ed and Laurel – ending with somewhat uneasy confirmations of the status quo. In the third play Alan (Arnold's boyfriend in the second play) has been killed by queerbashers; Ed moves in with Arnold and, together with David, a gay youth Arnold is adopting, they constitute an alternative family; Laurel is reportedly on her own and distressed. The situation is disturbed by the annual visit of Mrs Beckoff, Arnold's widowed mother, who scarcely tolerates his gayness and is angry and scornful when he compares his loss of Alan to her loss of her husband.

The validation of the teenage sexuality of Alan and David is still surprising and dissident. In other respects the politics of Arnold's household are debatable, in a way familiar to gay cultural analysis. Either Arnold, Ed and David subvert heterosexual marriage (and attitudes like that of Mrs Beckoff), or they create their own autonomous adaptation of it, or they attempt, slavishly, to copy it. 'All I know is whatever this is, it's not a Grade-B imitation of a heterosexual marriage', Arnold declares.[22] Of course, the issue is not so easily set aside; but I don't mean to evaluate these readings – all three are available and the play challenges us to explore their implications (that is the subcultural work I am endorsing).

In any event, there is a success of one kind or another for gay men, over or within the sex–gender system, and it is at the expense of Laurel and Mrs Beckoff. This is figured in the fact that Laurel appears only in the second play, Mrs Beckoff only in the third: they are pushed to the margins by the structure of the narrative (in the film Mrs Beckoff appears throughout – affording more of an entry-point for straight audiences – but she doesn't influence the story in any additional way). In fact, the action of the play might be perceived as a homosocial exploitation, with the men using the women as a means to get their own act together.

Laurel is a well-meaning person, trying to make out in a difficult world like the rest of us, but it is hard not to feel that she asks for trouble. This is not the first time she has become entangled with a bisexual man, she says (p. 32), and she seems to deceive herself with the language of therapy to make her wishes sound as if they will come true; her belief that she and Ed 'have few secrets and a great deal of openness' is shown to be complacent (p. 39). Fierstein cunningly raises the stakes by having Arnold define his 'marital' and 'parental' roles through and against the determined heterosexism of his mother. 'What loss

did you have?' she demands. 'You fooled around with some boy
. . .? Where do you come to compare that to a marriage of thirty-
five years?'

> ARNOLD: . . . How dare I say I loved him? You had it easy, Ma.
> You lost your husband in a nice clean hospital, I lost mine out
> there. They killed him there on the street. Twenty-three years
> old, laying dead on the street. Killed by a bunch of kids with
> baseball bats. (*MA has fled the room. ARNOLD continues to
> rant.*) Children. Children taught by people like you [she is a
> teacher]. 'Cause everybody knows that queers don't matter!
> Queers don't love! And those that do deserve what they get!
> (pp. 69–70)

Even after years of training in literary criticism, I confess to being
naively moved by this exchange.

For the emotional and political survival of Arnold and gay
men, Arnold has to have all the best lines. He has to be allowed
to win the argument with Mrs Beckoff. And for Arnold to win in
the action as well as the argument, Laurel has to lose Ed. To be
sure, there are innumerable texts which show same-sex
partnerships losing out to heterosexual relations, from *The
Merchant of Venice* and *Twelfth Night* to *David Copperfield* and
In Memoriam, to *Women in Love* and *Look Back in Anger*. But it
would be better if our success were not at someone else's expense.
In Fierstein's play *On Tidy Endings* (the film *Tidy Endings*, 1988)
the partner and ex-wife of a man who has died from AIDS quarrel
over him, but they are levelled up, in a way that confronts
orthodoxy (gay men get AIDS) when it is disclosed that she is
herself HIV-positive.

I can envisage ways of cleaning up the politics of *Torch Song
Trilogy*. Laurel would have to have other valuable things going
on in her life, and the stance of Mrs Beckoff would have to be
taken by Arnold's father instead. But it wouldn't work as well. If
Laurel were smarter she wouldn't marry Ed, and only a mother
can say 'You think that's what we brought you into the world
for? Believe me, if I'd known I wouldn't have bothered' (p. 72).
So although we can see that the text is tilted against the women,

it must be hard for most gay men to dislike Arnold or the trilogy (they may, however, dislike Ed, for this text, like others of the period, registers bisexuality as bad faith).

Yet there is more. Arnold doesn't just take the man from Laurel, he takes 'the feminine'. Stage directions require him to speak in the manner of Bette Davis, Blanche du Bois and Mae West (pp. 16, 29, 81); 'There are easier things in this life than being a drag queen. But, I ain't got no choice. Try as I may, I just can't walk in flats' (p. 6). He takes the 'feminine' stance of bravely suffering and waiting for his man – that's what the torch songs he performs are about ('Something about taking all that misery and making it into something'; p. 46). Arnold is very ready to admit the intensity of his feelings (not a manly trait), and it is to him that Laurel turns for comfort and insight when her relationship with Ed is in difficulty. She, conversely, according to Arnold, would 'make a great lesbian' (p. 37).

Now, there is, or should be, no offence in male effeminacy as such. But Arnold doesn't just share feminine attributes; he doesn't just, by pushing women out of the action, marginalise them. He seizes the feminine for himself (Dil is made to do this in *The Crying Game*); he is the better woman. It is Arnold who has a son (to David he is 'Ma'; p. 79), and Ed is made to agree that Arnold in drag is the more beautiful woman (p. 19).

As I have argued in *The Wilde Century* and chapter 3 above, 'feminine' and 'masculine' are cultural constructs; the masculine/feminine binary was a historical wrong-turn in western culture; it would be better if we could do without all that. Indeed, Arnold anticipates the end of drag queens: 'Once the ERA [Equal Rights Amendment] and gay civil rights bills have been passed, me and mine will find ourselves swept under the carpets like the blacks done to Amos, Andy and Aunt Jemima' (p. 6). However, those liberal reforms have not yet occurred. As matters stand, the claiming and/or repudiating of supposed masculine and feminine attributes constitutes among gay men a myth larger than that of the queer literary gent and his bit of rough, or even of HIV and AIDS.

Subordinated groups make their culture in the space seized

from, or made available by, the dominant; that is what it is to be subordinate. They replay its motifs in distinctive forms, sometimes reinforcing dominant arrangements, sometimes embarrassing them. Misogyny in *Torch Song Trilogy* is a response to a sex–gender system which invites Arnold, in order to assert his right to love, to perceive himself as feminine; meanwhile, the feminine is, anyway, an oppressive cultural construct, a mark of gender inferiority. Gay men, as well as women, have reasons both to retain and to resist gender hierarchy.

There is no magic wand for this; no new theoretical move. We just have to try very hard to get our myths to do what we want for us without damaging people we respect. Insofar as cultural work may effect a radical political intervention, that is how it will occur.

6 Conforming to type: the closet and the ghetto

Bruce Bawer shares David Leavitt's mistrust of purposefully gay writing:

> It is, of course, wrong to speak of great homosexual writers or artists of the past as being the special heritage of gay people. Every writer or artist – male or female, black or white, gay or straight – is part of the common human heritage; the obvious corollary to the misguided idea that a gay writer belongs specially to gay readers is that a straight writer's work belongs *less* to a gay reader than to a straight reader.[1]

I think that we should speak of 'writers or artists of the past' however we want, that 'the common human heritage' is predominantly heterosexist, and that, as a matter of fact, gay readers often *do* feel excluded from heteronormative works.

Thus far my leading arguments have been that we have to entertain more varied and permeable lesbian and gay identities, and that we need a purposeful, informed and critical subculture. In the present chapter and the next I investigate two partly complementary topics, conformity and transgression, as they are broached by contrastingly conservative and radical commentators, and as they illuminate the development, in fiction and commentary, of our subcultural myths.

Extreme behaviour

Bawer's principal goal in *A Place at the Table* is to distinguish 'mainstream' and 'subculture-oriented' gays. In a nice turn of phrase, he nominates his two types prisoners of the closet and the ghetto respectively (p. 36). His allegiance is with the mainstream. He wants gay men to be able to sit down at the table with everyone else. Bawer's definition of 'subculture' is different from mine, but, partly for that reason, it will be instructive to explore his ideas further, discussing also, as he does, novels by Mary Renault, Andrew Holleran and David Leavitt.

Bawer's goal, in effect, is to deny that his lifestyle and commitments as a gay man might exclude him from 'American' values, which he glosses as those of 'middle-America'. With far less qualification than Larry Kramer or David Wojnarowicz, whom I discuss in chapter 2, Bawer believes that 'America is basically a tolerant nation in which a misunderstood and persecuted minority's best chance lies in not sowing antagonism but in attempting to sow understanding' (p. 47). The extreme behaviour of subculture-oriented gays is what distresses these decent folk: they 'succeed only in making the homophobes' positions look legitimate to many middle Americans'. This must be opposed, for 'if gays are ever to be incorporated fully and freely into American society, the world has to be shown who the real fringe is, and who it isn't' (p. 193). For 'the truth is that homosexuality is not a problem and should not be seen as one' (p. 50). Bawer believes mainstream gay men can rely upon 'democracy' to gain 'acceptance', because 'to attempt to place restrictions on individual liberty and the right of others to pursue happiness is, quite simply, un-American' (p. 139).

The price of Bawer's project is this: 'One might imagine a gay couple that most heterosexuals would not even recognize as gay' (p. 34). We may be treated the same as everyone else, in other words, so long as we *are* the same as everyone else. Bawer does not consider whether this involves 'restrictions on individual liberty'. He asserts that subculture gays 'conform almost perfectly to every stereotype' – but intends no irony when declaring that the 'lifestyle' of mainstream gays is 'indistinguishable from that of most heterosexual couples in similar professional and economic circumstances' (pp. 33–4). That sounds pretty conformist and stereotyped to me.

As a thoroughgoing version of 'subculture-oriented gays' Bawer evokes a man who

lives in a small walk-up apartment in a gay ghetto like
Greenwich Village or West Hollywood or San Francisco's
Castro district. He holds down a job that is marginal or at least
vaguely artistic; he socializes almost exclusively with other
homosexuals; he dines in gay restaurants, dances at gay clubs,
drinks at gay bars; and his reading matter consists largely of
gay-oriented magazines and of novels by and about gays. His
'lifestyle' (if you want to use that word) would probably be
considered aggressively non-conformist by most Americans, his
politics uncomfortably left-wing; his manner of dress would
probably draw stares on the main street of the average
American town or city. (pp. 33–4)

I want to dismantle this picture from both ends. On the one hand,
it is not safe to assume the cohesiveness of this as a gay subcultural
image; on the other, it is not an image entirely distinctive to gay
men.

First, it is revealing of the state of US politics that Bawer does
not make reference to people who hold left-wing opinions while
being straight and/or while living in mainstream ways. Mainstream gays, he says, voted twice for Reagan and twice for Bush
(p. 34); he doesn't remark that this makes them a minority (most
US people have so little respect for the system that they don't
vote at all). He doesn't allow that there are heterosexuals who
are critical of the system – who have 'a powerful sense of
antagonism toward the manners and mores of the mainstream
culture' (p. 69). He doesn't acknowledge the radical traditions
which have flourished in the United States, from Wobblies to Beats
to draft-resisters to right-to-choose campaigners (to mention just
mainly white movements), and which might equally be called
'American'. The defining of radicals as 'non-American' is a grossly
ideological manoeuvre, one that aspires to delegitimate far more
than les/bi/gay people.

Second, gays with strong subcultural allegiances do not
necessarily have radical political opinions. This should not cause
surprise: les/bi/gay people, in or out of what Bawer calls
subculture, manifest the same range of political attitudes as
straight people. Indeed, John Weir complains that in the United

States 'self-identified gay men are especially resistant to thinking about issues of class and race, and they steadfastly deny their sexism'.[2] Weir discerns a different division among gay men. He distinguishes – and objects to – 'the privileged upper tenth of the gay community, the class of urban artists and professionals who dictate gay politics to the rest of the country'. This, he shrewdly remarks, includes both Bawer and Queer Nation activists: both of these Weir considers 'mainstream'. Weir declares himself 'postgay', declaring that gay in the USA has come to mean white, affluent and selfish, whereas most gay men are poor, provincial and closeted, in the Marines, or at home with Mom and Dad and *Reader's Digest*. He concludes: 'A conservative is someone who wants to keep what he has. So is a gay man' (pp. 30–4).

As I remark in chapter 1, there is no good reason to expect gayness as such to produce enlightenment on issues of class and race. In fact, there are two obvious, and opposite, responses to the outsider-situation of les/bi/gay people: one is to embrace it and become a radical, the other is to prove that in every *other* respect you are as normal as can be. What is troubling about Weir's analysis is not that he sees a lot of conservatism, but that he sees only superficial and compromised radicalism. It may be that the politicising of gay men has gone badly wrong, particularly in the United States where single-issue political affiliation is the dominant mode. I am no longer sure about North-western Europe. I have often said that les/bi/gay activism is inconceivable here outside the general framework of a broad-left commitment. However, ongoing changes in the political landscape forbid me to assume that this is still the case. I return to this topic in chapters 9 and 10.

In my definition of subculture, conservatives are included so long as they regard themselves as sexually dissident. Although I disagree with Bawer (more angrily, probably, about Reagan and Bush than about lifestyles), his book is a subcultural contribution of the kind that I am calling for: it discusses the relations that we have among ourselves and with the mainstream, and invites us to consider how best we may negotiate new situations in the future. Indeed, Bawer's analysis and mine are complementary: while he thinks that we have to take determined steps to implicate ourselves in the straightgeist, I think that it is very difficult for us to extricate ourselves from it.

Placing the scene: Renault and Holleran

Bawer pursues his theme by discussing three mythic texts. Because the attitudes he discloses have always been widely held among conservative-minded gays, I take Bawer's treatments as starting points for considering these novels and the issues they raise. It will emerge that they work less well for his mainstreaming argument than he supposes; indeed, they allow us to observe faultlines in it.

Boldly, Bawer endorses Mary Renault's novel *The Charioteer*, calling it 'a wonder of a novel' (p. 201). For its time – set in World War II and published in 1953 – perhaps, it is. Bawer acknowledges difficulties with the book – suggestions that homosexuality is like a physical disability, and that it is caused by childhood trauma. He grants that Renault is 'oddly contemptuous' of women, who 'tend to be silly, innocuous, or overbearing', that she 'accepts a bit too readily the necessity of the closet and the notion that most heterosexuals can never be made to understand and accept homosexuality' (pp. 200–1). But, in Bawer's reading, the dismissal of subculture gays in *The Charioteer* and the movement of Laurie and Ralph into a discreet, monogamous couple make up for all that.

Laurie's basic decency, it appears, prevents him from locating himself in the effeminate, queer (their word) milieu which offers itself. 'They had identified themselves with their limitations; they were making a career of them. They had turned from all other reality, and curled up in them snugly, as in a womb.'[3] Laurie objects to the very word 'queer', as 'Shutting you away, somehow; roping you off with a lot of people you don't feel much in common with, half of whom hate each other anyway, and just keep together so that they can lean up against each other for support.' Ralph strongly agrees (p. 172). 'It's not what one is, it's what one does with it', he declares (p. 149).

However, in the mid-twentieth century even more than today, some kind of network was essential both for finding partners and for the beginnings of an affirmative gay identity. Renault and others (Radclyffe Hall in *The Well of Loneliness*, for instance) meant well when they sought to rescue same-sex passion as personal integrity by counterposing it with any kind of gay scene, but in so doing they restigmatised precisely those milieux that afforded some kind of opportunity for self-expression. In *The Charioteer*, despite the ostensible case against the subculture, this is virtually acknowledged. Ralph has found his partners through a discreet network of private parties, and that is where he and Laurie recognise each other as potential lovers. Indeed, it is suggested that knowledge of oneself as homosexual *at all* requires some kind of interaction with a more knowledgeable person. 'I know about myself', Laurie says. Then 'presumably you know about at least one other person', Ralph responds – and, indeed, 'There was a man at Oxford . . .' (p. 171). A central question in the novel is whether Laurie should enlighten Andrew – helping him to see the queer potential which is evident to others but which he does not himself discern. Laurie decides not to initiate Andrew, thus sacrificing his love. In fact, Laurie is in a double bind, because part of the attraction of Andrew is that, not regarding himself as queer, he is uncontaminated by the shabby queer milieu. Of course, this prevents their relationship from developing a sexual dimension, and hence Laurie settles down with (settles for) Ralph.

Despite all the attempts to manoeuvre past it, *The Charioteer* shows that you can't be queer without being queer. So, actually, Laurie has more in common with the others than he likes to think. While weak from loss of blood and scarcely conscious from morphia, he rejects Ralph (whom he doesn't recognise) as if he had propositioned him: 'Sorry dearie. Some other time' (p. 43). Like Risley, the Lytton Strachey character in E. M. Forster's *Maurice*, Laurie uses the name of Tchaikovsky to test the extent of Andrew's queer knowledge (p. 62). And his hypersensitive distaste for the scene is expressed through a notably queer intuition for the nuances of the pick-up, and a ready way with the smart, snobbish put-down. When Bunny says Ralph is at bottom 'an unfrocked scoutmaster', Laurie has no difficulty producing a bitchy response: ' "We didn't have a scout troop actually," he said. "But I think it's quite good. It keeps boys off the streets. Did you ever join one?" ' – implying that Bunny is discreditably lower-class (p. 228). Laurie means to register his rejection of Bunny's effeminate bitchiness, but he displays his own facility in the manner. Correspondingly, two of the apparently frivolous scene queers – Sandy and Bim – turn out to be war heroes after all.

Good and bad – mainstream and subcultural – homosexuals refuse decisively to separate out in *The Charioteer*. This is because if Renault was to represent homosexuals at all then she had to make them credibly *as homosexuals were reckoned to be*. Unless they were *a bit* stereotypical, they would simply not be plausible in a fiction. Alternatively, or as well, Renault had her own stake in all this. As we can see from the biography by David Sweetman, she was a lesbian who was irritated by femininity: 'She hated to find herself "trapped in female company". She resented any invitation that led to her being placed among the wives while the husbands enjoyed themselves elsewhere ... She simply did not wish to be a woman.' At the same time, she didn't much want to regard herself as a lesbian either; she and her partner steered away from other lesbian couples, and, in the limited social and intellectual context of English-speaking white South Africa, she spent a lot of time in a queer male milieu.[4] So, in her view, a decent queer man would be preferable to a silly woman. And even an effeminate man (or a manly woman?) may be a hero when circumstances invite it.

Moving on historically, Bawer invokes Andrew Holleran's *Dancer from the Dance* (1978). He approves of this novel only insofar as it indicates the limitations of subculture gays who spend their time hanging out together and cruising. In fact, that is what Holleran (now) thinks he was doing; 'it's a critique of all that stuff ... these are the pitfalls, these are the time wasting obsessions, these are the problems if you are going to be gay'.[5] Reading *Dancer* in that way depends a good deal on the opening and closing sections, which frame the inner novel and the main action. The supposed author declares: 'The point is that we are not doomed because we are homosexual, my dear, we are doomed only if we live in despair because of it, as we did on the beaches and in the streets of Suck City.'[6] He has abandoned New York for a rural life in 'the Deep South'; he signs himself initially with gallic, 'feminine' names, but in the last letter eschews such camping for the decent, all-American, 'Paul'. These framing letters 'place the subculture's view in its proper context', Bawer believes. Nevertheless, 'it's too easy for a casual reader to miss the point' (pp. 205–6).

Like other commentators, and consistently with his notion that subculturally-oriented gays are a simple, unitary group, Bawer takes *Dancer* as comprising everyone who cruises and spends time in discos. He criticises Holleran for endorsing 'the false dichotomy propounded by the gay subculture: out, proud, and promiscuous versus closeted, ashamed, and repressed' (p. 204). However, the gay men in *Dancer* are neither out (for instance to parents and employers) nor proud, and they present only a limited social class. They are privileged in wealth and education; they move among socialites, celebrities and millionaires, and are able to give large, expensive parties; they have a thoughtlessly exploitative attitude to racially disadvantaged groups. We are reading about a smart set; certainly there is no sign of the 'uncomfortably left-wing' about their politics (Bawer, p. 34). Their brittle futility is comparable with that in an earlier novel about 'American' values and class society, Scott Fitzgerald's *Great Gatsby* (David Rees and Mark Lilly make this point). Holleran himself was not altogether one of these people – he says he served drink on the Fire-Island-bound buses to finance his writing career.[7] Hence, perhaps, an ambivalence in his attitude towards them. The equivalent set in his second novel, *Nights in Aruba*, is placed by the narrator as 'simply living the routines of bohemian New Yorkers, who when I first arrived seemed the most self-possessed and glamorous creatures on earth'.[8]

In fact, it transpires that there are some other gay men. 'Do you realize what a tiny fraction of the mass of homosexuals we

were?' Paul asks in his final letter. He recalls the day they joined
a Pride march: 'That day we marched to Central Park and found
ourselves in a sea of humanity, how stunned I was to recognize no
more than four or five faces? (Of course our friends were all at
the beach, darling; they couldn't be bothered to come in and make
a political statement)' (*Dancer*, p. 249). There are couples, as
well. Indeed, they may be 'a success', Paul thinks, but they are
unpromising material for fiction: 'After all, most fags are as boring
as straight people – they start businesses with lovers and end up
in Hollywood, Florida, with dogs and double-knit slacks and I
have no desire to write about them. What can you say about a
success? Nothing! So you see I've written about a small subspecies
only, I've written about doomed queens' (p. 18). Holleran's view
here is entirely compatible with Bawer's: there are 'mainstream'
gays, and they are unremarkable – so unremarkable that you can't
get a good novel out of them.

The problem is that literary representation is left with gays
who are consumed with alienation and self-disgust. For Malone,
we read, recognising his gayness 'was as if he had finally admitted
to himself that he had cancer . . . he was doomed' (pp. 71–2). As
commentators have noted, such imagery, here and in Larry
Kramer's *Faggots* (1978), permits the story that, somehow, we
were asking for AIDS. In the 1970s, the story runs, younger gay
men all lived as if there were no tomorrow. We were *either*
thoughtlessly innocent *or* irresponsibly immoral; but now, since
AIDS, which has been almost good for us, we have suffered into
maturity. As Eric Rofes says, this story is unhelpful, offensive,
and untrue.[9]

What Bawer cannot afford to recognise is that these gay men
are deeply preoccupied with his 'middle-American' values. If, as
he suggests, Malone is 'motivated by self-hatred' (p. 203), this is
not his personal hang-up, and still less the result of finding a gay
subculture. Malone is distressed not because he has chosen,
wilfully, to live outside Bawer's mainstream, but because he has
failed to kick free from the 'American' values that entail his
exclusion. He has been raised a Christian (a Catholic), and has
been subjected to systematic disqualification of *any* expression of

gayness. He 'believed in some undefined but literal sense that the body was the temple of the Holy Ghost', and hence that homosexuality is 'God's joke. His little joke. To keep us human. To humble the proud' (pp. 74–5). On Sunday Malone feels

> so utterly alone, he could not imagine anyone being sadder. Tears came to his eyes as he sat there. This day, Sunday, was his favorite of the week; this day, Sunday, a family always spent together in the evening as they came home from their various errands for a cold supper and a perusal of the Sunday paper; this day, Sunday, the softest, most human, tenderest time. (*Dancer*, p. 69)

Malone suffers not from inclusion in a gay subculture – in fact the subculture that he finds is only a small and limited segment of gay subculture – but from mainstream rejection.

A Holleran protagonist does attempt a return to 'middle America' in *Nights in Aruba*, the next novel. The narrator, Paul again, withdraws from New York to stay with his parents in a rural Florida town – because of guilt, his sister says.[10] When his mother asks 'Are you homosexual?' he feels impelled to deny it (p. 156). There is no prospect at all for gay life, mainstream or otherwise; even a gay friend who also spends time in the district is not much of a companion because he is afraid of being 'seen with another bachelor' (p. 210). If the chic New York scene is demoralising, getting round the table with middle America is impossible.

What both Bawer and Holleran disclose is the strength of pressure to conform to conventional notions, and the impasse that the gay man of conservative temperament must experience. For homophobia rarely occurs by itself. Most often it is accompanied by a swathe of illiberal attitudes. It is produced as an integral part of the mainstream values that Bawer wants us to admire and depend upon. 'Everyone in this country believes, deep down in their heart, that to be happy you must have a two-story house in the suburbs and a FAMILY – a wife and 2.6 kids and a station wagon and a big dog and an elm tree with a tire hanging from it on a rope', Paul says (*Dancer*, p. 15). If this is the case, then the dream of finding a place at their table must be largely frustrated. Any significant degree of assimilation would have to be accompanied by substantial, radical, nationwide reform. We have to develop the radical potential of gay men, therefore, not persuade them to respect a system that depends on their exclusion.

The choice of engaging with the scene or withdrawing to a conventional, non-gay family context is still structuring Holleran's thought in his story 'Sunday Morning: Key West', which Edmund White publishes in *The Faber Book of Gay Short Fiction* (1991). Roger has become a virtual recluse, he says, after going back home to tend his father after a stroke; revisiting Key West, his memories and perceptions are dismissive of the gay community there, and dominated by the AIDS crisis. When he and his former lover, Lee, enter a delicatessen for lunch he sees 'a room where gay men had collected like the grease of a million hamburgers, a million love affairs'.[11] This unpleasant vision is strongly established in the narration; nonetheless, Lee does indicate another perspective. At the beach Roger and he seem to have picked up where they left off, except that Roger 'noted, however, a difference – Lee was cheerful in the midst of troubles: his lover's illness, the hospitalization of a friend. Like everyone in the middle of the fray, he had a vivacity those trying to keep it at a distance did not' (p. 346). It dawns upon the reader (anyway, this reader) that Roger is offering the jaundiced vision of a man who is severely depressed, probably from trying to live in middle America, and that Lee is getting much more from commitment to his community, trivial and smashed as it largely is. Roger is stirred by Lee's situation. Instead of going to the beach he looks through Lee's old scrapbook and keeps vigil opposite the house of Lee's sick lover. Yet he restates this personal, human, communitarian feeling in terms of Jesus-on-the-cross religiosity, and his concluding thought is that he will avoid Key West next year. For readers, however, it is possible to take Lee's view. We don't have to go Roger's way, any more than we do Malone's.

Equal opportunities

Despite my rather intricate analysis of *Dancer*, I have to acknowledge that it has often been read as indicating the potential of male gay life, and that the picture it offers is not encouraging. David Leavitt says he encountered it as a young man and

> saw only, and with a kind of ashen horror, my future, or what I feared my future was going to amount to: relegation to some marginal role in a world where supermen possessed of almost blinding physical perfection preen, parade, ignore, dismiss. Seventies gay male culture did not have very much patience for the ugly man, the old man, the man with a small dick, or a potbelly or no hair on his head.[12]

The subcultural response, of course, is to write some more novels offering other representations, and that is what Leavitt has been doing. For Bawer, Leavitt is on the right lines: his 'heroes go through a period of sexual adventure but then fall in love, become monogamous, and look forward to a quiet, contented domestic life' (Bawer, p. 207). Actually, that is not altogether correct. Paul and Ted in Leavitt's story 'Houses' seem made for each other, but Paul feels unable to part from his wife; and Andrew in the story 'When You Grow to Adultery' appreciates hugely his easy place in Allen's family, but is betraying Allen.[13]

Up to a point Bawer is right about *Equal Affections* (1989), the instance he adduces. 'Sometimes I think the most political thing a gay man or woman can do is to live openly with another gay man or woman', Danny's sister says.[14] Danny gets billetted on Walter, a Yale law student, and they simply take to each other (no nasty gay scene). Luckily, money eases their path – 'as is common with lawyers, they quickly grew rich' (p. 23; Holleran's Malone also studied law at Yale; it must be fun there). However, life together is losing its shine. As is their habit after eight years, Danny and Walter watch a pornographic video (Bawer doesn't mention this as part of the 'American' good life). 'They pull their pants up and move to opposite sides of the house, each thinking about order, contentment, each wondering whether they are

sinking.' Danny wonders: 'So what is it, then, this sudden
conviction that everything he imagined would stave off disaster is
itself on the verge of blowing up?' (p. 26).

Walter is even more uncertain. 'Their suburban life, the life he
had urged Danny into, seemed absurd to him sometimes, even as
he cherished its rituals. What right did they have to such a life?
he asked himself. As if two men could be married, like anyone
else! How the neighbors must snicker behind their backs!' (p.
76). Walter is bored with domesticity and plans to abandon his
job and Danny. He imagines that he will 'find someone else –
someone fresh and young, as Danny had once been' (p. 78).
Meanwhile, he spends his time, and more, talking dirty with other
gay men on the internet; he likes the anonymity. This makes him
even less interested in Danny; he admits that he is 'addicted to
pornography' (p. 137). Eventually, a contact disconcerts him by
declaring his love, although he hasn't even seen Walter: 'I've seen
you. In my imagination I've seen you. And isn't that better? That
way nothing can spoil you for me. That way you'll always be
perfect.' 'But I'm not perfect,' Walter is moved to reply, 'And that
isn't love' (p. 139). He finds himself 'suddenly flushed with
affection' for Danny; 'I'm back', he tells him (pp. 241–2). In a
rather simple way, Walter opts for life.

The seductiveness of the internet is an up-to-date theme, but it
also enables Leavitt to evade some of the more awkward
consequences if Walter had engaged in more direct diversions with
other men. If he had gone cruising it might have been more
difficult for Leavitt plausibly to retrieve the partnership from
(self-)disgust; if he had taken a lover the feelings of this third
party would have been an issue. Further, Danny and Walter are
scarcely moved to talk about their situation, so there are no hard
words to swallow or forgive; perhaps Danny is more into
conformity than he, Walter wonders – 'But he never asked Danny
if that might be true. Such fundamental matter was the marrow
of their lives; it was too tender to bear conversation' (p. 78).

This reticence in the face of potential disturbance mirrors the
reticence, on gay matters, of the novel. For while Danny's mother
dies, his father moves in with another woman, and his sister has

a career as a singer, becomes lesbian and embarks on a pregnancy, nothing much is allowed to happen to Danny and Walter. It is often said that we need fiction in which lesbians and gay men are unremarkable, but something else is going on here. Leavitt is restraining the activities of the gay partnership.

The subtext in *Equal Affections*, I think, is AIDS. Neither Danny nor Walter, we are reassured, had 'ever done more than dip his toes in the great, cold, clammy river of promiscuity' (p. 25). So they are testing negative, we are to suppose; and none of their acquaintance is reported as sick or dying within the action of the novel. However, when his sister says she is to have a child by artificial insemination, Danny's first thought is: 'he is a gay man – well, has he had an AIDS test?' (p. 129). The prospect of an unconventional 'family' is policed immediately by an unconsidered, indeed inconsiderate, panic. Further, the central story is of Danny's mother, Louise, who for fifteen years has fought off recurring cancer. Her death is like a displaced version of AIDS (because of her treatments she is 'immunocompromised' and hence 'susceptible to all sorts of viruses and bacteria'; p. 173).

Perhaps Leavitt would like to write the book Bawer would like him to write – about how peaceful, monogamous pairing is, in principle, the best way to live. But, properly enough, he can't unravel ideas of gay relationships from ideas of the epidemic. If some gay men feel that their options are limited to solitary pornography and a boring partnership, Leavitt allows us to see, that is the emergency response of a damaged subculture, not an illustration of Bawer's programme. Furthermore (how many times must we say it?), the sensible response to AIDS is not monogamy but safer sex.

Despite his belief in 'the common human heritage', Bawer does write about Renault's and Holleran's novels from the point of view of a gay readership. *The Charioteer*, for instance, 'holds a valuable message for gays in the 1990s: don't ask for a medal; don't feel sorry for yourself' (p. 201). But he addresses *Equal Affections* obliquely, in the terms set by an article in *Vanity Fair* by James Wolcott, who mocks Leavitt and his partner for their suburban domesticity. In fact, Wolcott's case is cheap because it relies upon passages which, in the novel, are placed as humorous and/or problematic. Leavitt does invite gay men to reevaluate conformity.

What bothers Bawer is that Wolcott's comments are 'a remarkable illustration of the gay subculture's influence on sophisticated liberal views of homosexuality' (p. 207). Whether Leavitt significantly addresses the options for gay men takes second place to how the matter has been represented to 'the hundreds of thousands of affluent young urban heterosexuals' who read *Vanity Fair* (p. 208). The right response, surely, is (1) that it is not their business, and (2) that straights – as indeed Leavitt suggests – have little to teach us about the management of personal relationships.

What Bawer cannot afford to entertain is the thought that homophobia may be not an unfortunate, arbitrary awkwardness, but an intrinsic part of the 'mainstream' ethos which he wants to join. Nevertheless he cannot but allow a gap to open between his experience as a gay man and his wish to be 'incorporated fully and freely into American society' (p. 193). The difficulties Bawer encounters in his analyses indicate the difficulty of sustaining an assimilative stance while taking les/bi/gay issues seriously. Repeatedly, after castigating some aspect of radical gay culture, he veers round and complains that *all* gays get a bad time from the straight system. On Lesbian and Gay Studies, for instance, he exhibits a knee-jerk, right-wing hostility to programmes about which he evidently knows nothing. But then he adds: 'A properly constructed course in Gay Studies might provide [gay] students with an opportunity to contemplate the distinctive social, psychological, and ethical issues posed by the fact of being homosexual in a society that doesn't accept homosexuality and to recognize the breadth of personal and professional options open to them' (p. 210). Which is pretty much what we have been doing.

Finally, with notable honesty, Bawer allows his book to culminate in a wedding between straight friends whom he has believed to be really close and understanding. These good Americans do not pause to consider that they may offend him when they have it proclaimed that marriage between a man and a woman is 'the only valid foundation for an enduring home'; and through some strange oversight Bawer and his partner get omitted from the photographs (p. 261). 'People *can* be accepting', Bawer plaintively comments (p. 263), but he cannot avoid a sense of oppression very like that which moves gay radicals.

Bawer broaches, but does not resolve, the ultimate question about what les/bi/gay cultural workers should be doing. He compares the situations of other minorities in North America:

> A Haitian reading Philip Roth, say, or a Mississippian reading Naguib Mahfouz may find certain aspects of the novelist's culture exotic and baffling and even irksome, but certain things are universal: envy, sloth, greed, lust, ambition, the love of beauty, the fear of death, and above all the human attachments – boy-girl romance, parental affection, marital strife – on which most novels center. But can even the most gifted gay novelist count on straight readers to respond as desired to a novel about two young men falling in love? (p. 198)

This is a surprising conclusion; the more conventional claim, for someone who thinks there is a place for us at the mainstream table, would be that les/bi/gay people fall in love like other people and hence their writing is 'universal' as well.

But Bawer is on another tack. 'To most straight people', he adds, 'gay life is at best a mystery, at worst an object of revulsion, and the Gay Novel therefore a largely minority taste' (pp. 198–9). In order to scare us away from purposeful gay writing and into acquiescence with the straightgeist ideology of literature, Bawer reminds us that we excite revulsion. However, if that is the case, we may as well conclude that there can be little prospect of assimilating ourselves to people who are disgusted by us, or of finding a satisfying place in their fiction. Our better move would be to pursue writing that will help us to deal with all that homophobia.

The problem, Bawer almost says, is not how we fall in love, but how we have sex. *Dancer from the Dance* makes the point: 'if you were a family man going home on the 5:43 to Chappaqua,

I don't think you'd want to read about men who suck each other's wee-wees! Even if people accept fags out of kindness, even if they tolerate the poor dears, they don't want to know WHAT THEY DO' (pp. 14–15).

Compare a postcard currently circulating, which shows, as it were, a promotional still for the horror-film *The Homosexual Lifestyle*. Over a grotesquely screaming face it says:

> They worked at their jobs!
> They shopped for groceries!
> They even went to the movies!
> They lived . . .
>
> ### The homosexual lifestyle
> SEE . . . them do their laundry!
> HEAR . . . them order from the local take-out!
> FEEL . . . your spine tingle as they watch TV![15]

Right. There is nothing extraordinary about the way lesbians and gay men do all that. But then, few people say there is. What disconcerts the straightgeist is the way we do sex, and any analysis that doesn't include that is not going to reach the parts that count.

7 How transgressive do we want to be? What *about* Genet?

Jean Genet and Leo Bersani are on the other extreme of the argument from Bruce Bawer (in the previous chapter): they suggest that our sexuality outlaws us, not just from conventional mores, but from genial human society. Bersani is dismissive of assimilationist politics, and relishes the extent to which gay sex is transgressive. In his essay 'Is the Rectum a Grave?' he argues that the image of a man being fucked with his legs in the air triggers the ultimate anxiety of the male: that he might enjoy the psychologically-destructive ecstasy of taking his sex like a woman.[1] In his important book *Homos* Bersani criticises the Queer movement not because it draws attention to dissident sexualities, but because it blurs our image and disperses our potential for disturbance.

Homos culminates with a discussion of Genet's *Funeral Rites* (1947), which Bersani admires because it 'stands in sharp contrast to the tame demand for recognition on the part of our own gay community'.[2] Genet certainly presents same-sex practices explicitly. Furthermore, according to Bersani, *Funeral Rites* welcomes the thought that, to ordinary, decent, humane ways of thinking, gay sex is treacherous, sterile, and incompatible with intimate human relations. Genet was refused a US visa in 1965 and again in 1975 under the regulations designed to control moral turpitude, affiliation with a proscribed organisation, and sexual deviation.[3]

Why homos are treacherous

Bersani does well to confront us with Genet, for gay men have tended, complacently, to co-opt his literary distinction while skating past his ideas and attitudes. He is a part of our subcultural myth which we have neglected to work on. Indeed, he is a problem for anyone who wants to approach literature as a reservoir of profound truth (rather than as a tool for thinking with). *Funeral Rites* presents an unabashed continuity between Genet's enthusiasm for gay sex and his enthusiasm for Hitler and the Third Reich: 'It is natural for the piracy, and ultra-mad banditry of Hitler's adventure, to arouse hatred in decent people but deep admiration and sympathy in me.'[4] And this is not in the early 1930s, where some naive writers and artists may be excused for endorsing fascism because they didn't know what it was really about; this is in 1944, at the moment of the Liberation of France from Nazi Occupation. Queer activists may want to disconcert 'decent people' and SMers may want to play with the regalia of fascism (I return later to that), but 'ultra-mad banditry of Hitler's adventure' offers the Third Reich as something like Bonnie and Clyde. If we want 'literature' to challenge customary attitudes, *Funeral Rites* does that. But how can we use this kind of transgression?

Genet is not, Bersani rightly insists, attempting some kind of ironic exposure of fascism. He is not interested in redeploying dominant terms in a vein of parodic excess, as a way of getting readers to address their complicity in oppressive norms (*Homos*, p. 152). Nor does an 'explanation' of his work as an exemplification of existentialist self-assertion help us. This may confer straightgeist acceptance, as a highbrow (and hence allowable) exploration of the (alleged) limits of the 'human condition', but for gay men there is no novelty and little reward in being told that we represent a desperate extreme of human experience.

Bersani challenges us to confront not just Genet's 'proclaimed indifference to human life as well as a willingness to betray every tie and every trust between human beings', but, further, his enlisting of homosexuality as 'the prototype of relations that break with humanity, that elevate infecundity, waste, and sameness to requirements for the production of pleasure' (*Homos*, p. 172). He focusses on 'Genet's original and disturbing notion that homosexuality is congenial to betrayal and, further, that betrayal gives homosexuality its moral value' (p. 153).

The question Bersani poses, then, is something like this: What is it about homosexuality that makes it the quintessence of treachery, and how does Genet show us the truth of that? Of course, to an anti-essentialist such a question is problematic: it sounds as if there is an underlying essence to homosexuality (and Bersani invokes some Freudian propositions as if they represent human truths). Further, as I have argued, we should expect mythic subcultural texts such as Genet's to be valuable for thinking with, rather than as authorities.

If there is a central treachery of *Funeral Rites*, it is that the narrative sets out to mourn the death of a young man, Jean D. (in actuality Jean Decarnin) whom Genet loved, but swerves aside almost immediately to quite a different project. Jean was a Communist and a Resistance fighter; he was shot in 1944 by the collaborationist Militia during the uprising against the Germans that anticipated the Liberation of Paris. *Funeral Rites*, written shortly afterwards and published in 1947, mainly explores and celebrates the existence and sexual experience of the Militia boy who is imagined as having killed Jean. Riton, Genet calls him. Watching a newsreel film of the arrest of a young militiaman, Genet finds: 'My hatred of the militiaman was so intense, so beautiful, that it was equivalent to the strongest love. No doubt it was he who had killed Jean. I desired him' (p. 48). This act of treachery in the narrative composition of *Funeral Rites*, Bersani argues, is continuous with the treachery of Hitler and the Militia collaborator, the personal treacheries cultivated by Genet in his life and writing, and an alleged treachery in homosexuality itself.

Genet also invests imaginatively the sexual experience of Erik, a German soldier; in the culminating scene, on the rooftops of Paris from where remnants of the German forces fought their last stand, he has Erik fucking Riton. And Genet fantasises Paolo, Jean's half-brother, having sex with Hitler. Furthermore, in an act of identification with these fascists, the first person 'I' of the narrator in these scenarios moves across, without signal, into the first person of the character – Riton, Erik, Hitler. Genet acknowledges these things of darkness as his own.

Bersani focusses upon two passages in particular. In one, Paolo is being rimmed by Hitler. For Bersani, rimming shows 'how betrayal is inscribed within homosexual love itself', in that 'the other is momentarily reduced to an opening for waste and to the traces of waste' (pp. 157–8). In the other passage, Riton is being fucked by Erik from behind. The position is significant: 'If the two standing males had looked at each other, the quality of the pleasure would not have been the same', Genet says (*FR*, p. 232). Bersani reads this as a refusal of face-to-face intimacy – as 'anti-relational'. For Genet, he argues, rimming and fucking from behind represent gay treachery because they 'mythically emphasize the sterility of a relation from which the woman's body is excluded' and 'the anti-relationality inherent in all homo-ness' (*Homos*, p. 164).

Bersani acknowledges readily that rimming and *coitus a tergo* may be heterosexual practices also, but he believes they are specially associated with gay men. Fair point. But what is alarming about his view of rimming and sterility is, first, that it supposes the priority of reproductive over recreative sex (this was, of course, the Nazi case against homosexuality); and second that, so far as I can see, this view is not expressed in *Funeral Rites*. Genet does link homosexuality to death in a letter written some years later, in response to Sartre's prompting.[5] But Bersani's question – 'Could it be this failure to produce life, the absence of a reproductive site in (and exit from) the male body, as well as the "wasting" of sperm in the partner's digestive tract or rectum, that makes Genet refer to the love between two males as incomparable?' (pp. 159–60) – receives no answer in *Funeral Rites*.

Unfortunately, posing such a question alongside Genet's text allows readers to suppose that some essential, and essentially treacherous, property of gayness has been uncovered and authorised by Genet. This effect is exacerbated by Bersani's reference to Freudian notions such as Sándor Ferenczi's, that in sexual intercourse with a woman a man seeks unconsciously to return to his mother's womb (I don't know what is supposed to be in it for the woman): hence 'Genet's fantasized ascent into Jean through his anus is a savage reversal of this coming back to a life-nourishing site in the mother's body', and rimming 'replays the origins of life as an original death' (p. 159).

Bersani's second point is about 'the anti-relationality inherent in all homo-ness' (p. 164). As he says, in our culture the ideal image of sexual expression is two people finding themselves by looking deep into each other's eyes (which, I suppose, is one of the attractions of the legs-in-the-air position which Bersani invokes in 'Is the Rectum a Grave?'). Rimming, then, and fucking from behind, may present a refusal of this humane relation – a 'renunciation of intimacy' (p. 170).

According to Bersani, Erik and Riton's *coitus a tergo* gives them access to solitude and hence ties in with Genet's wider beliefs about transgression. Genet 'embraces crime *in order to* be alone', Bersani argues. Thus a singular possibility emerges: a redefinition of 'evil' (Genet's term) not as a refusal of the good, 'but as a turning away from the entire theater of the good, that is, a kind of meta-transgressive *dépassement* of the field of transgressive possibility itself' (p. 163). This would be a remarkable achievement, since conventionally evil is defined against good and transgression is limited by the boundary that it would cross; this has seemed to be a truism about how these concepts get constructed, in social interaction. Bersani credits Genet with moving beyond structure and beyond the social. *Funeral Rites* 'seeks to detach evil from its oppositional relation to good, from its dependence on a transgressive mode of address', Bersani says. 'It would replace the rich social discursiveness of good-and-evil with what might be called the empty value of solitude, a value that literature, always circulating within a symbolic network, can only name' (p. 168).

The invocation here of the power of literature to allude to an ultimate realm of experience, somehow beyond culture, signals familiar territory. Rather surprisingly, however, Bersani does not leave Genet, alone and beyond value, on some final, mysterious promontory of the imagination. Instead, he credits him with a project of cultural healing that would have appealed to a queer Matthew Arnold (if you can entertain such an idea): perhaps Genet's homosexuality 'allowed him to imagine a curative collapsing of social difference into a radical homo-ness, where the subject might begin again, differentiating itself from itself and thereby reconstituting sociality' (p. 177). In other words, if I apprehend Bersani's complex thought here, a point of sameness and solitude might be reached from which difference and the social might be reconstituted on new, unprecedented terms. Quite what this would be like, we cannot expect to know – 'Erik and Riton are positioned for a reinventing of the social without any indication about how such a reinvention might proceed historically or what face it might have' (p. 171).

A symmetry has emerged: Bruce Bawer (I showed in the previous chapter) thinks we are disgusting to decent, god-fearing folk but hopes they will forget about it if we keep our houses nice, look after our pets, and don't publish too many novels about gay sex. Leo Bersani also thinks we are disgusting to those people, probably in principle, but argues that this will enable us to break through to a profound new concept, beyond the social as it has been understood. (I think we should spend less energy worrying about what straights think, and if that makes us transgressive it is doubtless just as well.)

In a moment I will consider whether a disintegration and reconstitution of sociality is feasible or desirable. First, I must remark that the description of Erik and Riton fucking is not altogether anti-relational. Bersani reads it as 'this quickie on a Paris rooftop' (p. 165), but it is a good deal more substantial than that:

> If the two standing males had looked at each other, the quality of the pleasure would not have been the same . . . but the bodies in the figurehead which they formed looked into the darkness, as one looks into the future, the weak sheltered by the stronger, the four eyes staring in front of them . . . They were projecting the frightful ray of their love to infinity. Erik and Riton were not loving one in the other, they were escaping from themselves over the world, in full view of the world, in a gesture of victory. (*FR*, p. 232)

'The weak sheltered by the stronger': I don't think embracing from behind is necessarily anti-relational at all; what people call 'making spoons' is often thought to involve a valuable kind of closeness. Thom Gunn's volume *The Man with Night Sweats* (1992) opens with 'The Hug', which finds the poet and his domestic partner of thirty-plus years in bed together after a party. The poet's sleep is broken by a hug, 'Suddenly, from behind'. 'It was not sex', he says,

> but I could feel
> The whole strength of your body set,
>   Or braced, to mine,
>   And locking me to you.

Gunn calls it 'The stay of your secure firm dry embrace'.[6] When you both face the same way, you both face the same danger; Erik and Riton are looking out towards the people who mean to kill them.

Genet's impetus here, I believe, is not to do with an (anti-)relationality or treachery of Erik and Riton *as homosexuals*, but with Riton's relation with France. For the Militia boys were traitors – 'They were considered to be worse than whores, worse than thieves and scavengers, sorcerers, homosexuals, worse than a man who, inadvertently or out of choice, ate human flesh. They were not only hated, but loathed' (*FR*, p. 69). Hence their solitude; and their best response, as elsewhere in Genet, is to take *pride* in such infamy. Riton's homosexual experience is understood by him in those terms. As he begins to move toward Erik in sexual love,

> Suddenly the true meaning of his treason became apparent to him. If French rifles had been aiming at him for days, it was in order to prevent him from isolating himself at the top of the rock which all eyes had seen him climb to with that extraordinary mountaineer . . . He was in love with a man. He quivered with pleasure at the thought of being so near the goal.
> (p. 137)

In fact, homosexuality is only partly the expression of Riton's solitary outlaw condition; it is also a threat to it: Erik speaks 'so tenderly that Riton was flooded with disgust. He was being torn from his proud solitude' (p. 109). The two conditions – solitude and sexual sharing – collide when Erik and Riton stare out together into the darkness.

If Genet had established the substance of this defiant attitude towards France and conventional morality already by 1939, the German Occupation afforded supreme opportunity for its development. For in this context, who were the traitors? On the one hand, many of those fighting in the Resistance 'for France' were Communists, and hence regarded as destructive of established social relations. On the other hand, any continuation of ordinary life required an element of collusion with the occupying forces; after all, it was not at once obvious that Germany was going to lose the war. Time and again, some kind of collaboration was necessary. In December 1943 Genet frantically mobilised friends who had influence with the fascists to prevent his committal, as a persistent thief, to a concentration camp.[7] The episode in *Funeral Rites* where Pierrot is terrified by the Militia into identifying leaders of a prison revolt, who are summarily executed merely on his say-so, occurred again and again when the authorities exacted reprisals. The distress of the Occupation has not been resolved in French history and culture.

It is during those war years that Genet writes *Our Lady of the Flowers*, *Miracle of the Rose* and *Funeral Rites*, looking back at his formative experiences in the reformatory at Mettray, from a present spent partly in prison, and in a France that is, in effect, a gigantic reformatory or prison. Genet remarks in *The Thief's Journal*: 'Only the German police, in Hitler's time, succeeded in being both Police and Crime. This masterly synthesis of opposites, this block of truth, was frightful, charged with a magnetism that will continue to perturb us for a long, long time.'[8] The attraction of the Militia boys for Genet is clear enough. 'They were birds of a feather that would never include squares who wore glasses, noncoms of the destroyed army, hollow-chested bureaucrats, but only former thugs from Marseilles and Lyons', he tells us (*FR*, p. 188). Thus they represent – as against Jean and the high-minded Resistance – the tough boys whom Genet had longed for in Mettray and in prison. The Militia 'seemed the materialization of what every thief desires: that organization, that free, powerful society, which was ideal only in prison' (p. 188).

Genet admires Hitler as he admires the bosses in Mettray and the prisons, for he has dominated France. Genet believed that effeminate queers get fucked by real men; that was the assumption in Mettray. France has been dominated by Hitler, the hoodlum who beats all the others. This is figured when Paolo is compelled by Hitler to have sex with him. In *Miracle of the Rose* Genet compares the submission required in the reformatory and an alleged attachment of France to its shame: 'I realize that I loved my Colony [ie. Mettray] with my flesh just as, when it was reported that the Germans were preparing to leave, France realized, in losing the rigidity they had imposed on her, that she loved them. She squeezed her buttocks. She begged the supplanter to remain inside her.'[9]

For Bersani, Genet 'transforms the historical reality of Nazism into a mythic metaphor for a revolutionary destructiveness which would surely dissolve the rigidly defined sociality of Nazism itself' (permitting, as we have seen, 'a reinventing of the social'; *Homos*, p. 171). I think, rather, that *Funeral Rites* shows the historical appeal of Nazism as a logical conclusion of the kind of relations experienced by Genet at Mettray. If there is an element of treachery here, it is not intrinsic to homosexuality, and the Mettray scenario does not constitute the necessary, or best, way of being gay.

The Mettray scenario

My ultimate disagreement with Bersani's account of *Funeral Rites*, authoritative as in many ways it is, is this. Genet sets up the book as a stand-off between his love for Jean and his fantasy investment with Militia hoodlums. He deflects from one to the other. But if he evinces considerable imaginative investment in the hoodlums, he also asserts, throughout, the validity of his relation with Jean. By seeking the treachery in homosexuality *as such*, rather than in the deflection, Bersani overrides this distinction.

It is surely important that neither of the key passages analysed by Bersani – the rimming nor the fuck on the rooftop – involves Jean. The rimming of Paolo by Hitler is violent – 'I wanted to tear the muscles of the orifice to shreds and get all the way in, like the rat in the famous torture' (*FR*, pp. 127–8). When, in another passage, Genet rims Jean the tone is quite different: 'I saw the eye of Gabès become adorned with flowers, with foliage, become a cool bower which I crawled into and entered with my entire body, to sleep on the moss there, in the shade, to die there' (p. 236).

Again, although (in my reading) the fucking of Erik and Riton is more affectionate than Bersani suggests, the fucking of Genet and Jean is far more loving. Jean murmurs, afterwards: 'I love you even more than before'; 'I kissed the back of his neck with a warmth that must have reassured him', Genet writes (the back, notice). Jean confesses: 'I was afraid you wouldn't love me any more ... afterward.' It was this fear, Genet realises, that made Jean say 'I love you even more than before': he was seeking reassurance of their love (p. 55). Genet then makes Riton use these same words to Erik: 'I love you even more than before' – but it is the difference that counts. Genet comments: 'This phrase was offered to me three months ago by Jean, and I put it in the mouth of a militiaman whom a German soldier has just buggered.' The difference is that whereas these words were the ground upon which Genet and Jean understood each other with special intimacy, '*Erik did not understand*' (p. 236, my emphasis). There are two kinds of gay relationship: those where the two people understand each other intimately, and those where they don't. Homosexuality is not anti-relational as such.

To be sure, *Funeral Rites* has a great deal more to say about Riton than about Jean, and, anyway, violent and alienated elements in these fantasies cannot be quarantined from Genet's relations with Jean. The distinctiveness of Genet lies in the way he broaches extreme ideas and attitudes, and Bersani's pursuit of them to some of their conclusions is exciting as well as salutary. Nevertheless, I do want to take seriously Genet's statement that he is writing 'At a time when the death of Jean D. ravages me, destroying everything within me or leaving undamaged only the images that enable me to pursue doomed adventures' (*FR*, pp. 70–1). There are other images in Genet, other kinds of adventure that he might pursue, he is saying, though at the moment their possibility is 'damaged'. Again: 'It was to that purity, to the grandeur of that death, to my child's [ie. Jean's] calm, silent courage that I wanted to dedicate the story which best expresses the secret iridescences of my heart, but the characters I find in it are what I adored in the past, what I still love, but what I want to mutilate hatefully' (p. 89). The murder of Jean leaves Genet at the mercy of (partly) residual desires which he would prefer to handle differently. After the rooftop love-making of Riton and Erik, the French boy shoots the German and stamps on his body.

Genet is negotiating between modes of relating which he learnt in the reformatory at Mettray and in prison, and newer, more amiable kinds which he was developing, with Jean especially. The set-up in Mettray was that big boys had little boys and, according to Genet, there was ample intensity. But the relationships were ultimately coercive and always subject to the whims of the big boys and the warders, and the big boys didn't admit to being queer. Genet therefore experienced emotional intensity together with immense insecurity, and with hatred and self-hatred for homosexuals. That is what his investment in Riton is about.

As Edmund White explains, the Mettray relationships and those that derive from them (as described in *Our Lady of the Flowers* and *Miracle of the Rose*) are structurally skewed:

> Often in Genet's novels each of the male lovers in a couple functions under a different set of rules. The 'heterosexual' partner regards his lover as a 'pal', no competition for a real woman, whereas the 'homosexual', while pretending to be just a pal, secretly imagines that someday they'll marry or that they are already married.[10]

To be sure, hoodlums are entirely thrilling for Genet, but they are straight-identified and despise queers; they rarely permit affectionate expression and in some instances they deny sexual expression as well. In the Mettray scenario, he is condemned to unrequited love and only intermittent sexual satisfaction.

Consider, then: the prospect of a more-or-less requited love – and with a notably 'good' Frenchman – was figured, probably for the first time, by Jean. But he was killed by Militia hoodlums such as Genet still desired, and Genet has anyway been inclined to welcome the idea of bourgeois France getting fucked over by Hitler. So one part of Genet is destroyed by the other. No wonder he dwells upon treachery. The process is therapeutic, however: at the end, Genet declares that Jean has won: 'Jean D.'s death thus gave me roots. I finally belong to the France that I cursed and so intensely desired. The beauty of sacrifice for the homeland moves me' (*FR*, p. 231). Something like the Mettray scenario appears in another prison – in *Kiss of the Spider Woman* (chapter 3 above). There it is viewed critically and alternative ways of being gay are indicated. In *Funeral Rites* the relationship with Jean is the alternative.

Genet did not give up on these themes. They are explored again in *The Thief's Journal*, where Stilitano is the faithless criminal object of Genet's doomed love, but the alternative, toward the end of the book, is Lucien – Lucien Sénémaud, whom Genet met in 1945. Like Jean, Lucien returned Genet's love; when he married, Genet supported the family and built them a house.[11] In *The Thief's Journal* Genet finds that his love for Lucien is drawing him away from thieving and towards conventional morality. He ponders: 'How much more intoxicating to the point of dizziness, falling and vomiting, would be the love I bear him, if Lucien were a thief and a traitor. But would he love me then? Do I not owe his tenderness and his delicate merging within me to his submission to the moral order?'[12] There are alternatives, Genet says. If you want someone to be nice to you, it's better not to choose a treacherous, sterile, anti-relational, fascist hoodlum.

How transgressive do we want to be?

Bersani credits Genet with using the terms of the dominant culture 'to exploit their potential for erasing cultural rationality itself' (*Homos*, p. 153). It is not clear what would lie beyond 'cultural rationality', but I don't think it could be very pleasant. Bersani reassures us that 'neither territorial politics nor any specific genocidal ideology plays a part in Genet's fascination with Nazism'. Rather, he sees and respects 'a myth of absolute betrayal – the betrayal of all human ties, the attempted murder of humanity itself' (p. 167). In my view, that 'myth' is not something other than fascism, but an evocative summary of it; for Nazi genocide and aggression were legitimised by an ideology that dehumanises the other. When Bersani asks us to confront, as Genet's 'political radicalism', his 'proclaimed indifference to human life as well as a willingness to betray every tie and every trust between human beings' (p. 172), he has not found in Genet something for which fascism might be a metaphor, but a distillation of fascism. 'The Nazism of *Funeral Rites* is not a cause', Bersani says; 'it is the apocalyptic appearance in history of an impulse to erase history' (p. 169). But history is where people occur.

Bersani wants to recover 'the anti-relationality inherent in all homo-ness' (p. 164), and hence to 'bypass the social' (p. 179). But this cannot be; there is no human life beyond the social. Genet says he sought 'to remain outside a social and moral world' and 'chose to be a traitor, thief, looter, informer, hater, destroyer, despiser, coward' (*FR*, p. 157). Yet what is striking about almost all the identities on that list is that they *are relational*. Betrayal, thieving, looting, informing, hating, destroying and despising all entail social involvement. They do not constitute, even in fantasy, a mode of being beyond the social. They are not solitary; indeed, we rarely see the Genet narrator on his own. When he says 'outside a social and moral world' he actually means in a criminal subculture.

It is a commonplace of post-structuralist criticism that transgression is always in danger of being limited by that which it transgresses. Hans Mayer holds that in negating bourgeois values Genet fails to get beyond them. Elizabeth Wilson, writing generally about transgression, says it involves the crossing of a boundary – which sets up a new boundary which may in turn be crossed; so 'the transgressive spiral tends to become simply cyclical and circular, going neither up nor down but simply biting your own tail, or to put it more elegantly, disappearing up your own orifice'.[13] Perhaps such an engulfment would not altogether displease Genet. That is why Bersani wants to credit Genet with a more complete repudiation of the social – because otherwise 'social revolt is doomed to repeat the oppressive conditions that provoked the revolt' (*Homos*, p. 172).

In my view such structural repetition is indeed a danger, but it is not a 'doom'; it has to be confronted *in the social*. As with the tendency of hybridity to slide back into the formations it would displace (chapter 2 above), and the tendency of the market to (re)appropriate dissident imagery (chapter 9 below), the response has to be greater shrewdness, mobility and determination. The ineluctable problem with transgression as an idea is that it is individualist and voluntarist; too closely allied to the romantic gesture out of an exalted, solitary engagement within the profoundly troubled self. We would do better to decide, together, who we are, where we want to be, and what strategies are going to help us get there. This is what I am calling a project of shared subcultural work.

Placed alongside the dark forces that Bersani has invoked, this programme may seem sanguine. He too, I know, believes in everyday amiability; he just doesn't see it measuring up against 'revolutionary destructiveness'. Nonetheless, I want not only to resist the idea that homosexuality is distinctively treacherous, but also to reassert the general potential of political action. The Occupation turned the generally positive word *collaboration* into a euphemism for treachery, but we should not accept that collaboration is a bad thing. Basically, there are co-operative relations and competitive ones. Raymond Williams, writing in the 1950s, located them as proletarian and bourgeois respectively.[14] In fact most of us are socialised so as to have broad access to both. In the 1970s anthropologist Richard Leakey pointed out that amity and co-operation must be as important in the survival of human societies as aggression and competitiveness. 'We are human because our ancestors learned to share their food and their skills in an honoured network of obligation.'[15] It is lamentable that we live in a political culture where such insights can be brushed aside by a facile invocation of market forces.

For transgression is not, of course, just a matter of literary taste or personal preference. In August 1996 *Gay Times* published a full-page advertisement for a company called RoB, who supply 'leather and rubber clothes, toys and twisted gear' (p. 23). The half-page pictorial display is in four quarters, labelled 'gagged', 'bound', 'whipped' and 'restrained', and showing appropriate sex toys – a mask, wrist straps, a whip, handcuffs. The main legend is: 'No, this isn't an ad for Amnesty.' (And there is a number you can phone to get the RoB catalogue, but I won't reprint it here.) This is somewhere near the pulse of what I have been talking about, isn't it? If Bersani is interested in 'erasing cultural rationality itself' (*Homos*, p. 153), Amnesty International is on the opposite tack: it is a supremely rational – virtually an Enlightenment – organisation. It registers appalling cruelties perpetrated by powerful people all over the globe, while maintaining a belief that drawing them to the attention of governments and reasonable people will work a positive change. Lately Amnesty has set up a section to campaign against oppression based on sexual orientation.

Whether the RoB ad is playful or offensive is disputable – the question was sensitive enough for the company to fund a page for Amnesty in the next issue of *Gay Times*.[16] Our uncertainty is to the point: how transgressive do we want to be? For fascism, as Elizabeth Wilson adds,

> had a very transgressive aspect to it. It wasn't just all about Kinder, Kirche and Küche with a bit of Jew-baiting thrown in: it was seriously queer. It could never have had the mass appeal it did had it not plugged into more than people's desire for authority: the emphasis on physical beauty, the covert homo-eroticism, the chiaroscuro, the intensity, the paganism and the dark romanticism speak of transgression as much as of conformity.[17]

True: many people, gay and straight, have a psychic engagement with these motifs. The biographer of the popular artist Tom of

Finland tells cheerfully how during the Nazi occupation of Helsinki Tom 'began to have the sex he had dreamed of with the uniformed men he lusted after, especially once the German soldiers had arrived in their irresistible jackboots'.[18] In *The Folding Star* by Alan Hollinghurst, Paul confesses that he enjoyed sex with a uniformed man whom he has observed to be in the fascist militia, involved actively in seeking out Jews.

What is especially interesting in the RoB ad is another component: the AIDS ribbon logo and the message 'Who says safe sex can't be great sex?' The ad aspires to modify and contain its transgressive appeal within a collaborative ethos. We are invited to channel our fascistic impulses into responsible sub-cultural routines. But is such negotiation of fantasy not the negation of queer sexuality?

In fantasy we may be inclined, in the manner Bersani attributes to Genet, 'to betray every tie and every trust between human beings' (*Homos*, p. 172). But that should not determine our socio-sexual relations. While it is only sensible to recognise that we do not choose our fantasies, and cannot do much to change them, we can negotiate their expression. In fantasy, responsible sex may be a contradiction in terms, but in the world of sociality we have choices and we may learn to handle our selves better. If we want to transgress it should be against the straightgeist, the State and capital, not each other.

Genet managed to find collaborators for his Mettray scenario. Lucien Sénémaud, as well as loving Genet, actually had the background and appearance of a young thug, got arrested for stealing, and identified as heterosexual. Again, Genet went on to recognise common cause with other subjects of French oppression, the Arabs of North Africa, the Levant and Palestine; if this involved an expression or a displacement of sexual interest, should that be a problem?

One last textual instance. A flyer, picked up in the Antelope pub in Warwick, for the In Touch Coffee Bar: 'At last, NEW to Leamington Spa'. The location is given, and the phone number and opening times. Special features are itemised:

- Hot & cold drinks, home made cakes etc.
- Meet new friends, relax, check us out!
- Second hand CD's, vinyl
- Fancy dress
- Leather, whips
- Print your own T-shirt
- Fancy a browse, just call in.

What more could anyone want?

8 Theory of cultural production

In earlier chapters I have explored aspects of identity, art and subculture through textual instances, trying to stake out, quite informally, a les/bi/gay cultural politics for the time of the post-gay. In this chapter I try to elaborate a more sustained theory of gay cultural production.

Cultural materialism

There are many valuable accounts of aspects of lesbian and gay culture, but there is no lesbian and/or gay theory of cultural production as such. The two theories of culture in Western societies are the *idealist* or *formalist*, and the *materialist*. The idealist supposes high culture – culture 'with a big C' – to derive from the human spirit, and hence to transcend historical conditions, constituting a reservoir of ultimate truth and wisdom and belonging thereby to all people indifferently.

Cultural materialists argue that the notion of an unchanging human reality inhibits thoughts of progressive change by perceiving oppression and injustice as 'the human condition' – tragic but inevitable. They declare that cultures are produced by people in history, and regard high culture with some suspicion, since it is almost certainly promoting particular interests behind the claim of universal relevance. For the terms 'art' and 'literature' are neither spontaneous nor innocent. They are bestowed by the gatekeepers of the cultural apparatus, and should be understood as tactics for conferring authority upon certain works. Art and literature are involved in the circulation of representations through which cultural norms come to seem plausible, even necessary, and hence in authorising or calling into question the prevailing power arrangements. They do not – cannot – transcend the material forces and relations of production. This does not mean that they have to be conservative. How far high culture is complicit with the dominant ideology, or available to a critique of it, depends on the instance and on what we do with it.

Until 1945, it was fairly apparent that big-C culture, though it claimed universality, was in fact predominantly a subculture of the middle and upper classes. After World War II, governments thought they could control the economic cycle of boom and slump, and hence produce a fairer society without having to interfere much with capital. As with access to housing, education, healthcare and social security, in all of which public funding was to redress the most extreme inequities of capitalism, the State would facilitate access to high culture for everyone. However, the end of the postwar boom showed that these goals were not to be so conveniently attained. On the right, it was objected that the economy prospers better when the deprived are left to fend for themselves, that subsidy for the arts had been sheltering a left-liberal interest group, and that the proper way to organise culture, like everything else, is the market. On the left, it was objected that notions of quality and universality had been, in practice, pushing to the margins already subordinated groups – the lower classes, women, racial and sexual minorities.

Hitherto, socialists too had tended to believe that everyone could share the one 'human' culture, but in the 1970s disillusionment with the operations of (allegedly) universal culture gave rise to cultural materialism. This is Raymond Williams' term, and his *Marxism and Literature* (1977) is a key text; the work of Stuart Hall is equally important, and the whole Birmingham Centre for Contemporary Cultural Studies which he directed.[1] Cultural materialists investigate the historical conditions in which textual representations are produced, circulated and received, often considering big-C culture alongside popular culture. They engage with questions about the relations between dominant and subordinate cultures, the implications of racism, sexism and homophobia, the scope for subaltern resistance, and the strategies through which the system might tend to accommodate or repel diverse kinds of dissidence. Their work is cognate with and illuminated by that of materialist-feminists.[2]

Cultural materialists start from the premise that any social formation has to reproduce itself. It has to do this in material terms – people have to have food and water, shelter and other protection. Also, it has to reproduce itself ideologically – through churches, schools, the family, the law, the political system, trades unions, the communications system, cultural institutions. If it did not, it would die out or be transformed. There are directly repressive apparatuses as well – the police, courts, prisons, army. But, above all, people get socialised into ways of thinking that facilitate maintenance of the system. Therefore it makes sense to speak of a 'dominant ideology': the central and most authoritative set of ideas and attitudes. The dominant ideology is very plausible (that is why it is dominant); because we have come to consciousness as individual subjectivities within its terms, it seems to be *natural, normal, god-given, the way things are, simply human.* Of course, it embraces normative ideas about gender and sexuality – which I have been calling, informally, 'the straightgeist'.

This analysis is disputed. For commentators such as Jean-François Lyotard and Jean Baudrillard, ideological authority in postmodern societies is so dispersed and so mediated through a bombardment of flickering (televisual) messages that no one version can be regarded as dominant.[3] However, I reply (i) that some ideologies are indubitably more powerful than others, and the dominant is, simply, the most powerful (it does not have to derive from any conspiracy among politicians and businessmen, or even to operate always in their interests, though since they control the circulation of ideas it is likely to); (ii) were there not such an effective ideology, people would not put up with social arrangements that are neither fair nor in their interests.

Although the dominant ideology is very powerful, it would be quite wrong to suppose that it is coherent, secure and unchallengeable. On the contrary, as Williams observes, its dominance depends on continuous processes of adjustment, reinterpretation, incorporation, dilution. For 'its own internal structures are highly complex, and have continually to be renewed, recreated and defended'.[4] Dominant ideological formations are always, in practice, under pressure from diverse disturbances. For conflict and contradiction stem from the very strategies through which dominant ideologies strive to contain the expectations that they need to generate in order to establish their dominance. Dissidence, then, derives not from our irrepressible humanity, but from pressures and strains which the social order inevitably produces within itself, even as it attempts to secure itself (hence the title of my book, *Faultlines*).[5] Thus gay rights campaigners are able to exploit laws of citizenship which were designed initially to guarantee the rights of property, and never envisaged as justifying queer goings-on. Les/bi/gay people, like other dissidents, are well able to perceive and assert their own interests, both within and in opposition to the dominant ideology.

Hence my attention to subculture. As I said in chapter 2, if the dominant ideology constitutes subjectivities that will find 'natural' its view of the world, subcultures constitute *partially alternative subjectivities*. In Ken Plummer's formulation, 'As gay persons create a gay culture cluttered with stories of gay life, gay history and gay politics, so that very culture helps to define a reality that makes gay personhood tighter and ever more plausible. And this in turn strengthens the culture and the politics.'[6] Hence also my attention to fictional, or 'literary', texts. Along with film, song, autobiography, and so on, they are places where our subculture and its myths are constituted and where they may be questioned and developed. Cultural materialism frames cultural production in terms of the constituency that may be engaged, rather than through mystified notions of universality.

This approach may not immediately persuade les/bi/gay people. First, insofar as big-C culture claims to be universal, it promises to include us. Actually, though, even with the current fashionable kudos of gay men, it does that hardly at all – and even less for lesbians. Second, high culture, traditionally, is one of the things gay men have been good at. It suits our 'gay sensibility'. However, if there is no ultimate general truth about humanity for Raphael, Haydn and Ezra Pound to manifest, there is no ultimate particular truth about homosexuality in Michelangelo, Tchaikovsky and Djuna Barnes.

According to Jack Babuscio, gay sensibility is organised around camp, and has four basic features: irony, aestheticism, theatricality and humour.[7] In *The Wilde Century* I trace these features to the model of the queer man – dandified, effeminate, leisured, aesthetic, flamboyant – that was personified by Oscar Wilde. This model has as much to do with class as gender – with the perception of the leisure class as effete, in contrast to the purposeful middle classes. Hence, in part, the elements of theatricality and ironic disjunction: camp includes a 'sorry I spoke' acknowledgment of its inappropriateness in the mouth of the speaker. Aestheticism fits the model because high culture is regarded, implicitly and perhaps residually, as a leisured preserve, and as feminine in comparison with the (supposedly) real world of business and public affairs.

Gay sensibility is a specific formation that we have pieced together in the conflicted histories that we have experienced; it derives from the resources that have been available to us, and from our determination to seize them and make them work for us. These are the mechanisms of all cultural production. Recognising this, as Andy Medhurst points out, does not make gay sensibility any less real for people who frame their lives partly through it.[8] Nevertheless, we do need to notice that straightgeist crediting of gay men with artistic talent has generally been on condition that we be discreet, thereby acknowledging our own unspeakableness. Decoding the work of closeted artists discovers not a cause for celebration, but a record of oppression and humiliation.

Organic intellectuals

A central argument of this book is that les/bi/gay people, because of rather than despite moving into the post-gay, need a more intelligent and purposeful subculture. The idea is not to establish any kind of party line; of course, we are divided in terms of class, gender and race, and experience the massive conflicts that derive from those divisions in capitalism and patriarchy today. This diversity makes it more, not less, desirable to explore our situations. We need to create many more opportunities to think hard about our confusions, conflicts and griefs. We have enemies, and we sometimes damage ourselves. We need to get our act together.

The body of theory that will enable me to discuss the roles of subcultural producers has been developed particularly around the concept of the intellectual. Antonio Gramsci's treatment is valuable partly because he acknowledges that all people are intellectual, while also specifying as a social category the people who perform the professional function of intellectuals. That category will comprise people whose work mainly involves pushing ideas around society – journalists, broadcasters and copy-writers, novelists, playwrights and film-makers, songwriters and performers, teachers and students. Of course, everyone is involved in some measure in moving ideas around; that is what happens in social interaction. But people with the professional function of intellectuals have distinct roles, and, I suggest, distinct responsibilities.

According to Gramsci, an emergent group needs intellectuals to help it define its own technical, political, economic and social activity. It will find already-established 'traditional' intellectuals; very likely they 'put themselves forward as autonomous and independent of any social group'; an obvious instance is the priesthood. An emergent group may co-opt some of these traditional intellectuals. Also, such a group may produce 'its own organic intellectuals', from within its own resources.[9] Lately, as Foucault has observed, these terms need reformulating. Most intellectuals are employed – usually to exercise particular skills, often by business or the State.[10] Even so, they may cultivate an 'organic' relation with a subcultural constituency.

My stress upon the scope for les/bi/gay cultural workers is not intended to disqualify my earlier arguments about how we may appropriate work that is not actually oriented towards us. Nor is it my thought, by any means, that the virtue of an artwork depends on the intention of the creator, or that work done by les/bi/gay people should be subject to special reverence. As I tried to show in chapters 4–6 particularly, mythic subcultural texts, regardless of their origins, are most valuable when we challenge them.

Unfortunately, artists and critics are often reluctant to accept that their work might be oriented purposefully towards a subcultural constituency. Listening to Cherry Smyth talking about the painters she prints in her powerful collection, *Damn Fine Art* (Cassell, 1996), it is depressing how many of them seem to wish *not* to be perceived as *a lesbian artist*. To be sure, 'lesbian' does propose certain boundaries, but so does 'artist'. To regard 'lesbian' as a limited and constricting kind of concept, and 'art' – apprehended here as access to galleries and the rest of the conventional apparatus of artistic production – as contrastingly free and ample, is strangely lopsided. Indeed, as I argued in chapters 1 and 2, the hybridity likely to result from involvement with such straightgeist formations may effect a drag back into conservative positions. Not that we can simply break free of the straightgeist; but we may attempt an emphasis.

I want now to discuss Neil Bartlett and Monique Wittig, because their achievements in gay and lesbian subcultures demand that their ideas be taken seriously.

In *Who Was that Man? A Present for Mr Oscar Wilde* (1988) and *A Vision of Love Revealed in Sleep* (1989), Bartlett uses 'we' to mean not the allegedly universal 'man' of art and human nature but 'we gay men' of subculture. At the start of *Who Was That Man?* he writes of the difficulty of 'using certain words, the most ordinary of words, because I wanted to give them meanings which this city doesn't normally allow. When I write "we" for instance, I mean we gay men.'[11] *A Vision of Love* invokes Simeon Solomon from the viewpoint of a gay performer and audience: 'What should I say when I meet him; how should we talk to each other? I mean, how did men like us talk to each other in those days?'[12] However, Bartlett has been arguing lately that gay theatre does not need to be confined to a subcultural fringe, so I was keen to interview him about this. 'The 1970s opposition between a fringe margin which is radical, and a conservative mainstream: I think that's a false diagram – historically false', he says. Gay theatre belongs, and has always belonged, 'in the mainstream'.

After all, if you remove Wilde, Rattigan, Maugham, Coward, Orton and Novello from the post-1900 British theatre profession – from the money-earning profession of theatre –

you're left with a pretty serious problem at the box office. And
if you remove [the mid-century producer] Binkie Beaumont then
you lose half of the actors you've ever heard of.[13]

But, I ask, wasn't this gay mainstream theatre a middlebrow,
boulevard affair of subterfuge and equivocation? Not altogether,
Bartlett explains:

> By 'mainstream' I mean those points of entry which the
> mainstream allows me, to its mechanics and economics, *by
> accident*; certain moments in Wilde, Rattigan, Maugham,
> Novello, Coward, but also Malcolm Scott, Douglas Byng,
> Frederick Ashton, Robert Helpmann, Angus McBean. It's not a
> tradition so much as a cluster of artistic flashpoints – points of
> aesthetic excess at which the mainstream becomes ripe for my
> evil purposes, for plucking. So my mainstream is very picky;
> one that most people wouldn't recognise. It is deeply queer,
> kinky, complicated, melodramatic, over-determined, disruptive
> and disrupted. (p. 218)

Bartlett believes he can rely upon his own vision to draw from
the mainstream whatever is excessive and hence disruptive in the
queer practitioners who have worked there, and to reorient such
materials so that they will re-present this vision in our own time.
In fact, he does regard this as a subculturally effective strategy:
'It's important to say: "Actually, this has happened before – gays
in the mainstream – and maybe we can draw lessons and strength
from the way it's happened before" ' (p. 215).

To be sure, the more we know about how sexual dissidents
have lived historically, the better. But I still want to ask who is
hearing what, for the idea of a mainstream tradition 'that most
people wouldn't recognise' is plainly paradoxical. The mid-
century theatre of Coward and Rattigan was characterised by a
sleight-of-hand whereby massaging the anxieties of conservative,
middlebrow audiences secured the box office, while an in-the-
know minority thrilled to dangerously dissident nuances. In those
circumstances there were, in effect, *two (simultaneous)
performances*, one for each audience. For the time, this was a

necessary and cunning way of insinuating subcultural awareness, but the effect was only nominally mainstream, since mainstream audiences didn't realise it was happening.[14] Further, it probably can't be done today because (as I remark in the next chapter) very many people are likely now to pick up queer nuances; and, anyhow, we don't much need it because we have many other ways of signalling to each other.

Bartlett has other important arguments: working conditions on the fringe are unfair and oppressive, and audiences are predictable and complacent, whereas boulevard theatre may offer notable artistic scope at the moment. Those are entirely fair points. The working conditions available to organic or subcultural intellectuals of subordinated groups are generally inferior, and no-one is entitled to demand that they forego other opportunities. Indeed, my case is not that there is nothing to be gained by working in the mainstream; on the contrary, we have to do what we can with all the chances that present themselves. But we should not undervalue purposeful subcultural work. If you get asked to do a play for the Royal National Theatre, fine; but don't take it for granted that this is better than working with Gay Sweatshop. Of the exhibition linked to his book *The Sexual Perspective*, Emmanuel Cooper declares: 'It's in a gallery in the West End, it's in the mainstream, and that's where it belongs. It must stand within the mainstream, and be judged within those terms.'[15] Well, it is pleasing that people in a position to visit the West End can see these pictures, but we should not imagine that their standards are somehow superior. And if the assumption is that they have just been waiting for our work to become good enough before letting it into their galleries, that is bizarre. Actually, some of our work will be of high quality, some not – like anyone else's – and we can assess that for ourselves if we want to. We don't need to depend on recognition by establishment gatekeepers.

These considerations apply also in Lesbian and Gay Studies: academics too like to enjoy mainstream approval, and the working conditions that follow from impressing senior colleagues, a fellowship committee, a university press. And consequently, as much as Derek Jarman and the Pet Shop Boys (see chapters 1 and

2 above), we are vulnerable to co-option. In particular, we are likely to feel obliged to run queer subcultural concerns through academic routines, which will be illuminating in some aspects but inhibiting in others. Again, my thought is not that young colleagues should risk their jobs through impetuously explicit sexual politics, but that we should try to use the expertise and authority of the academy, insofar as we have some of that, to work in and through sexually dissident subcultures. This will mean trying to write our academic work in more accessible ways, and looking for opportunities to present it in the lesbian and gay press.

Monique Wittig would seem to be a good instance of a materialist intellectual who has committed her work to lesbians and other women. Diana Fuss invokes her as 'first and foremost a materialist thinker who believes that nothing which signifies can "escape the political in this moment in history" '. Her most famous comment, that lesbians are not women, discloses 'the act of social construction implicit in the very naming of "women" '.[16] In her essay 'Paradigm' (1979) Wittig claims for lesbian subculture a considerable measure of autonomy:

> As lesbians we are the product of a clandestine culture that has always existed in history. Until the last century Sappho was the only writer of our literature who was not clandestine. Today lesbian culture is still partially clandestine, partially open, in any case 'marginal' and completely unknown to *the* culture. It is, nevertheless, an international culture with its own literature, its own painting, music, codes of language, codes of social relations, codes of dress, its own mode of work.[17]

This situation derives from the ancient world, where lesbianism, as represented in the poems of Sappho, developed not '*against* the other, but rather outside of it, coexisting with it. To the extent that its origin is to be found outside the patriarchy, one could call it an a-patriarchal, a-heterosexual culture' (p. 116). Hence 'Lesbianism is the culture through which we can politically question heterosexual society on its sexual categories, on the meaning of its institutions of domination in general, and in particular on the meaning of that institution of personal dependence, marriage, imposed on women' (p. 118). Wittig announces here a role for the lesbian organic intellectual.

To be sure, there are problems with the argument of 'Paradigm'. As Fuss points out, Wittig proposes a miraculous free cultural space, and homogenises lesbians; as Judith Butler observes, lesbian and gay commentators today are more likely to understand our cultures as 'embedded in the larger structures of heterosexuality even as they are positioned in subversive or resignatory relationships to heterosexual cultural configurations'.[18] A fully materialist account will need to ground lesbian subculture in the historical conditions in which lesbian writers have worked, investigating the scope for dissidence and co-option in relation to the dominant cultural arrangements and the diversity of same-sex passion among women. All this said, Wittig's argument in 'Paradigm' offers a challenging and important evocation of the viability of lesbian subcultural work.

However, Wittig does not reprint 'Paradigm' in her collection, *The Straight Mind and Other Essays* (1992). In the title essay in that volume she insists on 'the material oppression of individuals by discourses', instancing psychoanalysis, science, the mass media, pornography, films, magazine photos, posters, the social sciences, history: these 'discourses of heterosexuality oppress us in the sense that they prevent us from speaking unless we speak in their terms' (pp. 25, 27). But *literature* is not in that list: it is not specified, on a footing with those others, as an oppressive discourse.

In fact, in another essay, 'The Point of View: Universal or Particular?' (1980), Wittig revokes the position she took in 'Paradigm': she specifically disqualifies subcultural writing by lesbians, other women, and gay men. 'A text by a minority writer is effective only if it succeeds in making the minority point of view universal, only if it is an important literary text', she writes. A gay theme is a gamble at best: the risk is that 'the theme will overdetermine the meaning, monopolize the whole meaning, against the intention of the author who wants above all to create a literary work'.[19]

Of course, Wittig is right: if you take 'literature' as your reference point, it will draw you towards a 'universal', i.e. straightgeist (straight-mind), way of thinking. But why should the lesbian or gay man be wanting 'above all to create a literary work'? 'Art' and 'literature' are defined by the established gatekeepers as meaningful to heterosexuals (so Arlene Croce on dance, chapter 4 above). That is why we have terms like 'the gay novel' and 'lesbian art': the qualifications indicate that these are partial, incomplete kinds of art. So when Wittig exclaims that Proust's *Remembrance of Things Past* is a monument of French literature *even though* homosexuality is *the* theme of the book',[20] this is indeed correct: only special excellence can persuade the literary establishment to allow an *evidently* gay text into its higher reaches.

Wittig concludes in this vein: 'even if Djuna Barnes is read first and widely by lesbians, one should not reduce and limit her to the lesbian minority' (p. 63). That is not acceptable. There is no more *reduction* in being appreciated by a lesbian minority than there is in being appreciated by the minority who feel themselves to be addressed in the discourses of art and literature (and it is a minority – never forget that big-C culture discriminates primarily in terms of educational attainment). Bartlett makes the point: 'people say: "You're just writing for gay people and all your work is about being gay and isn't that incredibly limiting?" So you just look them in the eye: "No, not at all".'[21]

John Frow, in his book *Cultural Studies and Cultural Value*, challenges the idea of organic or subcultural intellectuals on the ground that the relationship between intellectuals and a posited working-class constituency has generally been nostalgic and sentimental. He quotes Stuart Hall's retrospective analysis of the Birmingham School: 'The problem about the concept of an organic intellectual is that it appears to align intellectuals with an emerging historic movement and we couldn't tell then, and can hardly tell now, where that emerging historical movement was to be found. We were organic intellectuals without any organic point of reference.'[22] Indeed, it hardly seemed then, and does not seem now, that either working-class or youth movements in Britain are about to become the kind of formation to which intellectuals can conveniently hitch their visions of revolutionary political opportunity. However, Hall does reassert his belief in some such project: 'the organic intellectual cannot absolve himself or herself from the responsibility of transmitting those ideas, that knowledge, through the intellectual function, to those who do not belong, professionally, in the intellectual class' (p. 268).

Frow's suggestion is that we bear in mind that 'intellectuals have interests and "tastes" which, like everyone else's, are shaped by their class position'. 'This is an institutional, not a personal question' (p. 6) – to do with the role of intellectuals in the social formation, not with their individual sympathies and predilections. Their cultural politics, therefore, 'should be openly and without embarrassment presented as their politics, not someone else's' (p. 169).

In my view that is right. Intellectuals are a kind of class, class fraction or social category, and there is a disjunction, by definition, between them and people of other classes, class fractions or social categories. Intellectuals may forge sympathetic identifications with workers or aristocrats, but insofar as they do this *as intellectuals* they are engaging with concerns that are not immediately or entirely theirs. An element of altruism is involved, and this is open to charges of romanticism. But the pattern is different when we consider allegiances of race, ethnicity, gender and sexuality. In such cases, although the intellectual still has a distinct social role, there is no necessary disjunction *in respect of the organising principle of the subculture* – sexuality, for instance. The gay intellectual shares much of the history and current circumstances of the gay worker or businessperson. The idea of an organic relationship between intellectuals and a sexual constituency involves no intrinsic self-deception or nostalgia. The les/bi/gay intellectual has a legitimate role in the formation of a critical subculture, especially insofar as s/he works through subcultural myths and media. None of this means that organic intellectuals will not cultivate a wider analysis of relations in capital and patriarchy; to the contrary, one task is to bring such an analysis to the subculture.

To be sure, with the elitist and exclusionary use of jargon in the academy on the one hand and commercial media exploitation of ideas on the other, les/bi/gay people generally have little reason to trust intellectuals, whatever their sexual politics. However, the point about the organic intellectual is that she or he is envisaged, not as telling anybody what to think, but as claiming space for cultural work; space in which to explore, in terms that make sense to us, questions that are – *inevitably* – ignored or manipulated elsewhere by others. For, as I have said, it is unwise to leave these matters within the control of people who, we know, do not like us. Sarah Schulman observes:

> Many of us were deeply shaken by the casual, passing notice that took place in the mainstream press, of Audre Lorde's life and death, and it underlined yet again the understanding that our leaders, our geniuses, and our teachers can live and die without the respect and acknowledgment that they merit because our lives are simply not as important as the lives of heterosexuals.[23]

We should not have been surprised. We have to develop our own structures of understanding and recognition.

9 Consuming sexualities

Compulsory consumption

The outline of materialist theory which I attempted in the previous chapter insists that cultures are always inserted in material conditions. In the last instance, those conditions are determined by the prevailing economic arrangements. This chapter considers changes in lesbian and gay subcultures as they respond to the pressures and limits of the current phase of capitalism.

The most persuasive account of the development of gay identity in capitalist societies until the 1980s is John D'Emilio's. Industrialisation divested the household of its economic independence and fostered the separation of sexuality from procreation. This eventually allowed the space in which men and women, especially of the middle class, might 'organize a personal life around their erotic/emotional attraction to their own sex'. Socio-economic conditions, therefore, produced the 'social space' in which to be lesbian or gay.[1] The dislocations of World War II made gay subculture more distinct and confident, and primed early gay institutions – social and campaigning – so that some people were ready to respond to the riot at the Stonewall Inn with 'Gay Liberation'.

If capitalism thus facilitated gayness as we know it, why has it been having so much difficulty accommodating us? Because the change in the family that made space for gayness produced also an anxiety about the consequences for socialising and sustaining the workforce, D'Emilio argues. Hence it has seemed necessary to promote the family as the seedbed and shrine of privatised emotion, and to encourage suspicion and hatred of rival patterns of living and relating. So 'while capitalism has knocked the material foundation away from family life, lesbians, gay men, and heterosexual feminists have become the scapegoats for the social instability of the system' (p. 12).

Since D'Emilio wrote that account, in 1979–80, capitalism has moved towards a new relation with gay men and lesbians: we have become, in some aspects, targeted consumers. Danae Clark draws upon an article written in the *New York Times Magazine* in 1982, showing how advertisers were trying to incorporate a gay appeal without alienating larger markets. They put in covert hints which we might be expected to pick up – as we have been doing for decades among ourselves. This covert strategy has been called 'gay window advertising'.[2] By 1986–7, Frank Mort notes, an explicit gay component in marketing for British men was being recognised in articles in the *Guardian* and *City Limits*.[3] Gay men were supposed to have more disposable income – the 'pink pound' – and to be inclined towards tasteful – expensive – goods and services. In 1988 in *Gay Times* Peter Burton placed the pink pound as a hostile media concept; he noted that Hitler incited anti-Semitism by suggesting that Jews were rich. But generally the gay press welcomed the advertising revenue.[4]

London's 'gay village' around Old Compton Street developed from about the same time. This was not continuous with the 1940s bohemian Soho, Mort shows. Gay men came in the wake of media and marketing businesses, as 'specially commissioned market research pointed to the growing demand for a distinctly gay milieu in the centre of London', and local businessmen undertook 'carefully targeted advertising'.[5] Lately, lesbians too are being more explicitly targeted.

Not only do we spend our pink pounds, we enhance the product image. Polly Toynbee points out that when companies such as Absolut vodka, Häagen-Dazs and Benetton advertise in gay magazines they 'are saying a lot more about themselves beyond wanting to sell to the gay market. They are making a style and position statement designed to appeal to others, particularly the young. Gay is cool, gay is chic.' An IKEA furnishings ad showing two men buying a table together 'says IKEA is the sort of stylish shop where cool gay people would buy their tables, and that IKEA is sophisticated enough to be associated with up-front gayness.'[6]

The asymmetry is striking: in a period of new stigmatisation consequent upon HIV and AIDS, with minimal civil rights precariously balanced in the popular vote, the market has leapfrogged the earnest work of activists and conferred upon us the legitimation of glossy representation in national media.

Two factors in the immediate conjuncture seem to be licensing this development. One is that capitalism is in a rampant phase. Despite a world slump, attempts to evade or ameliorate capital have foundered – from the centralised control of the Soviet Bloc to social-democratic New Zealand. Multinational corporations are expanding, exuberantly or desperately, into the most recalcitrant markets. This is the impetus that reaches even lesbians and gay men. As Bill Short remarks, 'according to one marketing magazine at least, we gays are the last untapped market of capitalism. And when most markets are failing, this is news indeed.'[7]

The other factor is the weakening of respect for traditional authorities and decencies. Consider how the communal 'spirituality' of Sunday is getting reconstituted as the family going shopping together. Only market forces count, we are told. Those who invoke the 'postmodern' often declare that there are no more grand ideological narratives (somewhat like Daniel Bell, back in 1960, proclaiming 'the end of ideology'). However, they offer instead a universal *process*: the market affords the proper framework through which to comprehend and pursue every kind of activity. This ideology is so grand that they do not see that they live inside it. Gay men offer a fairly precise marketing niche, we have a certain disposable income, and our culture is not very anxious about hedonism. Up to a point, these factors embrace lesbians as well, though they experience the economic disadvantages of all women in paid employment.

We need to keep the pink pound in proportion, though. When Nick Kamen undid his fly buttons and took off his Levi 501 jeans in the launderette, in 1986, young gay men enjoyed the image and bought the jeans. But sales for the product rose by 700–800 per cent in a few months – far more than could be attributed to young gay men.[8] Gay consumption is a relatively incidental effect of a far larger project: the legitimising of youthful male narcissism and the drawing of young men into personal consumption. When I was a lad – well, we didn't have lads then, I must have been a scholarship boy or a teenager; when I was young, a common mode of aggressive male street assertion was the demand: 'Are you looking at me?' Women and effeminate men got looked at, not boys. In the 1980s, young men were persuaded to look at themselves and to allow themselves to be looked at by others. Media theorists stopped asserting that women are the only object of the male gaze. And fly buttons were back in.

Heterosexuality may have seemed compulsory when Adrienne Rich wrote about it in 1980, Donald Morton argues, but now the obligation is to consume and non-heterosexuals are becoming unremarkable. It is not, as D'Emilio thought, that the capitalist system is unable to accept homosexuality: the backlash against the queer is not 'from capitalism itself', but from older social relations that fitted earlier stages.[9] Homophobia is a quaint left-over and probably dysfunctional, Morton says; it is what Raymond Williams calls a 'residual' formation.[10] Morton entertains a thought which is surprising to most gay activists in the time of AIDS: that we are *not* significantly out of step with capitalism in the West.

Some might think this good news, but for Morton it is a dangerously seductive invitation to collaborate with an oppressive economic and political system. Queer theorists are particularly complicit. They celebrate the fluidity of the subject, which suits the marketing business very well; they present the moment-to-moment desperation of capitalism as analogous to gay cruising and as the best kind of life; they glamourise the 'risk' in S/M practices in the language of stock-market trading in derivatives.[11] British gay activists have long been suspicious of business. For Paul Hegarty, Queer turns its back on socialist analysis:

In the Seventies, our left stance made us wary of the capitalist profit-maximising motives of bar and club culture. It seemed to us that it was constructed as an alienating and individualised pleasuredrome which gave unsatisfactory highs and kept the

punters coming back for more. But of course that alienating
anonymity was part of its success. It was easy to participate in
this culture in a completely uninvolved way. But queer politics
is about consumption of style and being sexy. I consume,
therefore I am queer. Indeed, consumption of style now means
that the queerer you are the better and sexier you are.[12]

The significant contrary position comes from the *Marxism Today*,
'New Times' school, who have challenged socialists to acknowledge that there are attractive elements in the New Right emphasis
on individual consumption. Frank Mort argues: 'Advertisers and
marketers are not simply the slaves of capital. They are the
intermediaries who construct a dialogue between the market on
the one hand and consumer culture on the other.' Market
segmentation is a 'bid to come to terms with the cultural agenda
of the 1990s'; it correlates with the rise of 'new social movements.
For the fracturing of solid market blocs read the break-up of
postwar class certainties and the eruption of quite different
political subjects with alternative agendas: women, gays, the
elderly, etc.'[13] So that's where we come in; but who is using whom?

My view is in certain circumstances we have some economic
leverage, and we should use it. This may be specially true of our
power to boycott companies (such as Marlboro cigarettes) who
evince homophobic policies. But it is reckless to jump from that
to the notion that all we have to do is look trendy and keep our
houses nice, and soon our problems will be all over bar the
screaming. For short-term advantage the market will encourage
forces that the system may not endorse in the medium term
(capitalist publishers print Marxist texts; Williams calls this
asymmetry).[14] But while some gay men are being fêted in some
quarters for stylish dress, dancing and music, and lesbians are
said to be good at sport as well, all this is notably like the situation
of Blacks, suggesting that there are earmarked sectors of economic
and cultural activity where dangerous out-groups may be
accommodated. Further, the pink pound is arousing resentment,
most seriously among friendly but notably impoverished groups
such as lone parents. And many les/bi/gay people are poor and/or

unwilling to present the kind of image that pleases advertisers.

However and on the other hand, if twentieth-century homo-sexual identity is, as Foucault argues, in part a reverse discourse – taking up the stigmatised image and making our own assertion from it – then it should be possible for les/bi/gay people to deploy our status in the market for at least some of our own purposes. Clark allows that lesbians may politicise or reappropriate market images; I quoted earlier her case that 'lesbians *as lesbians* have developed strategies of selection, (re)appropriation, resistance, and subversion'.[15] Even covert window advertising may be fun, Clark says, just as lesbians enjoy the playful subversion of camp: 'By claiming this unarticulated space as something distinct and separable from heterosexual (or heterosexist) culture, lesbian readers are no longer outsiders, but insiders privy to the inside jokes that create an experience of pleasure and solidarity with other lesbians "in the know".'[16] She notes that indifference or hostility towards fashion was once an emblem of refusal, but now lesbians are asserting personal freedom as well as political commitment. Most lesbians and gay men believe that they have not chosen their sexuality; all the more reason, perhaps, why they should want to choose how they will manifest it. For there is no magical alternative space for les/bi/gay people to occupy; we have to make our own use of the resources that we can muster.

Marketing manoeuvres

Nick Kamen taking off his 501s in the launderette was screened nationally in cinemas and on television – not in gay space. Nevertheless, the gay appeal was plain enough. The young man was allowing an erotic gaze; jeans and T-shirts have been our uniform since Marlon Brando and James Dean; there is special focus upon Kamen sliding out his broad leather belt; the soundtrack song, 'I Heard It Through the Grapevine', suggests an in-crowd with secret knowledge. And, as Mark Simpson points out, the boy is doing his own washing; 'He is single, unafraid, flouting respectability and passively inviting our gaze: he is "queer" – his sexuality is outside regulation.'[17]

On the other hand, jeans, T-shirts, James Dean and Marlon Brando have a general, straightgeist 'American' significance, and 'Grapevine' has been widely popular since it was a number-one hit in 1968. The Kamen figure, Simpson concludes, is 'not *that* queer'. And he is watched by giggling young women who frame the view of him, 'to reassure the boys buying homoeroticism that they are making a heterosexual identification' (pp. 99–100). He is there for gay men if we want; the ad does nothing to discourage that; but it doesn't acknowledge it either.

This is *window advertising* – opportunity for covert gay decoding in a straightgeist context. Clark objects:

> gay window advertising can be described as a practice of 'ining'. In other words, this type of advertising invites us to look *into* the ad to identify with elements of style, invites us *in* as consumers, invites us to be part of a fashionable '*in* crowd', but negates an identity politics based on the act of 'coming out'. Indeed, within the world of gay window advertising, there is no lesbian community to come out to, no lesbian community to identify with, no indication that lesbianism or 'lesbian style' is a political issue.[18]

In window advertising, lesbians and gays do not appear in queer spaces (in bars or gyms with numbers of us in evidence). Such marketing may raid our images but it aspires to reconstitute us, as consumers, around the product; anything that we might be doing for ourselves – our subculture – becomes redundant.

The launderette ad dates from 1985–6. As advertisers begin to address lesbians and gay men more directly, many people get to recognise that queer inferences may be drawn. Now it is more difficult to produce covert window advertising: if there is an allusion to us, it tends either to be determinedly positive, or places us as inferior – which I call 'exploitative'.

In this section I mean to attempt a grammar, as it were, of marketing strategies. I shall be discussing how advertisements seem to be asking to be read, in the context of the site in which they appear. I do not suppose that such reading is inevitable; to the contrary, the 'wrong' reading may easily occur, because the

reader has not the cultural formation that is supposed by the
advertiser. Apparently seductive images in a gay lifestyle magazine
may be perused hostilely by a straight reader, a gay socialist, or a
potentially gay person uncomfortable with his or her sexuality.
Nevertheless, I mean to identify some principal tendencies.

An example of *positive* imaging would be the television
advertisement which was reported to be in production for
Guinness in 1995. What seems to be a wife clearing up around
her husband as he gets ready to leave for work (you don't see the
full figure) turns out to be another man when they are seen kissing
goodbye on the doorstep. After a great deal of media attention,
Guinness denied ever having intended to use the ad, though *Gay
Times* saw and described a copy.[19] Despite the media stir about
the pink pound, positive imaging is still rare outside the gay press.
Greg Woods shows how, even in a relatively adventurous shopping
catalogue, 'neither men's dressing gowns nor their underwear can
be promoted without the admiring and endorsing gaze of an
otherwise supernumerary female model'. Even 'what is
promisingly called a "2-man" tent is pictured being used by a
straight couple'.[20]

Catalogue shopping does tend to be a family affair, but in the
'Spring Fashion Special' (March 1995) of *GQ*, a lifestyle magazine
aimed mainly at straights, most of the stylish young males are
either by themselves or with females. There are exceptions,
though. In one feature several aeroplane pilots besport themselves,
but queer potential is partly controlled by manly connotations
(not just of machines and danger: in one shot three boys are
jumping for a rugby ball, in another one boy is arguing a technical
point with a sceptical colleague; pp. 108–15). Another feature
shows two Asian boys who look alike and are symmetrically posed
(pp. 146–7). This is the twinning or doubling effect pioneered by
Benetton (discussed below). By presenting two males who are so
close as to be nearly identical, twinning acknowledges same-sex
partnerships, even allowing a touch of kinky narcissism. At the
same time, it invites the thought that these men are brothers –
and therefore (as family ideology has it) not available for sexual
relations. Twinning both incites and controls intimacy (the Asian

boys are not touching). The only image in this number of *GQ* that could be called altogether gay-positive depicts Dolce and Gabbana together in an intimate stance – but they are designers rather than models, and known to be gay (p. 68).

Dolce and Gabbana appear in similar mode in another straight lifestyle magazine, *Arena* (July/August, 1995, p. 25). Elsewhere in this number of *Arena*, male models are solitary or with women, but there is one striking exception: a fashion shot where two young men (overdressed, it seems to me) sit side by side on a couch, so studiously casual and not noticing each other that they *must* be cruising; also, they are not noticing a picture above their heads showing statues of semi-naked women (p. 122). Positive imaging is evidently possible in these fashion contexts, and may be expected to increase.

The problem with positive imaging is that it tends to deploy cleaned-up versions of us. Lisa Peñaloza remarks 'the pervasive images of white, upper-middle class, "straight looking" people at the expense of those more distanced from and threatening to the mainstream, such as the poor, ethnic/racial/sexual minorities, drag queens, and butch lesbians.'[21] Michael Cunningham has noted this effect in films. Once, he remarks, he looked forward to film representations of gay men as 'ordinary, everyday people'. But, looking at *The Sum of Us*, *Priest* and *Philadelphia*, Cunningham observes 'A new kind of gay character . . . He's masculine but not macho. He's unassuming, decently dressed, devoted to his work. He's a regular guy . . . about as threatening as a game-show host.'[22] The deal is: acceptance for the straight-acting at the price of dumping embarrassing brothers and sisters. Anna Marie Smith shows how New Right discourse has begun to invoke the 'good homosexual' – the kind who, unlike the 'dangerous queer', makes him- or herself indistinguishable from heterosexuals.[23] We might compare the process through which certain Black people become 'acceptable'.

In *exploitative* imaging we are invoked in order to be relegated or repudiated. In a Levi ad of 1992, a young man in jeans dives into a sequence of private swimming pools, admired by women and frowned upon by their husbands; finally he is joined on the high board by a fantasmatic young woman and they dive together. There is a male admirer also: gays do like handsome young men in wet jeans. But he is 'an undesirable faintly ridiculous old queen', Simpson observes – this ad 'goes much further than *Launderette* in its attempt to bleach out any homosex stain'.[24] But that is not quite right. The gay reference is there and it is not hard to see. What is removed is any gay-*friendly* implication. Further, the soundtrack song is Noël Coward's 'Mad About the Boy' – which, for decades, encapsulated a moment at which the closet door began to swing open . . . but in the ad it is sung by a woman. *However*, on the other hand yet once more, the singer is Dinah Washington, who is something of a camp icon.[25]

Why does this ad make a gay reference at all? It is placed so as to allow awareness of a demi-monde of queer eroticism, while reasserting that heterosexuals have the monopoly on legitimate sexual interest in handsome young men in jeans. bell hooks calls this kind of exploitative manoeuvre 'the commodification of Otherness' and analyses, in the context of race, how out-groups may figure in straightgeist marketing:

> it is offered as a new delight, more intense, more satisfying than normal ways of doing and feeling. Within commodity culture, ethnicity becomes spice, seasoning that can liven up the dull dish that is mainstream white culture. Cultural taboos around sexuality and desire are transgressed and made explicit . . . The 'real fun' is to be had by bringing to the surface all those 'nasty' unconscious fantasies and longings about contact with the Other embedded in the secret (not so secret) deep structure of white supremacy.[26]

An extreme instance is surely Benetton's idea, that a picture of a man dying with AIDS would capture the consumer's interest. Perhaps they took their cue from *The Face*, manual of trendy consumption, which announced in May 1985: 'The AIDS scare has reinvested a fashionable, almost mundane homosexuality with taboo, rendered it marginal again. Despite the frank admissions and frantic gender-bending of pop stars in the not-so-gay Eighties, acceptance of homosexuality has now joined the other liberal causes in retreat.' 'This is printed only half legibly in white against a double-page enlargement', Simon Watney reports, 'together with appropriately "scientific" looking charts of incidence, the words of the text dissolving into the image of the virus, which stares out like a huge eye.'[27] Even our deaths may be marketed. If gay imagery is a way for the straightgeist to explore its exotic fantasies, then its continuing success depends on us staying roughly where we are.

As I finish writing in January 1997 there is a Wrigley's chewing gum advertisement on television, in which two (identical) young men appear to be embracing. However, it is evident that this is a mirror effect – from another angle we see one man embracing one woman – as he should. Some of these ads are, I suspect, testing the water: probably we will see a lot more casual same-sex imaging in the near future, and probably it will continue to improve our visibility. If I seem unappreciative of these openings, it is because I fear we are in danger of being excessively grateful for a few crumbs from the table.

I have discussed window, positive and exploitative uses of gay imagery. Two others are the subcultural, which appears mostly in gay media and helps us to establish and develop our own activities, concerns and institutions; and the assimilative, which addresses us insofar as it appears in gay outlets, but is couched in straightgeist terms.

The most effectively *subcultural* ads are not about AIDS, or about discos and phonelines; they acknowledge that les/bi/gay people have needs similar to those of other people, but in distinctive ways. The long-running advertisement in papers such as *Gay Times*, *Pink Paper* and *Capital Gay* for Ivan Massow Associates, financial advisers, is an instance. 'You are different', the copy runs –

> because you probably don't need to plan for school fees
> because you can't get 'married persons' allowances
> because you need pension plans that can pay out to same sex partners

because most life insurance companies will treat you unfairly or give you products that aren't appropriate for your needs.[28]

This invokes, almost in the manner of a manifesto, the main areas of fiscal discrimination complained of by gay men in Britain (though only the more affluent will have thought of school fees as the first problem). However, the gay allegiance of Ivan Massow & co. is not just a matter of precise pitching at a market niche. The accompanying photograph, under the banner 'we are different', shows ten men who look plausibly like financial advisers, but they are cavorting in their underwear in slightly exaggerated versions of characteristic gay poses (rather in the manner of a Bruce Weber photograph). This is our kind of joke; they offer themselves from within our subculture.

In its appeal to insider knowledge, subcultural imagery resembles window advertising, but it is not covert. Subcultural ads tend to appear in the gay press, and to present us in our own terms. Wings of Desire say they are 'The world's most exclusive chauffeur limousine service'. Their full-page ad in *Gay Times* (April 1996, p. 27) shows a Bentley coupé in dark red, waiting outside a pricey-looking apartment building. Also in dark red, and waiting, is a uniformed young chauffeur. The subcultural inflection is in his posture: he is slouching sulkily against the bonnet, holding a cigarette in a bored manner. For a conventional, straightgeist image, he should smarten himself up; this is supposed to be an exclusive Mayfair chauffeur service. But the transgressive posture admits a familiar gay fantasy of the subordinate, available young man; instead of smartly holding the door open, offering access to the limo, he offers access to himself.

In US magazines such as *The Advocate*, a high proportion of subcultural advertising involves health insurance and health products – solemn promises that our last wishes will be respected, and excessively fit-looking men declaring that they keep up their cell count by consuming nutritional supplements. PWAs are becoming a niche market. Increasingly these topics appear now in British papers.[29]

Assimilative marketing typically runs straight and gender-non-specific ads in les/bi/gay papers. Indeed, magazines have been founded in the hope that they will attract such advertising – though an insider tells me that sometimes the space is given free, so that the magazine will appear to have straightgeist endorsement.

The opening editorial of *Attitude*, in May 1994, makes this pitch:

> Not every person profiled in these pages is gay. Not every contributor to this magazine sleeps with someone of the same sex. In these post-Queer times, we're really not interested in policing boundaries . . . How do you judge a gay magazine? The answer must surely be – in exactly the same way that you judge any magazine. That is, by the standard of its journalism, the quality of its design, the strength of its opinions, its sheer entertainment value. (p. 7)

We are the same as anyone else, we neither need nor warrant any special attention. Nonetheless, we are expected to buy the magazine, so the inside front cover features a notably positive ad by Benetton. Two men, evidently identical twins, are embracing; they illustrate 'United colors of Benetton'. The colours are a pinky-mauve and turquoise, so these two affectionate boys are transgressing gender stereotypes (which say pink for a girl, blue for a boy – though in this case rather a pastel blue).

Elsewhere in this number of *Attitude*, though, the gay reader is expected to identify him- or herself with the common lot; we are assimilated to a straightgeist market. The presentation of a Citroën estate car (pp. 82–3) has no gay angle, and neither does Absolut vodka on the back cover. In fact, Citroën stress the amount of space in the car, which might be more appropriate for a family magazine. Perhaps there is a pun for gays in the main caption: 'now with improved load holding'.

Some ads in *Attitude* cultivate a particular device: imaging that is gender-non-specific. This is quite a feat, when you consider how much marketing hitherto has depended on hetero-normative gender stereotyping. A double-page spread for Glenmorangie highland whisky presents a lake and mountain landscape. This beautiful water goes into the whisky, we may infer, producing 'tranquillity'. The view is taken from behind a pair of identical, symmetrically-placed, *empty* chairs, with two glasses beside them. We may place in these chairs a tranquil same-sex couple, or a mixed couple if we prefer.[30] Again, a double-page spread for Cuervo Especial tequila shows in one panel a pair of symmetrical alligators (twins). One grasps in its jaws the valued bottle – probably they are playing. The message: 'Drink Cuervo Gold today'. The other panel just has a pair of shoe-trees: '– Because tomorrow. . . ?'[31] Tomorrow you die, and alligators may be made into shoes; we may play and share with a partner today but who knows what lies in wait? The thought may apply to straights or gays – the pairing in the ad is gender-non-specific (I have to say, though, that I don't understand the intended appeal – the concept strikes me as surprisingly distasteful). These ads run in straight magazines as well. One more pair: a Smirnoff ad has ornamental ducks winging their way across a wall.[32]

If we are not repudiated in such imaging, neither are we entirely recognised. Assimilative marketing supposes that gay men are like anyone else of the class, age, gender and race that is being addressed. In fact, as soon as we appear with our pink pounds, that very claim to attention is used as a reason for pushing us back out of sight again.

The anti-subcultural tendency of assimilative imaging is acknowledged by Pas Paschali, editor of *Attitude*, at the end of the first year of publication:

> Of course, it has been a controversial move, but where else was gay publishing to go but out of the ghetto and into the real world? Gay publishing came of age with *Attitude*. For the first time it has been acknowledged that we as gay men don't live in a cultural vacuum, that there is a two-way relationship between our subculture and the dominant culture. That we are not inward-looking and are able to break the bounds of the ghetto.[33]

Paschali writes of a 'two-way relationship' between 'our subculture and the dominant culture', but his impetus is all one way: 'out of the ghetto and into the real world'.

Assimilative imaging surely has a place; insofar as we may want to select one brand of vodka rather than another, or vodka rather than whisky, we may not be very different from hetero-sexuals. In the New York lifestyle magazine *Out*, subcultural ads run happily alongside assimilative ads. But it will be evident that my inclination is to welcome subcultural marketing because it makes for the elaboration and cohesion of lesbian and gay social subcultures.

Some readers may object that this preference involves a wish to corral gay men into one kind of stance. That is not so. I have said in earlier chapters that the gay identity that we have cultivated hitherto is too narrowly conceived, and will argue in a moment that commercial gay subculture may also be unhelpfully restrictive. Nevertheless, we need to feel very safe before we trade the shelter of subculture for the pleasure of being in style. The task, complicated as it may be, is to find a framework within which we can be both more various and more purposeful.

It is often imagined that the alternative is for us each to be an individual. As David T. Evans says, consumer capitalism invites us to see ourselves as 'unique individuals with needs, identities and lifestyles which we express through our purchase of appro-priate commodities'.[34] But that is not how marketing actually works. Consider the zip fly: it surely has a good claim to be one of the indisputable improvements to human life devised in the wretched twentieth century. Yet we can be persuaded – each as an individual making his or her own authentic choice – to buy Levi 501s and return, *en masse*, to buttons.

Reproduction and pleasure

Mass production in its classic form required the State, the churches and much of civil society to police our sex lives. Antonio Gramsci remarks:

It is worth drawing attention to the way in which industrialists

(Ford in particular) have been concerned with the sexual affairs of their employees and with their family arrangements in general. One should not be misled, any more than in the case of prohibition, by the 'puritanical' appearance assumed by this concern. The truth is that a new type of man demanded by the rationalisation of production and work cannot be developed until the sexual instinct has been suitably regulated and until it too has been rationalised.[35]

Much of the traditional hostility toward gays seems to be sited on this ideological terrain: we disturb the assumption that parenting a heterosexual family, working round the clock in household and factory, and rearing children suitable for the labour force is the natural way to live. To be sure, we are not the only ones producing this disturbance. In the late 1950s, Barbara Ehrenreich has shown, some men began to succumb to the temptation not to bother with family responsibilities; lately, many women prefer to manage without a man in the house if they can afford to. Paul Hoch identifies 'the fundamental reason why political and sexual deviants are so often equated, why commies are called queers: on the conscious and, more importantly, the subconscious level, both groups attack the work ethic and its psychic structures of authority'.[36]

Western ideas of sexuality, as I said in chapter 3, have been dominated by reproduction as opposed to recreation. Reversing this priority was one of the goals of the 'liberalisation' of 'sex' that we associate with the 1960s, and one of the initial goals of Gay Liberation. This was thought to be a revolutionary pro-gramme: 'The societal organization of the sex instinct taboos as *perversions* practically all its manifestations which do not serve or prepare for the procreative function', Marcuse argued. Were it otherwise, the body would become 'an instrument of pleasure. This change in the value and scope of libidinal relations would lead to a disintegration of the institutions in which the private interpersonal relations have been organized, particularly the monogamic and patriarchal family.'[37] However, as has often been shown, the 1960s agenda tended overall towards 'promoting, even rejuvenating, the heterosexual coital imperative'. Women who declared and/or acted otherwise were separated off as 'new women' – and became the focus of purposeful marketing in magazines such as *Playgirl* and *Cosmopolitan*.[38] They were precursors, in other words, of the gay man with his pink pounds. However, most women, for economic if not other reasons, were inhibited from taking this route.

But perhaps it is different now. If classic, Fordist capitalism tied reproductive sex to the economic productive system, whereas post-Fordist society is organised around consumption, then recreational sex may be the mode of the future. And les/bi/gay people, complete with safer-sex habits that ensure there will be no transmission of anything, may be the vanguard of the coming phase in capitalism and the good life.

George Orwell in *1984* anticipated a strengthened State, run by a privileged managerial cadre, engaged continually in remote wars, and bombarding its citizens with ideological messages. All that was prescient enough. What perhaps was not, was Orwell's supposition that the State would maintain an artificial scarcity, wasting resources in war so as to keep people poor and hence subservient. As Marcuse pointed out in 1955, scarcity is not (as Freud along with most classical economists had supposed) an absolute determinant of human societies. Actually we experience 'a specific *organization* of scarcity' which has been '*imposed* upon individuals – first by mere violence, subsequently by a more rational utilization of power'.[39] What is new in the Western economies at the present conjuncture, and what fuels the idea of consumer societies, is that we appear not to be in a situation of overall scarcity. The problem is not resources, but their distribution.

In the 1960s, impressed with the rate of technological change, we began to envisage a regime of abundance: we imagined that everyone might work a 3-day week. The problem, I think, was that this might make it difficult to keep many of us committed to regular work at all – people began to 'drop out'. 'Under the reign of plenty,' Hoch suggests, 'the whole organisation of work and consumption considered necessary under the regime of scarcity begins to be felt as increasingly oppressive, and the various ethics of masculinity based on alienated work and competition might well begin to crumble.' Writing in the 1970s, Hoch thought that the outcome might be a classless society:

> If the increasing economic surplus above people's subsistence needs should lead to a widespread perception of the non-existence of scarcity, there would no longer seem to be any reason to compete, no moral value attaching to competing – ie no work or production ethics – and no reason to allow winners in a competition – thus, no social classes.[40]

Technological change has indeed made abundance possible, but it is not being shared round. Instead, those in work, especially career-oriented work, are striving obsessively or in terror of dismissal for six-and-a-half days a week, and millions of others are not employed at all, or are in part-time or casual labour. The function of this pattern, or anyway the effect, is to select for work the strivers – including women, though they must strive even harder. They can toil until they break down or become obsolete, then be replaced by new, younger people. This is Will Hutton's 30–30–40 society. The first 30 per cent are *disadvantaged* – the unemployed or economically inactive; then there are the *marginalised* and the *insecure*, without effective job-protection – many part-time, casual, and fixed-contract workers, and many of the self-employed. That leaves 40 per cent who are relatively secure and hence *privileged*, though many of these are quite poorly paid. The outcome of 'the Thatcherite programme' is that 'more than half the people in Britain who are eligible to work are living either on poverty incomes or in conditions of permanent stress and insecurity'.[41]

The strivers are rewarded with consumption, when they have time, but the others have little reason for being good citizens, and when specially provoked, or just bored, are inclined to break up the place. This is the faultline in New Right ideology: having declared that the market is the only and necessary pattern for all kinds of relations, ideologists find themselves lamenting that people seem to lack moral principles, a work ethic, responsibility and respect for authority.[42] They will not save water in a shortage, as they used to when water was a publicly-owned utility rather than a way to make a quick profit. So the purportedly non-interventionist State attempts to reassert ideological authority (Thatcher's 'Victorian values'); to displace its disarray onto racial and sexual minorities, unemployed people, travellers, and so on; and to discover pretexts for undermining trade union activity, cancelling civil liberties, gagging the media, introducing electronic surveillance and strengthening the security forces. For the supplement to the Ideological State Apparatuses, of course, is the Repressive State Apparatuses. The State resorts more to violence – unemployment, poverty, the police, prison.

Zygmunt Bauman discusses an argument of Pierre Bourdieu, that we now experience a new mode of domination: the substitution of seduction for repression, public relations for policing, advertising for authority, needs-creation for norm-imposition. So if our societies cannot legitimate themselves, it doesn't matter: the consumer is enchanted into acquiescence.[43] However, this analysis needs qualification. First, it is not new – it is part of what Marcuse was saying. Second, we still have plenty of repression, policing and authority. Third, as Bauman observes, many people are too poor to join in:

> The 'tragedy' of consumer society is that it cannot reproduce itself without reproducing inequalities on an ever rising level and without insisting that all 'social problems' must be translated into individual needs satisfiable through the individual consumption of market commodities; by doing so, it daily generates its own handicapped, whose needs cannot be met through the market and who therefore undermine the very condition of its reproduction. In a truly dialectical manner, consumer society cannot cure the ills it generates except by taking them to its own grave. (p. 187)

For, actually, it is not possible to run an economy on consumption. As several UK chancellors have found, consumer-led growth sucks in imports, producing a balance of payments crisis, high interest rates, a falling exchange rate and low investment.

Marx noted that production is mediated and completed by consumption but, nonetheless, 'production is the real point of departure and hence also the predominant moment'.[44] Consumption has not displaced production, and the people who best know this are the global corporations who control production. They drive the marketing campaigns that persuade us to consume what they produce. As Judith Williamson remarks, while we are encouraged to organise our very identities through consumption, attempts to gain a stake in the control of production are strongly resisted.[45]

We should not take the 'pink pound' at face value, therefore. Recent work in the United States suggests that gay men earn less than heterosexuals, especially if you allow for levels of educational attainment. Probably this is because we are discriminated against by employers and because, as Short suggests, we gravitate towards jobs where we feel our sexuality can be accommodated.[46] Think how many lively and interesting gay men you know who have come to believe that their career aspirations should be limited to bar, catering and shop work. Other US research indicates that explicitly lesbian and gay couples are more likely to be mocked and ignored by shop staff, and are more likely to be refused hotel reservations.[47]

Many lesbian and gay people are living in poverty, and even more in chronic insecurity, scarcely eligible even for the regulatory humiliation of the benefits system. For many, the invitation to express gayness through style-marking fashion items is a seduction they cannot afford. Those unable to join in are doubly excluded: both from heteronormalcy and from prestigious subcultural motifs. They may resort to casual labour, sometimes prostitution, in order to maintain identity.

What is ultimately worrying about the concept of pink pounds is that no-one is interested in how we earn them. We just have them, because of the irresponsible (not looking after families) nature of gayness. Our work doesn't matter; we can sit around in wine bars reading glossy magazines and stay out all hours without harming the economy. Gay production isn't required. In fact, the occupations that are popularly associated with us, or where we have traditionally shown expertise and commitment, either have poor pay and/or job security (shopwork, catering, nursing), or require us to conceal our gayness (teaching, therapeutic professions, entertainment), or are part of the pink economy and therefore trivial (design, decor, care of the body). We ourselves, even, are doubtful of our capacity to do anything more demanding or responsible than consume. We are suspicious of our professionals, and of our activists; a friend doubts that a gay builder will be any good. We are celebrated as consumers because it is not important.

Consider also that, traditionally, work is masculine and consumption feminine. Consumption has been the mark of the frivolous, 'effeminate' leisure class. According to Thorstein Veblen, writing in the time of Oscar Wilde, leisure-class women were supposed to undertake a good deal of conspicuous expenditure, especially in respect of dress. The resulting status should accrue to men, though; the consumer herself was hardly a responsible agent.[48] For the *Evening Standard*, not much has changed. In 1988 it came up with a new acronym for an envied category of over-privileged consumers: MINK – Male Income, No Kids. Peter Burton observed the implication of 'idle femininity (albeit in a male body) wrapped if not in expensive furs then at least surrounded by expensive possessions'.[49] As Evans remarks, the development of gay consumer potency has been linked with 'virilisation' in our subculture. However, he adds, 'gay men are still not to be confused with the real thing. "New" styles of homosexual manliness are not conventionally masculine, but "masculine" to a quite studied and specifically homosexual purpose.'[50]

If all that is on the right lines, we might expect leisure consumption by lesbians, who are perceived as deficient in femininity rather than as misapplying it, to be regarded as a dangerous declaration of independence – since such purchases by women are neither for the family nor to attract men. How far the system will be able to celebrate lesbian consumption remains to be seen.

To note that the idea of a society based on consumption is a fantasy, and that it may attempt to reinsert gay men into a reactionary structure, is not to deny all progressive potential in the current situation. There does appear to be some weakening of the taboo on recreational sex, and it is associated with commodification and niche marketing. However, whether this is going to be empowering for les/bi/gay people, or more complicated in its consequences, is questionable.

First, destabilising an aspect of the dominant ideology will not have a progressive outcome unless it is accompanied by a new, radical consciousness. It will be a task for activists to promote this. Second, if free-market consumption does indeed (partly) promote recreational sex, it may nevertheless not help us to see how we should develop it. As I argued at the end of chapter 3, we have to find an accommodation that will enable us to repudiate the gender hierarchy, sexism and homophobia of the ideology of reproduction while sustaining love relationships, friendships, nurturing of children, care of the sick, appreciation of the elderly, and something partly like our families, pretended and otherwise. The market is not going to tell us much about all that.

Limited liabilities

These questions are not distinctive to les/bi/gay people: feminist theory has been grappling with them for some time, Angela McRobbie observes, and they arise in Black cultures also, Paul Gilroy remarks.[51] What is distinctive about the relation of les/bi/gay people to commodification is that other modes of identity formation are less available. In practice, of course, we identify ourselves in numerous ways, across a vast range of social interactions – negative as well as positive, often without other people realising that this is happening. We are not constructed entirely by fashion and music; in fact, complaints about 'the commercial scene' (abbreviated to 'the scene', as if there were no other) are almost as standard, in gay culture, as commodification itself.

Nonetheless, there are innumerable aspects of social practice, which other people take for granted, in which we are *not* allowed to discover ourselves. To the contrary, we are expected to pretend that we don't exist. In this situation, we are at special risk of being constituted overwhelmingly through a very limited range of the spectrum of social practice.

As Evans explains, the Wolfenden Report of 1957 deployed a new distinction: between legality and morality. 'Male homosexual citizenship is predicated on the conjunction of individual consenting adult freedoms including, indeed particularly, those of a consuming market, and the reinforced stigma of immorality which bans this citizen from the "moral community" and polices him into privacy.'[52] Despite the decriminalising of some homosexual practices in private, an aura of immorality remains, seeming to justify the withholding of various rights of citizenship – not just those that involve public display, in fact, but familial and quasi-familial rights (partnerships, child-rearing, entertainment in the home – magazines, TV and video). These are facets of the private sphere which, in the public/private ideology of Wolfenden, is where lesbians and gay men are supposed to be licensed. But privacy is too valuable to be conceded to us: moral policing seeks to establish more carefully just which private privileges we are to be allowed.

Hence the key deficiency in government policies on HIV and AIDS advice: the State cannot bring itself to recommend safer gay sex practices – because it cannot bring itself to recommend *any* gay sex practices.

The point is not that consumption fails to appeal to 'the whole man'. Rather, because this is the main ground that has been conceded to us, we are particularly vulnerable to pressures of fashion and the media. Commodification is not just one of the pressures upon gay men; it aspires to create our world (and lesbians too may recognise aspects of this regime). 'We are forced to prove we exist by projecting a gay image or lifestyle', Short observes.[53] This may be particularly true for youngsters finding their way into gay subculture: like some pre-feminist women, they may be persuaded to respect only a narrow image of the permissible self. If this is happening, then it is peculiarly unfortunate that they should escape the tyranny of the straightgeist only to succumb to another set of narrow demands.

Cornel West has written boldly of the nihilism that he believes is pervading Black communities in the current phase of capitalism:

> Aside from the changes in society as a whole, developments like hedonistic consumerism and the constant need of stimulation of the body which make any qualitative human relationships hard to maintain, it is a question of breakdown in resources, what Raymond Williams calls structures of meaning. Except for the church, there is no longer any potent tradition on which one can fall back in dealing with hopelessness and meaninglessness.[54]

This is recognisable enough if we translate it into gay terms; the difference is that West is able to speak of the 'breakdown' of a 'potent tradition' that previously existed. So bell hooks, quoting this passage, is able to urge African-Americans to set against consumerist nihilism the dignity and community that preceded integration.[55] Les/bi/gay people have been working on our histories, but we haven't found much in the way of a compensatory lost community to draw upon or revive. The way forward, I believe, is to develop a far fuller range of practices in les/bi/gay civil society.

Now, 'civil society' is a contentious term in political theory. It generally denotes the ensemble of personal, commercial and industrial relations, as distinct from the legal and political institutions of the State that govern those relations. It is a valuable concept insofar as it helps us to envisage a strengthening of non-State institutions against the power of the State. However, *by so much as it does that*, it allows three dangerous suppositions. One is that there is a realm of personal and political freedom, guaranteed by democratic institutions and traditions in Western societies, where we may manage ourselves. Gay people have every reason to know that there is no such free space – for, as I have said, the State does not concede us even privacy, and the civil sphere is dominated by institutions historically hostile towards us (the family, churches, the education system, business, organised labour). Second, focussing upon 'civil society' may allow the organisation of capital and labour to appear as one institution among others, conceptually on a par with hospitals and voluntary organisations. While those institutions should not be undervalued, they plainly do not have the determinative force of capitalism. Third, the concept 'civil society' allows the supposition that the market constitutes a space of freedom, as against the coercion of the State.

In fact, as Ellen Meiksins Wood observes, the rights encoded in civil society are, overwhelmingly, those of property, and its market mechanisms are coercive: 'No ancient despot could have hoped to penetrate the personal lives of his subjects – their life chances, choices, preferences, opinions and relationships – in the same comprehensive and minute detail, not only in the workplace but in every corner of their lives.'[56]

The good news in market capitalism, Meiksins Wood says, is that, unlike some other systems, it does not aspire entirely to control extra-economic identities. There is space to move. The bad news is that the system moves in on the identities that we fashion and exploits hierarchies of all kinds: it is 'likely to co-opt whatever extra-economic oppressions are historically and culturally available in any given setting'.[57] So capitalism may not specifically produce HIV and AIDS, for example, but it manages to thrive on the consequent scapegoating.

My point, therefore, is not that civil society may be played against itself and the State in a neo-pluralist, post-everything, free play of the market; but that we should cultivate a wider subcultural infrastructure. Then the element of commodification may take a better proportion in our self-understandings.

A network of wider les/bi/gay association is there already – you can see it in the back pages of our press. There are organisations concerned with sport and outdoor activities, party politics, Christian and other religions, humanism, personal growth, historical research, bisexuals, parents and children, racial and ethnic groups, employment rights, censorship, anarchism, pen-pals, HIV and AIDS. They are in small print, and rarely get into the news and features pages; they are not glamorous, not expensive, not of much interest to advertisers. And there is the commercial sector as well – not just escorts, masseurs and phone lines, also travel and holidays, legal and financial services, building and decorating, cleaning and gardening, counselling and pet care. We need to develop these resources, and to give them credit for the contribution they can make to our self-understanding. Probably this can't be done without a stronger *local* les/bi/gay press.

Sometimes it is supposed that the organisation of gay culture around bars and clubs facilitates our allegedly insatiable appetite for sexual adventures. In fact bars and clubs may encourage some men to maintain a pin-up approach, looking for the unique appearance of their ideal image, rather than encouraging attentiveness to erotic nuances that may arise in a fuller range of interactions. But the main point is that heterosexuals have many other opportunities to form partnerships, through friendship networks, informal associations and, above all, through work – in fact through civil society. Les/bi/gay people need those opportunities as well.

It is not that hiking with the Gay Outdoor Club is better than dressing up and sitting in a wine bar. In fact, our lads of Old Compton Street today are reviving gay tradition as recorded in one of my favourite bits of Quentin Crisp, who as a youngster sat in the Black Cat café ('Au Chat Noir') with a group of boys, making up, combing each other's hair and conversing in a 'stylised cattiness'; from time to time they 'waltzed round the neighbouring streets in search of love or money or both. If we didn't find either, we returned to the café and put on more lipstick.' This café actually was, Crisp says, in Old Compton Street![58] It is not that hiking is better, but that having a range of les/bi/gay activities, knowing that we have them, and appreciating their contribution to our identities, gives far greater depth and density to our subculture.

For many British leftists and activists, such a development of civil society will mean reassessing the role of business. For when we planned a lesbian and gay centre in Britain, we always sought public funding; and why not? – we are as entitled to it as anyone else. But we scarcely thought to ask for help from gay businesses; in fact, a good deal of the point was to get away from 'the scene'. This was a mistake. On the one hand, there is no reason to expect the State to help us; it is not, as was imagined in the postwar settlement, a bulwark against capital. Rather, it is capital's primary institution – seventeen years of Conservative rule showed us that. On the other hand, a market may be – sometimes still is – a friendly place, where people meet up and exchange goods and services. It is a fairly recent phase of capitalism that has made the idea of a market merely impersonal and exploitative – a pretext for not being kind to each other.

Of course, a gay businessperson may rip you off like anyone else. For, as Nicola Field points out after interviewing several gay entrepreneurs, 'there is no boss who can afford to put the interests of his or her workers before the pursuit of profit in competition'.[59] At the same time, the provision of goods and services within the community is not an unworthy occupation; the Castro activist Harvey Milk became prominent by running a strategically sited photography shop. A couple of guys setting up with a van as plumbers and taking on an apprentice is not the military-industrial complex. As I have said, there is no magical way for les/bi/gay people to exit from the economic and political system, or even from any significant part of it.[60]

So probably it doesn't matter too much if Pride these days seems more like a carnival than a political demonstration. Except at moments of crisis, marches are mainly for the self-validation of the people in them anyway, and a carnival is a traditional mode of self-expression. It is not just that a commercial slant makes Pride far larger and more exuberant than it otherwise would be, or that it draws in people who would be suspicious of student- or party-political rhetoric; it is not just that it is sensible to recognise clubs and pubs as principal points of gay socialising. Including commercial interests is better because it thickens up our subcultural networks.

Even so, some of that old-fashioned political stuff needs to be kept going. In Brighton, the trustees of Pride decided in 1995–6 'to change the emphasis from politics to a fun "Mardi Gras" style event open to all our community and supporters'; they experienced 'a great response from local and national business'.[61] This air of inclusiveness was somewhat qualified by the composition of the trustees: five (white) men and no women. I asked about this, and was told that it hadn't really occurred to the trustees as an issue; also, probably, the gay clubs and pubs which provided the floats, and the businesses who provided the sponsorship, are male-oriented. But it does seem that Brighton Pride still needs just a little 'emphasis' on that boring old 'politics'.[62]

The corollary of the anti-commercial stance among UK activists has been that gay entrepreneurs have assumed little responsibility for the wider situation of gays. In the United States, les/bi/gay businesses are typically at the centre of new subcultural ventures. This is changing in Britain, especially in relation to prestige events like Pride and arts festivals (It's Queer Up North, Glasgay). But it needs sustaining into the everyday commerce of civil society. It is still common to find a big man sitting *inside* the door of a gay club – not that there is any 'trouble'; it doesn't seem to strike anyone that there should be a big man *outside* the door, to make sure that people get safely away from a marked district. We should try to expand the scope of decent, local, les/bi/gay businesses, and ask more of them as a subcultural resource. That would be a positive use of our pink pounds.

Conclusion for socialists and others

To be sure, a call for the further development of les/bi/gay civil society is hardly revolutionary. Once upon a time, the New York Gay Liberation Front declared in its founding statement:

> Gay Liberation is a revolutionary homosexual group of women and men formed with the realization that complete sexual liberation for all people cannot come about unless existing social institutions are abolished . . . we are creating new social forms and relations, that is, relations based upon brotherhood, co-operation, human love and uninhibited sexuality. Babylon

has forced us to commit ourselves to one thing . . . revolution.[63]

But that was 1969. We didn't get it together – too many snags –
and since then it has been a discouraging time for socialists and
other progressives. As we turn the millennium there seem to be
two choices: (1) prepare for a future revolutionary conjuncture;
(2) regard socialism, for the time being, as a relative condition –
to be achieved in fits and starts where circumstances are
propitious. Either way, a good strategy will be to nurture and
sustain dissident groups, and to work with the opportunities that
occur.

In summary, there are three ways of thinking about the
commodification of lesbian and gay subcultures.

(1) It is good for us because it allows us to have fun while
    strengthening our identities. However, our gain, in that
    case, is at the expense of humankind, since it tends to
    endorse and strengthen capitalism; and, anyway, we should
    not trust the system. Tony Kushner remarks: 'it's entirely
    conceivable that we will one day live miserably in a
    thoroughly ravaged world in which lesbians and gay men
    can marry and serve openly in the Army and that's it.
    Capitalism, after all, can absorb a lot.'[64]

(2) Les/bi/gay commodification and its corollaries are
    undermining some of the traditional oppressions that we
    associate with capitalism (specially the emphasis on
    reproduction). However, the consequences will be
    progressive only if our movement is politicised. D'Emilio
    suggests that we should be working with other people who
    are living outside traditional family limits, to build an
    alternative affectional community.[65]

(3) Commodification is at least partly bad for us because it
    confines our identities by deriving them from too narrow a
    base. However, we may develop les/bi/gay civil society so
    as to ameliorate its disadvantages.

Readers coming from other political traditions may wonder what
the fuss is about: if the market wants to put gays on the same

kind of footing as other people, isn't that a good start? However, the case against capitalism is not that it promises no pleasure – far from it – but that the pleasure, if it indeed eventuates, is always paid for, sometimes by oneself, sometimes by other people.

10 Gay and after

Boundary games

Constructionism, in lesbian and gay thinking, calls for a recognition that categories such as 'gay', 'lesbian' and 'heterosexual' do not demarcate *essential* differences. They are not intrinsically 'human' and do not represent an individual, ultimately metaphysical, selfhood (like the soul). We may well believe, however, that they do demarcate differences that our societies find necessary in their current formations. And that is surely correct – for to write as though cultural categories were a semiotic game, without location in the actual structures which make some people powerful and others weak, some rich and others poor, some legitimate and others shameful, is to attempt a merely abstract, and conservative, exercise. The differences that our cultures mark do constitute the scope for our lives.

But this is not to say that we are confined by those categories. Boundaries are always permeable: that is the key insight of poststructuralist theory. They do denote a point at which a line is experienced as necessary, but that very need signals a point of vulnerability. The boundary is the place where the most urgent ideological work occurs; it is a region of conflict, where confusion reigns and the unequivocal is usually over-emphatic. If only for the sake of perversity, boundaries are going to be crossed (consider again Genet and the Nazis, chapter 7 above).

In the Latin American sex–gender system, as I showed in chapter 3, the key distinction is between the inserter and the insertee – the *activo* and the *passivo*. However, there is evidence that sometimes the *maricónes* ('effeminates') of Mexico are called upon, privately, to play the 'masculine', inserter role (the denial that accompanies such transgressions makes it difficult to track the spread of HIV).[1] In Brazil, the insertee role is ascribed to cross-dressed *travestis* by the dominant sex–gender ideology, but often they are asked to perform the inserter role. Despite, and because of, the assertion of boundaries that is drag, neither the sexuality nor the gender of the *travesti* is beyond negotiation; in fact, his/her skill is to respond strategically to the wishes of clients in their explorations of gender boundaries and the power relations that they encode. Hence, for the most part, *travestis* are not interested in sex-change operations; the juxtaposition of female and male attributes is part of their allure. Andrea Cornwall calls this 'boundary flux': 'The dissonance generated through boundary flux gives *travestis* the scope to enact a range of gendered identities in different situations.'[2]

In Black townships in South Africa, same-sex practices seem to be governed by a sex–gender model like that in Latin America. *Injongas*, by definition, penetrate *skesanas* and everyone seems to like it that way. But 'some *injongas* will confess that they actually also enjoy a receptive role in sex. They will not admit this openly and it would be disastrous if the *skesanas* found out.'[3]

If observing the sex–gender categorisation in different countries discloses not only the *diversity* of human practices and identities, but also their *mobility*, then we have to acknowledge, I think, that the metropolitan concepts of straight, gay and lesbian have afforded us clarity at the expense of flexibility.

This has happened for good reasons. Lesbians and gay men have needed identities to cohere around; and straight-identified people, where they have been prepared to countenance gays at all, have preferred to reduce the chances of contamination by placing us as a separate category of person. We should now entertain the thought that we have got ourselves slotted into a system that offers us limited lifestyles and minimal civil rights at the cost of amenability to State regulation and market exploitation.

To put this provocatively, we might consider whether men who have sex with men are on to something. Heterosexually-identified men who log into gay sex when they feel like it are, surely, the ones who fool the system. They do not reveal a dissident lifestyle on the computers of the electoral register, taxation and social security offices, credit card and insurance companies, banks. They are not seduced by advertising into spending money on designer clothes and standing around in discos. They are not shamed by the gay press into working out in gyms, attending earnest queer movies and contributing to AIDS charities. Commentators have proposed that camp lays bare the operations of ideology, but, as plausibly, it is men who have sex with men who effectively blur and resist conventional categories. They are the dissidents; they are both pre- and post-gay.

Of course, that is not all there is to say. Generally men who have sex with men are vulnerable to exposure – as gay men were before they decided to anticipate such embarrassment by coming out more or less of their own accord. Also, but not necessarily, they risk upsetting their partners more than most of us end up doing. Nonetheless, I am not entirely tongue-in-cheek about this: there are more ways than we normally allow of relating to both conformity and transgression in the prevailing sex–gender system and some of these ways have positive potential; our subcultural work, both fiction and commentary, has tended to overlook or marginalise them.

The part of Tony Kushner's *Angels in America* that gets quoted is not the anxieties about ethnicity, AIDS, religion, self-hatred and coming out; these are all well done, and they lead to a 'proper' resolution: the purposeful embracing by the 'good' characters of a conventional gay identity. Louis and Prior do this, Joe moves towards it. The distinctive figure is Roy Cohn, the corrupt, powerful and homophobic attorney who says the term 'homosexual' doesn't refer to him because he can pick up the phone and call the President's wife: 'Homosexuals are not men who sleep with other men. Homosexuals are men who in fifteen years of trying cannot get a pissante anti-discrimination bill through City Council. Homosexuals are men who know nobody and who nobody knows. Who have zero clout. Does this sound like me, Henry?'[4] If you want to shout 'But Cohn, you monster, *you are gay*', then you are missing my point. Kushner enables us to see that it has, in fact, been entirely possible to engage in same-sex relations through the 1970s and 1980s while having very little to do with gay subculture. Homosexual or gay identity is an affiliation, comparable, say, to being a baptist or on the left (it may feel like we didn't have much option about our sexualities, but many people have that feeling about religion and politics).[5] If you don't feel gay, then you aren't (though your behaviour may suggest that you aren't straight either).

In *Angels in America*, to be sure, Cohn's kind of adjustment does not appear attractive. That is because Kushner sets it up so that refusal of gay identity correlates with political and judicial corruption; conversely, Joe's coming out aligns with his resistance to Cohn's inducements. Of course, I don't really disagree with Kushner; Cohn has not found a better way to live. But this representation of him may provoke us to think again about the scope for sexual expression in our societies. For his culture has in fact overlapped with ours, even if we don't like to think so.

A persistent feature in attacks on the idea of les/bi/gay community is a dual denunciation: (1) it limits us by suggesting that we are all the same, (2) it can't work because we have nothing in common but our sexualities. Thus journalist Polly Toynbee greets the announcement of the 1994 *Out* series on Channel 4 television by wondering whether we want this flood of media resourcing – six whole programmes! She thinks we should not need special programmes in these liberated days, complains of 'the implicit notion that all gay people must share the same interests', and wonders whether lesbians and gays 'really all want to be defined primarily by sex', to have their 'life and achievement . . . reduced to this one aspect'.[6] The reply, of course, is that such objections are not raised in respect of, say, sports programming. Toynbee is not unfriendly to lesbians and gays, but the tendency of her argument is to allege that we are, at once, too various and too limited to attempt any common purpose, and hence to disqualify subcultural organisation and political activity.

In fact, I would go further – gay sexuality is not an inevitably cohesive force either. It too is diverse: there are different kinds of homosexuality. Probably that is why people who want to find 'the cause' are so easily confounded with counter-instances. Different homosexualities have different, perhaps multiple, causes. Our apparent unity resides in the shared condition of being *not-heterosexual*. Compare 'people of colour', whose collocation derives from being not-white. Even so, not-heterosexual, like not-white, is not an illusion. It is a real-world political category, in which people actually live. Its indeterminacy makes subcultural work more necessary, and potentially more productive.

The boundary which I have hardly addressed, it occurs to me as I draw my themes finally together, is between the sexual and the non-sexual. Like the rest of our society, I have been pre-occupied with modes of sexuality and with movement between them. But the line between the sexual and the non-sexual should not be taken for granted. In many of the instances of something-like-homosexuality which we collect from earlier centuries – David and Jonathan, Shakespeare and Mr W. H., the Ladies of Llangollen, Alfred Tennyson and Arthur Hallam – it is not really clear how far we are looking at friendship and how far at a sexual relationship. The reason, surely, is that they were not drawing quite the boundary that we draw. That is how it was for many women, Lillian Faderman argues, until the term 'lesbian' became current.[7]

Even in very recent times, changes in the boundaries of the sexual may be observed. When I was young, in my country and my class, kissing, other than between the affianced, spouses, and parents and children, indicated illicit and dangerous sexual attention. If, as your dinner guests prepared to depart, you were caught in the hallway kissing one goodbye while his or her partner was looking for their coat upstairs, the uproar would amount almost to pistols at dawn. Kissing signified either family or adultery. But no longer. First, in order to prove we can be as relaxed about these matters as the French are supposed to be, progressive-minded English people began friendly kissing on the cheek. Today, mouth-to-mouth resuscitation is in order among friends. Or, for that matter, footballers. Once again, we should not suppose that our local sex/gender arrangements begin to realise the scope of human possibilities.

At least three uncertainties

I complained in chapter 1 of the dismissive attitude towards gay culture in parts of Mark Simpson's collection, *Anti-Gay*. However, I do think we have to countenance contributions by Peter Tatchell, Lisa Power and Jo Eadie, who accuse lesbians and gay men of being frightened of indeterminate identities and trapped in an ancient stand-off with the straight world. These commentators are not coming all from the same position. Eadie presents as a card-carrying bisexual, whereas Power wants to be able to have some sexual relations with men without getting driven out of the category 'lesbian'. Tatchell relates sexual indeterminacy to the idea of Queer, arguing that people who settle for the conventional gay lifestyle are 'implicitly committed to the preservation of sexual difference and to solidity of the gay/straight dichotomy', and hence to a reformist, rights agenda. Conversely, 'strident, anti-assimilationist queer activists seek the extension of sexual freedom in ways that ultimately benefit *everyone*'.[8]

Unfortunately, the pattern is not quite so tidy, in principle or in the world. Obstreperous queerness may become a way of life as much as more peaceable kinds of gayness; civil disobedience may contribute to reformist goals (and has often done so); and, willy-nilly, activists may reinforce the gay/straight binary model that they aim to destroy. I don't mean to attempt to adjudicate among these complications. Rather, I want to complicate matters further by locating three large uncertainties in the current historical conjuncture – uncertainties which make it difficult to locate a single, right, strategy for sexual dissidents.

First, we don't have a consensus about how les/bi/gay people are placed at the moment, even in such a small and ideologically coherent space as England. 'Identification with being gay gives rosy reassurance, defining a sense of personhood, place and purpose', Tatchell says. 'There is no need for anyone attracted to people of the same sex to feel lost and uncertain.'[9] It seems to me that the problem columns of the gay press disclose a good many confused and distressed people; but then, I daresay lots of straight-identified people are confused and distressed as well. I will record, though, that I was shaken by my own response to the withholding of an equal age of consent in the UK parliamentary vote of 1994. Though I knew perfectly well that there would be a compromise and had long despised the trimming that would determine it, I discovered myself to be, albeit briefly, humiliated and tearful at news of this rejection. I mention this merely as a very minor instance of the kind of humiliation that is experienced today, even by case-hardened lesbians and gay men.

And how secure are our gains? I think of an almost forgotten moment, the early 1980s – when the pop charts featured Boy George, Divine, Marc Almond, Bronski Beat, Frankie Goes to Hollywood. You couldn't get into Lesbian and Gay Soc discos (as we called them then) for straight men checking out the scene and slopping their beer around. Then HIV and AIDS gave opportunity to the tabloids, the bigots and the New Right, and suddenly we were fêted no more. We cannot assume that current prospects are any less precarious, should history take a new turn against us. Bars, clubs and shops are vulnerable, Nick Walker remarks. 'Look to New York where the regime of a right-wing mayor has seen the end of some of the best gay clubs in the world. Of course, Old Compton Street has given London its gay village, but it has only done so for a short eight years.'[10]

A second uncertainty concerns the extent of homophobia. Heterosexuals are not all the same (if I seem to have been writing as if they are, that is because I have been trying to identify dominant tendencies). In many aspects, many people are only vaguely concerned about same-sex relations. However, a minority – perhaps of about the same size as the minority of lesbian and gay people – is rabidly homophobic (the situation with racial hatred may be broadly similar). Here are the queerbashers, the spiteful colleagues or siblings, the discriminatory employers, the poisonous gutter-press columnists. And the more space we claim for ourselves – gay villages and such like – the more they will resent us and the better they will know where to find us. Because this group is so relentless, it does damage quite disproportionate to its size.

This phobic minority may effect an irreducible minimum

pressure for the foreseeable future, if only because it maintains a bridgehead for attitudes that, among people generally, may be dormant but still available. For ideology is always conflicted and contradictory, and composed of residual and emergent, as well as dominant, elements; people may hold amiable libertarian attitudes while harbouring also ancient anxieties. They may give little thought to same-sex relations from one month to the next, but then be roused into traditional prejudices by hostile media treatment of a provocative instance (around parenting, perhaps). However far 'we' have come, there is plainly a major structural instability around sex and gender in our societies, and nothing can be taken for granted. As I remark in chapter 2, parents will repudiate their offspring because of gayness: something very powerful is going on there.

A third uncertainty involves the kind of society we expect ourselves to be inhabiting in the medium-term future. Tatchell allows perhaps fifty years for a change to legal equality in Britain and the USA, and considerably longer for the fading of 'prejudiced attitudes'.[11] Maybe, but what else is going to be happening? I don't think it can be denied that attitudes toward sexuality are tangled in with the general political and economic structure. Even if these connections are incidental – opportunist rather than intrinsic – it is hard to imagine such a key social marker as sexual preference becoming unexceptional. As gay commentators like to note, there have been and are societies where same-sex passion figures more amiably than in ours. But I can think of none where it is unremarked – a matter of indifference.

Plainly our economic and social system is undergoing important changes in structures of authority and legitimation. As I suggest in chapter 9, some of these may tend partly to license gayness. However, it is a mistake, I argue there, to suppose that we have moved, miraculously, into a situation of 'free play', in which we can all wear T-shirts with personalised logos and just be ourselves. To be sure, some old authorities have collapsed recently, but mostly they were merely quaint, and they have been replaced by others. Instead of the Crown we have the World Bank, instead of bishops we have tele-evangelists, instead of political leaders we have spin doctors, instead of scholars and literary critics we have market researchers and publicity agents. Among advanced students of English a new orthodoxy has emerged: a text which can be shown as presenting identities as multiple, provisional and shifting is good in principle. This notion enables smart readings but gains scant purchase upon the options that are actually available to people. The task is less to applaud and hasten the disintegration of residual identities – the market will take care of that – than to assess and exert some influence over the emergence of new ones.

If in the medium term we are to anticipate an unfettered global market economy, in which competition for resources becomes more urgent, the poor get poorer, and the rich install electric fences and armed guards around their homes (I have seen this in São Paulo, Johannesburg, Southern California), then we have to anticipate also persistent unrest among the excluded – from aggressive begging to robbery to riots, though probably not the revolutions that might really disconcert big business. Such a breakdown in social cohesion will be accompanied by more police, prisons and surveillance, and probably by a more strident scapegoating of out-groups.

Nor is this hostility the likely reaction just of the State and establishment institutions. Already we are seeing other oppressed groups cultivating 'fundamentalist' stances that threaten lesbians and gay men. Kobena Mercer mentions Minister Louis Farrakhan and the Nation of Islam and quotes Buju Banton's notorious 1992 hit, 'Boom bye bye ina de batty man head'. Mercer asks: 'Can you imagine Stevie Wonder or Bob Marley coming up with a lyric like that? What has happened over the last thirty years such that a counter-hegemonic vision of universal liberation has given way to a horrific mirror-image of the politics of resentment and retribution?'[12]

The more affluent among les/bi/gay people may be able to evade many of the effects of social disruption. But surely there can be little doubt that most of us would do much better in a society where respect for other creatures and for the environment were important values, and among ourselves thoughtfulness, fairness, co-operation, peace, generosity and love. It seems unlikely that a true advance towards sex and gender liberation can occur without progress on those wider aspirations.

At least three uncertainties, then. It is because so much of our situation is unclear that we experience such difficulty in evaluating the options before us. This book ends without resolving the tension between a call for purposeful subcultural work and an awareness that sexuality is more mobile and various than it has been convenient, historically, for our subcultures to handle. My case, still, is that we live in a dangerous world and cannot risk trying to manage without the social support and political organisation that derives from subculture; and that, at the same time, we need also to entertain more diverse and permeable identities.

The question of 'community' is often bizarrely posed, as if it should mean a wondrous unity – endless choruses of Tom Robinson's 'Glad to be Gay'. I have preferred the term 'subculture' because it doesn't connote cosiness. Of course, we manifest the divisions of class, gender, race, age and education that occur in the wider society. It would be absurd to expect otherwise. Such complexity is not a weakness; what would be enfeebling is if our subcultures were no more than clubs, bars and phonelines. In fact there are innumerable sites where we interact, create and re-create ourselves.

Not all of this diversity is good. We experience among ourselves serious racism, misogyny, ageism, snobbery. Les/bi/gay subcultures confer no spontaneous immunity to oppressive attitudes and practices; they are what activists, including organic or subcultural intellectuals, have to work on. The task is not to imagine an exclusive group of like-minded people, but to build on the diverse strengths of our constituency, to enlarge it, and to politicise it.

In the last analysis, our sexual identities are situated at the most sensitive friction points of sexuality, love, gender, power, intimacy, stigma, nakedness, risk, and vulnerability. They have been developed in the face of extreme hostility, not just from strangers, but from people whom we believed we could trust. They have the complexity and strength, and perhaps the brittleness, that derive from resistance – including, in most cases, our own resistance to our selves. In other words, they could hardly have a stronger basis in social interaction and in our subjectivities. If such identities are indeed compelling, there is no reason to expect them to be simple.

Notes

Notes to chapter 1

1. David Drake, *The Night Larry Kramer Kissed Me* (New York: Anchor, 1994), pp. 29–30. Dennis Altman seems to miss the point when he remarks: 'The long-haired androgynous look of the early seventies was now found among straights, and the super-macho image of the Village People disco group seemed to typify the new style perfectly': Altman, *The Homosexualization of America* (Boston: Beacon Press, 1982), p. 1.
2. Andrew Holleran, *Nights in Aruba* (1983; Harmondsworth: Penguin, 1991), p. 116.
3. On BBC2 on 1 October 1993.
4. Robert S. Liebert, *Michelangelo* (New Haven: Yale University Press, 1983), p. 91; see also pp. 44–6, 91–5, and cf. M. L. D'Ancona, 'The Doni Madonna by Michelangelo', *Art Bulletin*, 50 (1968), pp. 43–50.
5. Giorgio Vasari, *The Lives of the Painters, Sculptors and Architects*, trans. A. B. Hinds (London: Everyman, 1963), vol. 4, pp. 117–18.
6. Sunil Gupta, 'Black, *Brown* and White', in Simon Shepherd and Mick Wallis, eds., *Coming on Strong* (London: Unwin Hyman, 1989), p. 176. See also Russell Leong, ed., *Asian American Sexualities* (New York: Routledge, 1996).
7. Cherríe Moraga, *Loving in the War Years* (Boston: South End Press, 1983), p. 116.
8. See also Michael Warner, ed., *Fear of a Queer Planet* (Minneapolis: Minnesota University Press, 1993); Cherry Smyth, ed., *Lesbians Talk Queer Notions* (London: Scarlet Press, 1992); Leo Bersani, *Homos* (Cambridge, Mass.: Harvard University Press, 1995), prologue and chs. 1, 2; Murray Healy, *Gay Skins* (London: Cassell, 1996), pp. 172–86.
9. Walter O. Bockting and Eli Coleman, eds., *Gender Dysphoria* (New York: Haworth, 1992); Kate Bornstein, *Gender Outlaw* (New York: Routledge, 1994); Bernice L. Hausman, *Changing Sex* (Durham: Duke University Press, 1996); Richard Ekins, *Male Femaling* (New York: Routledge, 1997).
10. See Michael Baker, *Our Three Selves* (London: Gay Men's Press, 1985), pp. 216–20.

11. Sharon Rose, Cris Stevens et al., eds., *Bisexual Horizons*, (London: Lawrence and Wishart, 1996), p. 6. See also Sue George, *Women and Bisexuality* (London: Scarlet Press, 1993); Bi Academic Intervention, eds., *The Bisexual Imaginary* (London: Cassell, 1997).

12. Arlene Stein, *Sex and Sensibility* (Berkeley: University of California Press, 1997). See Lisa Power, 'Forbidden Fruit', in Mark Simpson, ed., *Anti-Gay* (London: Cassell, 1996).

13. Quentin Crisp, *The Naked Civil Servant* (New York: Plume, 1977), p. 56.

14. Jeffrey Weeks, *Coming Out* (London: Quartet, 1977), pp. 33–5.

15. Jeanette Winterson, *Written on the Body* (London: Vintage, 1993), p. 13.

16. Alan Sinfield, 'Who Was Afraid of Joe Orton?', *Textual Practice*, 4 (1990), pp. 259–77; in Joseph Bristow, ed., *Sexual Sameness* (London: Routledge, 1992), p. 182.

17. Marjorie Garber, *Vice Versa: Bisexuality and the Eroticism of Everyday Life* (New York: Simon and Schuster, 1995), p. 486.

18. Unpublished taped conversation between Zackie Achmat and Alan Sinfield, Johannesburg, July 1996. See Mark Gevisser and Edwin Cameron, eds., *Defiant Desire* (London: Routledge, 1995).

19. Toby Manning, 'Gay Culture: Who Needs It?', in Simpson, ed., *Anti-Gay*, pp. 107–8. John Weir, in his essay 'Going In' (in the same volume), declares himself 'postgay' but makes a partly different argument in a US context; see ch. 6 below.

20. Vera Whisman, *Queer by Choice* (New York: Routledge, 1996).

Notes to chapter 2

1. Peter Burton, *Gay Times*, 199 (April 1995), p. 24; Dennis Altman, *The Homosexualization of America* (Boston: Beacon Press, 1982), p. 29.

2. Eve Kosofsky Sedgwick, *Epistemology of the Closet* (Hemel Hempstead: Harvester, 1991), p. 85, and pp. 84–90.

3. Steven Epstein, 'Gay Politics, Ethnic Identity', in Edward Stein, ed., *Forms of Desire* (New York: Routledge, 1992), p. 255; Michael Warner, 'Introduction', in Warner, ed., *Fear of a Queer Planet* (Minneapolis: Minnesota University Press, 1993), p. xvii. See also Martin Duberman, *About Time*, revised edn. (New York: Meridian, 1991), pp. 404–5, 458–9.

4. See Simon LeVay, *The Sexual Brain* (Cambridge, Mass.: MIT

Press, 1993); Alan Sinfield, *The Wilde Century* (London: Cassell, and New York: Columbia University Press, 1994), pp. 177–84.

5. Edmund White, 'Gender Uncertainties', *New Yorker*, 17 July 1995, pp. 79–81, reviewing Marjorie Garber, *Vice Versa: Bisexuality and the Eroticism of Everyday Life* (New York: Simon and Schuster, 1995).

6. Didi Herman, 'The Politics of Law Reform: Lesbian and Gay Rights Struggles into the 1990s', in Joseph Bristow and Angelia R. Wilson, eds., *Activating Theory* (London: Lawrence and Wishart, 1993), pp. 251–2.

7. Cindy Patton, 'Tremble, Hetero Swine', in Warner, ed., *Fear of a Queer Planet*, pp. 173–4.

8. Herman, 'The Politics of Law Reform', in Bristow and Wilson, eds., *Activating Theory*, p. 251.

9. John D'Emilio, *Making Trouble* (New York: Routledge, 1992), p. 12.

10. Warner, 'Introduction', in Warner, ed., *Fear of a Queer Planet*, p. xxvi.

11. Henry Abelove, 'From Thoreau to Queer Politics', *Yale Journal of Criticism*, 6:2 (Fall, 1993), 17–28, pp. 25–6.

12. Hans Mayer, *Outsiders*, trans. Denis M. Sweet (Cambridge, Mass.: MIT Press, 1982), p. 18; Homi K. Bhabha, *The Location of Culture* (London: Routledge, 1994), p. 139.

13. T. H. Marshall, *Citizenship and Social Class* (Cambridge University Press, 1950), p. 47. See Alan Sinfield, *Literature, Politics and Culture in Postwar Britain*, revised edn. (London: Athlone, 1997), pp. 13–21. On relations between citizenship and gay organisations in France, see Bill Marshall, *Guy Hocquenghem* (London: Pluto Press, 1996), pp. 5–7.

14. See Alan Sinfield, 'Closet Dramas: Homosexual Representation and Class in Postwar British Theater', *Genders*, 9 (1990), 112–31.

15. Manuel Castells, *The City and the Grassroots* (London: Arnold, 1983), p. 163.

16. Steven Epstein, 'Gay Politics, Ethnic Identity', in Stein, ed., *Forms of Desire*, pp. 279, 282. See Herman, 'The Politics of Law Reform', in Bristow and Wilson, eds., *Activating Theory*, p. 251; Jo Eadie, 'Activating Bisexuality: Towards a Bi/Sexual Politics', in Bristow and Wilson, eds., *Activating Theory*, pp. 164–5.

17. Castells, *The City and the Grassroots*, pp. 162, 138–9.

18. Douglas Crimp with Adam Rolston, eds., *Aids DemoGraphics*

(Seattle: Bay Press, 1990), p. 138; Rachel Thomson, 'Unholy Alliances: The Recent Politics of Sex Education', in Bristow and Wilson, eds., *Activating Theory*, p. 228.

19. Castells, *The City and the Grassroots*, p. 171.
20. David Wojnarowicz, *Close to the Knives* (London: Serpent's Tail, 1992), p. 81. See Dennis Altman, *AIDS and the New Puritanism* (London: Pluto Press, 1986), ch. 8: 'A Very American Epidemic?'.
21. Randy Shilts, *And the Band Played On* (New York: St Martin's Press, 1987), p. 595.
22. 'Happy as Larry', Lisa Power interviewing Larry Kramer, *Gay Times*, 203 (August 1995), p. 49.
23. Bruce Bawer, *A Place at the Table* (New York: Simon and Schuster, 1993), p. 139; see ch. 6 below.
24. Shane Phelan, *Getting Specific* (Minneapolis: Minnesota University Press, 1994), p. 60.
25. Stuart Hall, 'New Ethnicities', in James Donald and Ali Rattansi, eds., *'Race', Culture and Difference* (London: Sage, 1992), p. 254.
26. Henry Louis Gates, Jr., *The Signifying Monkey* (New York: Oxford University Press, 1988), p. 237.
27. Stuart Hall, 'Cultural Identity and Diaspora', in Jonathan Rutherford, ed., *Identity: Community, Culture, Difference* (London: Lawrence and Wishart, 1990), p. 235; Hall, 'New Ethnicities', in Donald and Rattansi, eds., *'Race', Culture and Difference*, p. 258.
28. Stuart Hall, 'Deviance, Politics, and the Media', in Paul Rock and Mary McIntosh, eds., *Deviance and Social Control* (London: Tavistock, 1974), p. 293.
29. Paul Gilroy, *The Black Atlantic* (London: Verso, 1993), p. 4; Gates, *The Signifying Monkey*, p. xxiv.
30. Ganesh N. Devy, 'The Multicultural Context of Indian Literature in English', in Geoffrey Davis and Hena Maes-Jelinek, eds., *Crisis and Creativity in the New Literatures in English* (Amsterdam: Rodolphi, 1990), p. 353. I am grateful to Ashley Tellis for helping me with Devy.
31. Molefi Kete Asente, *Afrocentricity* (New Jersey: Africa World Press, 1988), p. 27.
32. Asente, *Afrocentricity*, pp. 57–8; Devy, 'The Multicultural Context', in Davis and Maes-Jelinek, eds., *Crisis and Creativity in the New Literatures in English*, p. 353. See Ron Simmons, 'Some Thoughts on the Challenges Facing Black Gay

Intellectuals', in Essex Hemphill, ed., *Brother to Brother* (Boston: Alyson, 1991), pp. 212–15.

33. Stuart Hall, 'Cultural Identity and Diaspora', in Rutherford, ed., *Identity*, p. 226; bell hooks, *Yearning* (London: Turnaround, 1991), p. 29.

34. Gates, *The Signifying Monkey*, pp. xxiii–xxiv.

35. John Weir, 'Going In', in Mark Simpson, ed., *Anti-Gay* (London: Cassell, 1996), p. 28.

36. Frank Mort, 'Essentialism Revisited? Identity Politics and Late Twentieth-Century Discourses of Homosexuality', in Jeffrey Weeks, ed., *The Lesser Evil and the Greater Good* (London: Rivers Oram Press, 1994), p. 202; Warner, 'Introduction', in Warner, ed., *Fear of a Queer Planet*, p. xvii.

37. Paul Monette, *Half-way Home* (New York: Crown, 1991), p. 262. See also Gregory Woods, *This Is No Book* (Nottingham: Mushroom Publications, 1994), p. 79.

38. Nicholson Baker, 'Lost Youth', *London Review of Books*, 9 June 1994, p. 6.

39. Cf. Sagri Dhairyam, 'Racing the Lesbian, Dodging White Critics', in Laura Doan, ed., *The Lesbian Postmodern* (New York: Columbia University Press, 1994), p. 31; Avtar Brah, 'Difference, Diversity and Differentiation', in Donald and Rattansi, eds., *'Race', Culture and Difference*, pp. 128–9; Sedgwick, *Epistemology of the Closet*, pp. 76–82.

40. Jonathan Dollimore, *Sexual Dissidence* (Oxford: Clarendon, 1991), p. 33.

41. Philip Roth, *Operation Shylock* (New York: Simon and Schuster, 1993), p. 157. See Alan Sinfield, *Cultural Politics – Queer Reading* (Philadelphia: University of Pennsylvania, and London: Routledge, 1994).

42. Homi Bhabha, 'The Third Space', in Rutherford, ed., *Identity*, p. 211.

43. Bhabha, 'The Third Space', in Rutherford, ed., *Identity*, pp. 216, 211. Some of these points, and others, are made by Ania Loomba, 'Overworlding the "Third World" ', *Oxford Literary Review*, 13 (1991), 164–91; Benita Parry, 'Signs of Our Times: Discussion of Homi Bhabha's *The Location of Culture*', *Third Text*, 28–9 (1994); and Robert J. C. Young, *Colonial Desire* (London: Routledge, 1995).

44. Bhabha, *The Location of Culture*, p. 88, and see pp. 111–21; Butler revises this argument in her book *Bodies that Matter* (New

York: Routledge, 1993), p. 125. Judith Butler, *Gender Trouble* (London: Routledge, 1990), p. 137.

45. Young, *Colonial Desire*, pp. 2–4; Karl Marx, *Manifesto of the Communist Party*, in Marx, *The Revolutions of 1848*, ed. David Fernbach (Harmondsworth: Penguin, 1973), p. 70.

46. Kobena Mercer, 'Black Hair/Style Politics', *New Formations*, 3 (Winter, 1987), 33–54, p. 49.

47. Danae Clark, 'Commodity Lesbianism', in Henry Abelove, Michèle Aina Barale and David M. Halperin, eds., *The Lesbian and Gay Studies Reader* (New York: Routledge, 1993), p. 199.

48. Rupert Smith, 'Jarman's Battle Royal', *Radio Times*, 23–9 January 1993, p. 28.

49. M. M. Mahood, *Poetry and Humanism* (London: Cape, 1950), p. 83.

50. Judith Cook, *At the Sign of the Swan* (London: Harrap, 1986), p. 107; quoted in Gregory Woods, 'Body, Costume, and Desire in Christopher Marlowe', in Claude Summers, ed., *Homosexuality in Renaissance and Enlightenment England* (New York: Harrington Park, 1992), pp. 73–4. See also Simon Shepherd, *Marlowe and the Politics of Elizabethan Theatre* (New York: St Martin's Press, 1986), pp. xii–xiii.

51. Paul Hammond, *Love Between Men in English Literature* (London: Macmillan, 1996), p. 53. See Bruce R. Smith, *Homosexual Desire in Shakespeare's England* (Chicago University Press, 1991), p. 221.

52. Smith, 'Jarman's Battle Royal', p. 28.

53. Marlowe, *Edward II*, V. i. 26–7, 153, 110–1, in *The Plays of Christopher Marlowe*, ed. Roma Gill (Oxford University Press, 1971).

54. Hence, I suspect, the sympathetic reading of the 'perfect shadows in a sunshine day' speech by a friend of Jarman such as Colin MacCabe; MacCabe, '*Edward II*: Throne of Blood', *Sight and Sound*, ns., 1:6 (September 1991), 12–14, p. 13; see also Kate Chedgzoy, *Shakespeare's Queer Children* (Manchester University Press, 1995), ch. 5; Martin Quinn-Meyler, 'Opposing "Heterosoc": Jarman's Counter-hegemonic Activism', in Chris Lippard, ed., *By Angels Driven* (London: Flicks Books, 1996).

55. Quoted in Chedgzoy, *Shakespeare's Queer Children*, p. 213.

56. See Dympna Callaghan, 'The Terms of Gender: "Gay" and "Feminist" *Edward II*', in Valerie Traub, M. Lindsay Kaplan and

Dympna Callaghan, eds., *Feminist Readings of Early Modern Culture* (Cambridge University Press, 1996).

57. Gayatri Chakravorty Spivak, *In Other Worlds* (New York: Methuen, 1987), p. 205; Jeffrey Weeks, *Invented Moralities* (Cambridge: Polity Press, 1995), ch. 3. See Gilroy, *The Black Atlantic*, p. 102, and Chris Woods, *State of the Queer Nation* (London: Cassell, 1995).

58. Simon Watney, 'AIDS and the Politics of Queer Diaspora', in Monica Dorenkamp and Richard Henke, eds., *Negotiating Lesbian and Gay Subjects* (New York: Routledge, 1995), p. 61.

59. Oscar Moore, *A Matter of Life and Sex* (Harmondsworth: Penguin, 1992), p. 234.

60. Weeks, *Invented Moralities*, p. 98.

61. Watney, 'AIDS and the Politics of Queer Diaspora', in Dorenkamp and Henke, eds., *Negotiating Lesbian and Gay Subjects*, p. 63; Edmund White, 'AIDS Awareness and Gay Culture in France', and Larys Frogier, 'Homosexuals and the AIDS Crisis in France: Assimilation, Denial, Activism', both in Joshua Oppenheimer and Helena Reckitt, eds., *Acting on AIDS* (London: Serpent's Tail and ICA, 1997).

62. *Radio Times*, 13–19 April 1996, p. 50.

63. Richard Rorty, 'A Leg-Up for Oliver North', *London Review of Books*, 20 October 1994, pp. 13, 15.

64. Hall, 'Cultural Identity', in Rutherford, ed., *Identity*, p. 225.

65. Sarah Schulman, interviewed by Andrea Freud Loewenstein (1990), repr. in Betsy Warland, ed., *Inversions* (London: Open Letters, 1992), p. 219.

66. hooks, *Yearning*, p. 29. See further Alan Sinfield, ' "The Moment of Submission": Neil Bartlett in Conversation', *Modern Drama*, 39:1 (Spring 1996).

Notes to chapter 3

1. For the use here of 'metropolitan', see pp. 6–7 above.

2. Manuel Puig, *Kiss of the Spider Woman*, trans. Thomas Colchie (London: Arena, 1984), p. 60.

3. Rebecca Bell-Metereau, *Hollywood Androgyny*, 2nd edn. (New York: Columbia University Press, 1993), p. 290. See also Keith Howes, *Broadcasting It* (London: Cassell, 1993), p. 437.

4. I am grateful to Robert Howes for help with this and many other aspects of the Latin American setting. See Howes' introduction

to Adolfo Caminha, *Bom-Crioulo* (San Francisco: Gay Sunshine, 1982).

5. Juanita Ramos, ed., *Compañeras* (New York: Routledge, 1994), p. xxvi.

6. Joseph Carrier, *De los Otros: Intimacy and Homosexuality among Mexican Men* (New York: Columbia University Press, 1995), p. 21 and ch. 1. For a comparable argument in respect of Islamic countries, see Alan Sinfield, 'Identity and Subculture', in Andy Medhurst and Sally Munt, eds., *Lesbian and Gay Studies* (London: Cassell, 1997).

7. Manuel Puig, *El beso de la mujer araña* (Barcelona: Seix Barral, 1976), p. 67; Carrier, *De los Otros*, pp. 11–13.

8. See Alan Sinfield, 'How to Read *The Merchant of Venice* Without Being Heterosexist', in Terry Hawkes, ed., *Alternative Shakespeares 2* (London: Routledge, 1996).

9. Ramos, ed., *Compañeras*, p. xxvi. See Gloria Anzaldúa, *Borderlands/La Frontera* (San Francisco: Spinsters/Aunt Lute, 1987); Cherríe Moraga, *Loving in the War Years* (Boston: South End Press, 1983).

10. Carrier, *De los Otros*, pp. 193–5; Carter Wilson, *Hidden in the Blood* (New York: Columbia University Press, 1995), pp. 21–3; Andrea Cornwall, 'Gendered Identities and Gender Ambiguity among *travestis* in Salvador, Brazil', in Andrea Cornwall and Nancy Lindisfarne, eds., *Dislocating Masculinity* (London: Routledge, 1994), pp. 123–4; Ian Lumsden, *Machos, Maricones, and Gays: Cuba and Homosexuality* (Philadelphia: Temple University Press, 1996), pp. xxiv–xxv, 29–32, 149–50. See Stephen O. Murray, 'The "Underdevelopment" of Modern/Gay Homosexuality in MesoAmerica', in Ken Plummer, ed., *Modern Homosexualities* (London: Routledge, 1992).

11. Federico Garcia Lorca, *Selected Poems*, trans. Merryn Williams (Newcastle upon Tyne: Bloodaxe Books, 1992), pp. 159–60. I am grateful to Vincent Quinn for this reference. See further Stephen O. Murray, ed., *Latin American Male Homosexualities* (Albuquerque: University of New Mexico Press, 1995).

12. See Alan Sinfield, *The Wilde Century* (London: Cassell, and New York: Columbia University Press, 1994), pp. 169–70 et passim.

13. Carrier, *De los Otros*, pp. 16–17; Cornwall, 'Gendered Identities and Gender Ambiguity', in Cornwall and Lindisfarne, eds., *Dislocating Masculinity*, pp. 113, 123. See Murray, 'The "Under-

development" of Modern/Gay Homosexuality in MesoAmerica', in Plummer, ed., *Modern Homosexualities*.

14. The quotation is from Puig, *Kiss*, p. 139, with reference to Freud, *On Narcissism: an Introduction*.
15. Martin Edwin Andersen, *Dossier Secreto* (Boulder: Westview, 1993), p. 196.
16. Lumsden, *Machos, Maricones, and Gays*, ch. 3.
17. Pamela Bacarisse, *Impossible Choices* (Calgary: University of Calgary Press, and Cardiff: University of Wales Press, 1993), p. 147.
18. Quentin Crisp, *The Naked Civil Servant* (New York: Plume, 1977), pp. 21, 56. See John Marshall, 'Pansies, Perverts and Macho Men: Changing Conceptions of Male Homosexuality', in Kenneth Plummer, ed., *The Making of the Modern Homosexual* (London: Hutchinson, 1981); Marjorie Garber, *Vested Interests* (New York: Routledge, 1992), pp. 137–41; Sinfield, *The Wilde Century*, chs. 6–8.
19. Hall Carpenter Archives, Gay Men's Oral History Group, *Walking After Midnight* (London: Routledge, 1989), p. 133 (and see p. 60).
20. Two helpful recent analyses are: David Forrest, ' "We're here, we're queer, and we're not going shopping": Changing Gay Male Identities in Contemporary Britain', in Cornwall and Lindisfarne, eds., *Dislocating Masculinity*; and Murray Healy, *Gay Skins* (London, Cassell, 1996), ch. 6.
21. See Sue-Ellen Case, 'Towards a Butch-Femme Aesthetic', in Henry Abelove, Michèle Aina Barale and David M. Halperin, eds., *The Lesbian and Gay Studies Reader* (New York: Routledge, 1993).
22. Cornwall, 'Gendered Identities and Gender Ambiguity', in Cornwall and Lindisfarne, eds., *Dislocating Masculinity*, p. 129.
23. Stephen O. Murray, *American Gay* (Chicago University Press, 1996), pp. 200–1.
24. Daniel L. Wardlow, ed., *Gays, Lesbians, and Consumer Behavior* (New York: Harrington Park, 1996), p. 110.
25. Mitchel Raphael, 'The Dancer Behind the Dance: the Andrew Holleran Interview', *Icon*, September 1966, 48–61, p. 60.
26. Michael Cunningham, 'Straight Arrows, Almost', *New York Times*, 7 May 1995, p. 42.
27. See Hans Huang, 'Be(com)ing Gay: Sexual Dissidence and Cultural Change in Contemporary Taiwan', unpublished MA dissertation, University of Sussex, 1996, p. 46. Here and

elsewhere, I am grateful also for the advice of Wei-cheng Raymond Chu; see his 'Homo and Other: Articulating Post-colonial Queer Subjectivity', unpublished D. Phil. dissertation, University of Sussex, 1998.

28. Pai Hsien-yung, *Crystal Boys*, trans. Howard Goldblatt (San Francisco: Gay Sunshine, 1990), p. 13.

29. *Crystal Boys*, p. 267. On the compatibility of national and familial ideologies, see Charles Stanford, 'Good Sons and Virtuous Mothers: Kinship and Chinese Nationalism in Taiwan', *Man*, n.s., 27 (1992), pp. 363–78.

30. Bret Hinsch, *Passions of the Cut Sleeve* (Berkeley: University of California Press, 1990), p. 171. Hinsch considers that Pai Hsien-yung offers a fair, though rare, representation of homosexuality in China (pp. 163–4); in my view the publication of *Neih-Tzu* was made possible by its stature as literature.

31. Richard A. Isay, *Being Homosexual* (Harmondsworth: Penguin, 1993), pp. 128–9.

32. Chris Berry, *A Bit in the Side* (Sydney: Empress, 1994), pp. 96–7. *Okoge* and *Twinkle* both appeared in 1992.

33. David F. Greenberg, *The Construction of Homosexuality* (Chicago University Press, 1988), p. 25 and ch. 2; Randolph Trumbach, 'Gender and the Homosexual Role in Modern Western Culture: The 18th and 19th Centuries Compared', in Dennis Altman, Carole Vance, Martha Vicinus, Jeffrey Weeks and others, *Homosexuality, Which Homosexuality* (London: Gay Men's Press, 1989).

34. This swing from equality to tragic doom occurs again at the end of the book: see p. 323.

35. '*Tong Chi* looking for *Tong Chi*'. I owe the reference and the translation to Hans Huang, 'From *Crystal Boys* to "Comrades" ': Towards a Trajectory of a New Queer Politics', unpublished paper, University of Sussex, 1996, p. 9. For the interpretation here I am indebted also to Wei-cheng Raymond Chu.

36. Murray, 'The "Underdevelopment" of Modern/Gay Homo-sexuality in MesoAmerica', in Plummer, ed., *Modern Homosexualities*.

37. Arjun Appadurai, 'Disjuncture and Difference in the Global Cultural Economy', *Theory, Culture & Society*, 7 (1990), 295–310, p. 296.

38. Martin F. Manalansan IV, 'In the Shadows of Stonewall: Examining Gay Transnational Politics and the Diasporic

Dilemma', *GLQ* (*Gay and Lesbian Quarterly*), 2 (1995), 425–38, p. 429.

39. Carrier, *De los Otros*, p. 8.
40. Jeffrey Weeks, *Coming Out* (London: Quartet, 1977), p. 196. See this section of Weeks's book for an assessment of London GLF.
41. See Kath Weston, *Families We Choose* (New York: Columbia University Press, 1991); John D'Emilio, *Making Trouble* (New York: Routledge, 1992), pp. 12, 14.
42. Simon Edge, 'Heterosexuals Must Get Their Act Together', *Gay Times*, December 1996, p. 52.
43. Michèle Barrett and Mary McIntosh, *The Anti-social Family*, 2nd edn. (London: Verso, 1991), p. 71.
44. Raphael, 'The Dancer Behind the Dance', p. 50.
45. Mark Simpson, 'Gay Dream Believer: Inside the Gay Underwear Cult', in Simpson, ed., *Anti-Gay* (London: Cassell, 1996), p. 7; see ch. 1 above.
46. Sigmund Freud, 'From the History of an Infantile Neurosis', *Standard Edition of the Complete Psychological Works*, ed. James Strachey, vol. 17 (London: Hogarth Press, 1955), p. 47.
47. Sigmund Freud, *New Introductory Lectures in Psychoanalysis*, trans. James Strachey, Penguin Freud Library, vol. 2 (Harmondsworth: Penguin, 1973), p. 152. For more careful discussion of these passages, see Sinfield, *The Wilde Century*, p. 167.
48. Christopher Robinson, *Scandal in the Ink* (London: Cassell, 1994), pp. 118–19. See Herbert Marcuse, *Eros and Civilization* (London: Penguin, 1969), pp. 49, 51–54, 201.
49. Camille Paglia, 'Junk Bonds and Corporate Raiders: Academe in the Hour of the Wolf', *Arion*, 3rd series, 1 (Spring 1991): 139–212, pp. 182, 206.
50. Camille Paglia, *Vamps and Tramps* (London: Viking, 1995), pp. 70–1.
51. See Anne McClintock, *Imperial Leather* (New York: Routledge, 1995); Robert J. C. Young, *Colonial Desire* (London: Routledge, 1995).
52. Walt Odets, *In the Shadow of the Epidemic* (London: Cassell, 1995), p. 195.
53. *Pink Paper*, August 9, 1992, p. 1.

Notes to chapter 4

1. Arlene Croce, 'Discussing the Undiscussable', *New Yorker*, 26 December 1994, 54–60, p. 60.
2. 'In the Mail: Who's the Victim?', *New Yorker*, 30 January 1995, pp. 11–12. See 'Dance this Diss Around: Homi K. Bhabha on Victim Art', *Artforum*, 33:8 (April 1995), 19–20.
3. Gregory Woods, *This Is No Book* (Nottingham: Mushroom Publications, 1995), p. 30. For discussion of this topic, see Alan Sinfield, *Cultural Politics – Queer Reading* (Philadelphia: University of Pennsylvania Press, and London: Routledge, 1994); Kate Chedgzoy, *Shakespeare's Queer Children* (Manchester University Press, 1995), pp. 181–94.
4. Douglas Crimp, 'AIDS: Cultural Analysis/Cultural Activism', in Crimp, ed., *AIDS: Cultural Analysis, Cultural Activism* (Cambridge, Mass.: MIT Press, 1988), pp. 2–5.
5. Simon Watney, 'Those Waves of Dying Friends: Gay Men, AIDS and Multiple Loss', in Peter Horne and Reina Lewis, eds., *Outlooks* (London: Routledge, 1996), p. 161.
6. Thom Gunn, *The Man with Night Sweats* (London: Faber, 1992), p. 80.
7. Raymond J. Ricketts, 'Working with Bill T. Jones', *Dance Now*, Autumn 1995, 47–53, p. 48.
8. Gregory Woods, 'AIDS to Remembrance: The Uses of Elegy', in Emmanuel S. Nelson, ed., *AIDS: the Literary Response* (New York: Twayne, 1992), pp. 156–8; Jeff Nunokawa, ' "All the Sad Young Men": AIDS and the Age of Mourning', *Yale Journal of Criticism*, 4:2 (1991), 1–12, p. 9. On how gays and lesbians identify distinctively with a range of cultural icons, see Alexander Doty, *Making Things Perfectly Queer* (Minneapolis: University of Minnesota Press, 1993), ch. 1.
9. Edmund White, *The Burning Library* (London: Chatto, 1994), p. 215.
10. Robert Baldick, *The First Bohemian* (London: Hamish Hamilton, 1961), p. 17.
11. David Wojnarowicz, *Close to the Knives* (London: Serpent's Tail, 1992), p. 229.
12. Croce, 'Discussing the Undiscussable', p. 59.
13. See David Bergman, *Gaiety Transfigured* (Madison: University of Wisconsin Press, 1991), p. 138; Woods, 'AIDS to Remembrance', in Nelson, ed., *AIDS: the Literary Response*, p. 164.

14. 'Courtesies of the Interregnum', in Gunn, *The Man with Night Sweats*, p. 73.
15. Wojnarowicz, *Close to the Knives*, pp. 166–7.
16. William H. Hoffman, *As Is*, in M. Elizabeth Osborn, ed., *The Way We Live Now* (New York: Theatre Communications Group, 1990), pp. 6, 29.
17. Buchanan managed to find a brief segment of *Tongues Untied* that shows only white people! See Kobena Mercer, 'Decolonisation and Disappointment: Reading Fanon's Sexual Politics', in Alan Read, ed., *The Fact of Blackness* (London: ICA, 1996), pp. 120–1.
18. Sarah Schulman in an interview with Andrea Freud Loewenstein (1990), repr. in Betsy Warland, ed., *Inversions* (London: Open Letters, 1992), p. 220.
19. I return to this topic in ch. 8; and see Alan Sinfield, *The Wilde Century* (London: Cassell, 1994, and New York: Columbia University Press, 1994), ch. 4.
20. Sarah Schulman in interview with Andrea Freud Loewenstein, in Warland, ed., *Inversions*, p. 222.
21. Woods, *This Is No Book*, pp. 79–80.
22. Quoted in Henry Louis Gates, Jr., 'The Chitlin Circuit', *New Yorker*, 3 February 1997, 44–55, p. 44.
23. *Gay Times*, August 1996, p. 76; and September 1996, p. 81.
24. Walt Odets, *In the Shadow of the Epidemic* (London: Cassell, 1995), pp. 102–3.
25. Eric Rofes, *Reviving the Tribe* (New York: Harrington Park, 1996), pp. 26–7, 33.
26. I owe this point to Raymond O'Neill of Dublin Gay Switchboard.
27. Edward King, *Safety in Numbers* (London: Cassell, 1993), ch. 1.
28. Dennis Altman, *AIDS and the New Puritanism* (London: Pluto Press, 1986), pp. 174–6. On the UK situation as distinctive, see also Philip Derbyshire, 'A Measure of Queer', *Critical Quarterly*, 36:1 (1994), 39–45, and Joshua Oppenheimer, 'Movements, Markets, and the Mainstream: Gay Activism and Assimilation in the Age of AIDS', in Joshua Oppenheimer and Helena Reckitt, eds., *Acting on AIDS* (London: Serpent's Tail and ICA, 1997).
29. Rofes, *Reviving the Tribe*, pp. 208, 210.
30. King, *Safety in Numbers*, pp. 142, 145–7, 155–60; Odets, *In the Shadow of the Epidemic*, pp. 195–204.

Notes to chapter 5

1. See *Gay Times*, December 1993, p. 42.
2. *Guardian*, 27 October 1993.
3. See Alan Sinfield, *Literature, Politics and Culture in Postwar Britain*, 2nd edn. (London: Athlone, 1997), ch. 5; Sinfield, *The Wilde Century* (London: Cassell, and New York: Columbia University Press, 1994), ch. 6; Joseph Bristow, *Effeminate England* (Buckingham: Open University Press, 1995), ch. 2.
4. Christopher Isherwood, *Christopher and His Kind* (London: Magnum, 1978), pp. 168–9, 194–6, 204.
5. T. C. Worsley, *Fellow Travellers* (London: London Magazine Editions, 1971), p. 7.
6. Stephen Spender, *The Temple* (London: Faber, 1988), pp. xi–xii.
7. David Leavitt and Mark Mitchell, eds., *The Penguin Book of Gay Short Stories* (Harmondsworth: Penguin, 1994), introduction, p. xix.
8. Janice A. Radway, *Reading the Romance* (London: Verso, 1987), p. 8. See Sara Mills, 'Reading as/like a Feminist', in Mills, ed., *Gendering the Reader* (Hemel Hempstead: Harvester, 1994).
9. Diana Fuss, 'Reading like a Feminist', in Naomi Schor and Elizabeth Weed, eds., *The Essential Difference* (Bloomington: Indiana University Press, 1994), p. 108.
10. Quoted in Marjorie Garber, *Vice Versa: Bisexuality and the Eroticism of Everyday Life* (London: Hamish Hamilton, 1996), p. 357; see pp. 355–64. Garber confirms my sense that Edward's death is reminiscent of AIDS deaths (p. 356). For a reassertion of Leavitt's interpretation of Spender, see W. Scott Thompson, *The Price of Achievement* (London: Cassell, 1995), pp. 54–5.
11. David Leavitt, *While England Sleeps* (London: Viking, 1993: withdrawn), pp. 33, 143, 155.
12. Nick Walker, 'Gay Capital of Europe', *Independent*, 6 July 1996.
13. Armistead Maupin, *Babycakes* (1984; London: Black Swan, 1988), p. 147. I owe this reference to Vincent Quinn.
14. Andrew Ross, *No Respect* (New York: Routledge, 1989), p. 231. See John Frow, *Cultural Studies and Cultural Value* (Oxford: Clarendon, 1995), pp. 155–61.
15. John McGrath, *The Bone Won't Break* (London: Methuen, 1990), p. 64.
16. Paul Gilroy, *Small Acts* (London: Serpent's Tail, 1993), ch. 8. See Richard Wright, 'How "Bigger" Was Born', in Wright, *Native*

Son (New York: Harper and Row, 1966), pp. xiii–xiv; Ron Simmons, 'Some Thoughts on the Challenges Facing Black Gay Intellectuals', in Essex Hemphill, ed., *Brother to Brother* (Boston: Alyson, 1991), pp. 212–15.

17. Alan Hollinghurst, *The Swimming-Pool Library* (New York: Random House, 1988), p. 37.
18. Leo Bersani, *Homos* (Cambridge, Mass.: Harvard University Press, 1995), p. 63.
19. Mary Renault, *The Charioteer* (London: New English Library, 1990), p. 207.
20. Dana Heller, *Family Plots* (Philadelphia: Pennsylvania University Press, 1995), p. 158.
21. See Nina Baym, 'Melodramas of Beset Manhood: How Theories of American Fiction Exclude Women Authors', in Elaine Showalter, ed., *The New Feminist Criticism* (London: Virago, 1986), pp. 71, 75.
22. Harvey Fierstein, *Torch Song Trilogy* (London: Methuen, 1984), p. 80.

Notes to chapter 6

1. Bruce Bawer, *A Place at the Table* (New York: Poseidon Press, 1993), pp. 209–10.
2. John Weir, 'Going In', in Mark Simpson, ed., *Anti-Gay* (London: Cassell, 1996), p. 29.
3. Mary Renault, *The Charioteer* (London: New English Library, 1990), p. 150.
4. David Sweetman, *Mary Renault* (London: Chatto, 1993), pp. 151–2, 127–8.
5. Mitchel Raphael, 'The Dancer Behind the Dance: the Andrew Holleran Interview', *Icon*, September 1966, 48–51, 60–61, p. 51.
6. Andrew Holleran, *Dancer from the Dance* (London: Cape, 1979), p. 249.
7. See David Rees, *Words and Music* (Brighton: Millivres Books, 1993), pp. 174–5; Mark Lilly, *Gay Men's Literature in the Twentieth Century* (London: Macmillan, 1993), pp. 191–4; Raphael, 'The Dancer Behind the Dance', p. 50.
8. Andrew Holleran, *Nights in Aruba* (1983; Harmondsworth: Penguin, 1991), p. 117.
9. Eric Rofes, *Reviving the Tribe* (New York: Harrington Park, 1996), pp. 102–5.

10. Rees in *Words and Music* (p. 176) notes the extent to which these characters reflect Holleran's own situation.
11. Andrew Holleran, 'Sunday Morning: Key West', in Edmund White, ed., *The Faber Book of Gay Short Fiction* (London: Faber, 1991).
12. David Leavitt and Mark Mitchell, eds., *The Penguin Book of Gay Short Stories* (Harmondsworth: Penguin, 1994), pp. xvii–xviii.
13. These stories are collected in David Leavitt, *A Place I've Never Been* (New York: Viking, 1990); 'When You Grow to Adultery' is also in White, ed., *The Faber Book of Gay Short Fiction*.
14. David Leavitt, *Equal Affections* (Harmondsworth: Penguin, 1989), p. 24.
15. 'The Homosexual Lifestyle' (Washington, DC: Dan Kaufman Graphics, 1992).

Notes to chapter 7

1. Leo Bersani, 'Is the Rectum a Grave?', in Douglas Crimp, ed., *AIDS: Cultural Analysis, Cultural Activism* (Cambridge, Mass.: MIT Press, 1988). I am grateful to Leo Bersani for reading and commenting on this chapter.
2. Leo Bersani, *Homos* (Cambridge, Mass.: Harvard University Press, 1995), p. 161.
3. Edmund White, *Genet* (London: Chatto, 1993), p. 549.
4. Jean Genet, *Funeral Rites*, trans. Bernard Frechtman (London: Panther, 1971), p. 106; cited hereafter in the text as *FR*. For gay unease with Genet see Mark Lilly, *Gay Men's Literature in the Twentieth Century* (London: Macmillan, 1993), ch. 6, and Christopher Robinson, *Scandal in the Ink* (London: Cassell, 1994), pp. 57–71.
5. The letter is quoted in White, *Genet*, pp. 441–4.
6. Thom Gunn, *The Man with Night Sweats* (London: Faber, 1992), p. 3.
7. White, *Genet*, pp. 273–4.
8. Jean Genet, *The Thief's Journal*, trans. Bernard Frechtman (Harmondsworth: Penguin, 1967), p. 157.
9. Jean Genet, *Miracle of the Rose*, trans. Bernard Frechtman (Harmondsworth: Penguin, 1971), p. 227. See White, *Genet*, pp. 186–7.
10. White, *Genet*, pp. 361–2.
11. On Lucien, see White, *Genet*, pp. 327–33, 361–5.

12. Genet, *The Thief's Journal*, p. 195.

13. Hans Mayer, *Outsiders*, trans. Denis M. Sweet (Cambridge, Mass.: MIT Press, 1982), pp. 255–8; Elizabeth Wilson, 'Is Transgression Transgressive?', in Joseph Bristow and Angelia R. Wilson, eds., *Activating Theory* (London: Lawrence and Wishart, 1993), p. 111.

14. Raymond Williams, *Culture and Society 1780–1950* (1958; Harmondsworth: Penguin, 1961), pp. 312–14.

15. Richard Leakey and Roger Lewin, *People of the Lake* (London: Collins, 1979), p. 125; also p. 213. See Alan Sinfield, *Literature, Politics and Culture in Postwar Britain*, 2nd edn. (London: Athlone, 1997), pp. 139–50.

16. The Amnesty ad plays rather adventurously upon 'chilli con carnage' as a recipe (so to speak) for how to rape women in Mexico: see *Gay Times*, September 1996, p. 71. On the Amnesty campaign against oppression based on sexual orientation, see p. 115 of the same issue. On gay fascism today, see Murray Healy, *Gay Skins* (London: Cassell, 1996).

17. Wilson, 'Is Transgression Transgressive?', in Bristow and Wilson, eds., *Activating Theory*, p. 114.

18. Valentine Hooven III, introduction, *Tom of Finland* (Köln: Benedikt Taschen Verlag GmbH, 1992), p. 6.

Notes to chapter 8

1. See Raymond Williams, *Marxism and Literature* (Oxford University Press, 1977); David Morley and Kuan-Hsing Chen, eds., *Stuart Hall: Critical Dialogues in Cultural Studies* (London: Routledge, 1996).

2. See Judith Newton and Deborah Rosenfelt, eds., *Feminist Criticism and Social Change* (New York: Methuen, 1985).

3. See Steven Connor, *Postmodern Culture* (Oxford: Blackwell, 1989), ch. 2.

4. Raymond Williams, *Problems in Materialism and Culture* (London: New Left Books, 1980), pp. 37–8.

5. Alan Sinfield, *Faultlines* (Berkeley: California University Press, and Oxford: Oxford University Press, 1992); see particularly pp. 35–42, 45–51, 291–9.

6. Ken Plummer, *Telling Sexual Stories* (London: Routledge, 1995), p. 87. See also Pat Califia, *Public Sex* (Pittsburg: Cleis Press, 1994), p. 21.

7. Jack Babuscio, 'Camp and the Gay Sensibility', in Richard Dyer, ed., *Gays and Film* (London: British Film Institute, 1977), p. 42. See Andy Medhurst, 'Camp', in Sally Munt and Andy Medhurst, eds., *Lesbian and Gay Studies* (London: Cassell, 1997).

8. Andy Medhurst, 'That Special Thrill: *Brief Encounter*, Homosexuality and Authorship', *Screen*, 32 (Summer, 1991), 197–208.

9. Antonio Gramsci, *Selections from the Prison Notebooks*, trans. Quintin Hoare and Geoffrey Nowell Smith (London: Lawrence and Wishart, 1971), pp. 5–10. I argue along these lines also in Sinfield, *Cultural Politics – Queer Reading* (Philadelphia: Pennsylvania University Press, and London: Routledge, 1994), ch. 4.

10. Michel Foucault, *Power/Knowledge*, ed. Colin Gordon (Brighton: Harvester, 1980), pp. 126–33.

11. Neil Bartlett, *Who Was That Man? A Present for Mr Oscar Wilde* (London: Serpent's Tail, 1988), p. xxii.

12. Neil Bartlett, *A Vision of Love Revealed in Sleep*, in Michael Wilcox, ed., *Gay Plays: Volume Four* (London: Methuen, 1990), p. 89.

13. Alan Sinfield, ' "The Moment of Submission": Neil Bartlett in Conversation', *Modern Drama*, 39 (1996), Special Issue on Lesbian/Gay/Queer Drama, ed. Hersh Zeifman, 211–21, p. 215.

14. See Alan Sinfield, 'Private Lives/Public Theatre: Noël Coward and the Politics of Homosexual Representation', *Representations*, 36 (Fall 1991), 43–63.

15. Emmanuel Cooper, 'Kaleidoscope', BBC Radio 4, 8 September 1994.

16. Diana Fuss, *Essentially Speaking* (New York: Routledge, 1989), pp. 41–2, quoting Wittig's essay, 'The Straight Mind', in Monique Wittig, *The Straight Mind and Other Essays* (Hemel Hempstead: Harvester, 1992), p. 25.

17. Monique Wittig, 'Paradigm', in George Stambolian and Elaine Marks, eds., *Homosexualities and French Literature* (Ithaca: Cornell University Press, 1979), p. 117.

18. Fuss, *Essentially Speaking*, p. 43; Judith Butler, *Gender Trouble* (New York: Routledge, 1990), p. 121.

19. Wittig, *The Straight Mind and Other Essays*, pp. 62, 64.

20. Wittig, *The Straight Mind and Other Essays*, p. 64. The italics are in the text.

21. Sinfield, ' "The Moment of Submission" ', p. 214.

22. Stuart Hall, 'Cultural Studies and its Theoretical Legacies', in

David Morley and Kuan-Hsing Chen, eds., *Stuart Hall* (London: Routledge, 1996), p. 267; see John Frow, *Cultural Studies and Cultural Value* (Oxford: Clarendon, 1995), pp. 128–9.

23. Sarah Schulman, 'A Modest Proposal' (1993), repr. in Schulman, *My American History* (London: Cassell, 1995), p. 275.

Notes to chapter 9

1. John D'Emilio, 'Capitalism and Gay Identity', in D'Emilio, *Making Trouble* (New York: Routledge, 1992), p. 7.

2. Danae Clark, 'Commodity Lesbianism' (1991), in Henry Abelove, Michèle Aina Barale and David M. Halperin, eds., *The Lesbian and Gay Studies Reader* (New York: Routledge, 1993), pp. 187–8, referring to Karen Stabiner in the *New York Times Magazine*, 2 May 1982, p. 80. See also David T. Evans, *Sexual Citizenship* (London: Routledge, 1993), pp. 104–13.

3. Frank Mort, *Cultures of Consumption* (London: Routledge, 1996), p. 16.

4. Peter Burton, 'Is It Really Pink?' (1988), in Burton, *Amongst the Aliens* (Brighton: Millivres, 1995), p. 128. The analogy with Jews is made also by Shane Phelan, *Getting Specific* (Minneapolis: Minnesota University Press, 1994), p. 135.

5. Mort, *Cultures of Consumption*, p. 165. See Jon Binnie, 'Trading Places: Consumption, Sexuality and the Production of Queer Space', in David Bell and Gill Valentine, eds., *Mapping Desire* (London: Routledge, 1995), pp. 195–9.

6. *Radio Times*, 6–12 August 1994, p. 24. On IKEA, see Anthony Freitas, Susan Kaiser and Tania Hammidi, 'Communities, Commodities, Cultural Space, and Style', in Daniel L. Wardlow, ed., *Gays, Lesbians, and Consumer Behavior* (New York: Harrington Park, 1996), p. 91.

7. Bill Short, 'Queers, Beers and Shopping', *Gay Times*, November 1992, 18–20, p. 18.

8. See Mort, *Cultures of Consumption*, pp. 112 and 107–13; Mark Simpson, *Male Impersonators* (London: Cassell, 1994), pp. 97 and 97–100.

9. Donald Morton, 'Queerity and Ludic Sado-Masochism: Compulsory Consumption and the Emerging Post-al Queer', in Mas'ud Zavarzadeh, Terese L. Ebert and Donald Morton, eds., *Post-ality: Marxism and Postmodernism*, Transformation, 1 (Washington: Maisonneuve Press, 1995), 189–215, p. 210. Cf.

Adrienne Rich, 'Compulsory Heterosexuality and Lesbian Existence', in Ann Snitow et al., eds., *Desire: the Politics of Sexuality* (London: Virago, 1984).

10. Raymond Williams, *Culture* (Glasgow: Fontana, 1981), pp. 203–5.

11. Morton, 'Queerity and Ludic Sado-Masochism', in Zavarzadeh, Ebert and Morton, eds., *Post-ality*, pp. 193–6, 212.

12. Paul Hegarty, 'I Consume, Therefore I am Queer', *Rouge*, 11 (1992), 18–19. See also Jeremy Seabrook, *A Lasting Relationship* (London: Allen Lane, 1976); Nicola Field, *Over the Rainbow* (London: Pluto Press, 1995); Chris Woods, *State of the Queer Nation* (London: Cassell, 1995), pp. 41–8.

13. Frank Mort, 'The Politics of Consumption', in Stuart Hall and Martin Jaques, eds., *New Times* (London: Lawrence and Wishart, 1989), pp. 167–9.

14. Williams, *Culture*, pp. 98–107.

15. Clark, 'Commodity Lesbianism', in Abelove et al., eds., *The Lesbian and Gay Studies Reader*, pp. 198–9. See also Evans, *Sexual Citizenship*, pp. 103–4; Richard Dyer, 'In Defence of Disco', in Dyer, *Only Entertain* (London: Routledge, 1992).

16. Clark, 'Commodity Lesbianism', in Abelove et al., eds., *The Lesbian and Gay Studies Reader*, pp. 194–5. See sidney matrix, 'Desire and Deviate Nymphos: Performing Inversion(s) as a Lesbian Consumer', in Wardlow, ed., *Gays, Lesbians, and Consumer Behavior*.

17. Simpson, *Male Impersonators*, p. 99.

18. Clark, 'Commodity Lesbianism', in Abelove et al., eds., *The Lesbian and Gay Studies Reader*, p. 196.

19. See *Gay Times*, September 1995, p. 57.

20. Greg Woods, 'We're Here, We're Queer and We're Not Going Catalogue Shopping', in Paul Burston and Colin Richardson, eds., *A Queer Romance* (London: Routledge, 1995), pp. 151, 155.

21. Lisa Peñeloza, 'We're Here, We're Queer, and We're Going Shopping! A Critical Perspective on the Accommodation of Gays and Lesbians in the U.S. Marketplace', in Wardlow, ed., *Gays, Lesbians, and Consumer Behavior*, p. 34.

22. Michael Cunningham, 'Straight Arrows, Almost', *New York Times*, 7 May 1995, p. 17.

23. Anna Marie Smith, *New Right Discourse on Race and Sexuality* (Cambridge University Press, 1994), pp. 204–39.

24. Simpson, *Male Impersonators*, p. 101.

25. I am grateful to Vincent Quinn for pointing this out to me, and for showing me some of the magazines discussed in this chapter.

26. bell hooks, *Black Looks* (London: Turnaround, 1992), pp. 21–2.

27. Simon Watney, *Policing Desire* (London: Methuen, 1987), p. 80. On *The Face*, see Mort, *Cultures of Consumption*, pp. 22–8.

28. See, for instance, *Gay Times*, September 1995, p. 33.

29. See Joshua Oppenheimer, 'Movements, Markets, and the Mainstream: Gay Activism and Assimilation in the Age of AIDS', and Sarah Schulman, 'Niche Marketing to People with AIDS', both in Joshua Oppenheimer and Helena Reckitt, eds., *Acting on AIDS* (London: Serpent's Tail and ICA, 1997). Oppenheimer's essay recognises the UK situation as distinct.

30. *Attitude*, December 1994, pp. 10–11.

31. *Attitude*, February 1995, pp. 12–13.

32. For instance in *Gay Times*, September 1995, pp. 8–9.

33. 'From the Editor', *Attitude*, May 1995, p. 8. Mort discerns an emphasis on ' "mixed" cultures' among opinion leaders in the Soho village (Mort, *Cultures of Consumption*, pp. 176–81).

34. Evans, *Sexual Citizenship*, p. 45; and see Clark, 'Commodity Lesbianism', in Abelove et al., eds., *The Lesbian and Gay Studies Reader*, p. 195.

35. Antonio Gramsci, *Selections from the Prison Notebooks*, trans. Quintin Hoare and Geoffrey Nowell Smith (London: Lawrence and Wishart, 1971), pp. 296–7.

36. Paul Hoch, *White Hero Black Beast* (London: Pluto Press, 1979), p. 87. See Barbara Ehrenreich, *The Hearts of Men* (London: Pluto Press, 1983).

37. Herbert Marcuse, *Eros and Civilization* (London: Penguin, 1969), pp. 49, 51–54, 201. This is in part the territory of Leo Bersani, 'Is the Rectum a Grave?', in Douglas Crimp, ed., *AIDS: Cultural Analysis, Cultural Activism* (Cambridge, Mass.: MIT Press, 1988), and of Jonathan Dollimore, 'Sex and Death', *Textual Practice*, 9 (1995), 27–53.

38. Gail Hawkes, *A Sociology of Sex and Sexuality* (Buckingham: Open University Press, 1996), p. 108 and ch. 7.

39. Marcuse, *Eros and Civilization*, p. 36.

40. Hoch, *White Hero Black Beast*, pp. 102, 154.

41. Will Hutton, *The State We're In*, revised edn. (London: Vintage, 1996), pp. 105–10.

42. See, for instance, Stephen Green, *The Sexual Dead-End* (London: Broadview, 1992), chs. 31, 32.

43. Zygmunt Bauman, *Legislators and Interpreters* (Cambridge: Polity Press, 1987), pp. 167–8, 178–87. See Pierre Bourdieu, *Distinction, a Social Critique of the Judgment of Taste*, trans. Richard Nice (London: Routledge, 1984).

44. Karl Marx, *Grundrisse*, trans. Martin Nicolaus (Harmondsworth: Penguin, 1973), p. 94.

45. Judith Williamson, *Consuming Passions* (London: Marion Boyars, 1986), pp. 230–1.

46. See Simon LeVay and Elisabeth Nonas, *City of Friends* (Cambridge, Mass.: MIT Press, 1995), pp. 109–10, 418; Peñaloza, 'We're Here, We're Queer, and We're Going Shopping!', in Wardlow, ed., *Gays, Lesbians, and Consumer Behavior*, p. 25; Short, 'Queers, Beers and Shopping'.

47. See Andrew S. Walters and Maria-Cristina Curran, ' "Excuse Me, Sir? May I Help You and Your Boyfriend?": Salespersons' Differential Treatment of Homosexual and Straight Customers', and David A. Jones, 'Discrimination against Same-sex Couples in Hotel Reservation Policies', both in Wardlow, ed., *Gays, Lesbians, and Consumer Behavior*.

48. Thorstein Veblen, *The Theory of the Leisure Class* (New York: Mentor, 1953), pp. 125–6.

49. Burton, 'Is It Really Pink?', in Burton, *Amongst the Aliens*, p. 127.

50. Evans, *Sexual Citizenship*, p. 100.

51. See Angela McRobbie, 'Looking Back at New Times and Its Critics', in David Morley and Kuan-Hsing Chen, eds., *Stuart Hall: Critical Dialogues in Cultural Studies* (London: Routledge, 1996); Paul Gilroy, 'Wearing Your Art on Your Sleeve', in Gilroy, *Small Acts* (London: Serpent's Tail, 1993), p. 256.

52. Evans, *Sexual Citizenship*, p. 100.

53. Short, 'Queers, Beers and Shopping', p. 20.

54. Cornel West, quoted in bell hooks, *Yearning* (London: Turnaround, 1991), p. 38. See also Gilroy, *Small Acts*, ch. 8.

55. hooks, *Yearning*, pp. 33–6.

56. Ellen Meiksins Wood, *Democracy against Capitalism* (Cambridge University Press, 1995), pp. 254–5. My argument here draws strongly upon ch. 8 of Meiksins Wood's book.

57. Meiksins Wood, *Democracy against Capitalism*, p. 267.

58. Quentin Crisp, *The Naked Civil Servant* (New York: Plume, 1983), pp. 22–3.

59. Field, *Over the Rainbow*, p. 81.

60. For a similar case, argued specifically against the Trotskyite left,

see Simon Edge, *With Friends Like These* ... (London: Cassell, 1995), pp. 19–23.

61. *Brighton Pride '96*, Official Magazine (Brighton: XYZ Publishing Co., 1996), p. 3.

62. I am grateful to Nimrod Ping, Pride trustee and secretary, for talking to me about this.

63. Quoted from the first issue of *Come Out* by Denis Altman, *Homosexual: Oppression and Liberation* (Sydney and London: Angus and Robertson, 1972), pp. 109–10.

64. Tony Kushner, 'A Socialism of the Skin', *The Nation*, 4 July 1994, 9–14, p. 9.

65. D'Emilio, 'Capitalism and Gay Identity', in D'Emilio, *Making Trouble*, pp. 13–14.

Notes to chapter 10

1. See Stephen O. Murray, 'The "Underdevelopment" of Modern/Gay Homosexuality in MesoAmerica', in Ken Plummer, ed., *Modern Homosexualities* (London: Routledge, 1992), p. 30; Joseph Carrier, *De los Otros* (New York: Columbia University Press, 1995), pp. 193–5; Carter Wilson, *Hidden in the Blood* (New York: Columbia University Press, 1995), pp. 21–3.

2. Andrea Cornwall, 'Gendered Identities and Gender Ambiguity among *travestis* in Salvador, Brazil', in Andrea Cornwall and Nancy Lindisfarne, eds., *Dislocating Masculinity* (London: Routledge, 1994), pp. 119–20, 129–30.

3. Hugh McLean and Linda Ngcobo, 'Abangibhamayo bathi ngimnandi (Those who fuck me say I'm tasty): Gay Sexuality in Reef Townships', in Mark Gevisser and Edwin Cameron, eds., *Defiant Desire* (London: Routledge, 1995), p. 167.

4. Tony Kushner, *Angels in America: Part One: Millennium Approaches* (London: Royal National Theatre and Nick Hern Books, 1992), p. 31. This scene is excerpted in M. Elizabeth Osborn, ed., *The Way We Live Now* (New York: Theatre Communications Group, 1990).

5. See Ed Cohen, 'Who Are "We"? Gay "Identity" as Political (E)motion (A Theoretical Rumination)', in Diana Fuss, ed., *Inside/Out* (New York: Routledge, 1991), pp. 84–5.

6. *Radio Times*, 6–12 August 1994, p. 24.

7. Lillian Faderman, *Surpassing the Love of Men* (London: Junction Books, 1981).

8. Peter Tatchell, 'It's Just a Phase: Why Homosexuality Is Doomed', in Mark Simpson, ed., *Anti-Gay* (London: Cassell, 1996), pp. 46, 48. See also, in the same collection, Lisa Power, 'Forbidden Fruit', and Jo Eadie, 'Indigestion: Diagnosing the Gay Malady'.
9. Tatchell, 'It's Just a Phase', in Simpson, ed., *Anti-Gay*, p. 45.
10. Nick Walker, 'Gay Capital of Europe', *Independent*, 6 July 1996.
11. Tatchell, 'It's Just a Phase', in Simpson, ed., *Anti-Gay*, pp. 43–4.
12. Kobena Mercer, 'Decolonisation and Disappointment: Reading Fanon's Sexual Politics', in Alan Read, ed., *The Fact of Blackness* (London: ICA, 1996), p. 121.

Index